STREETS OF SIN

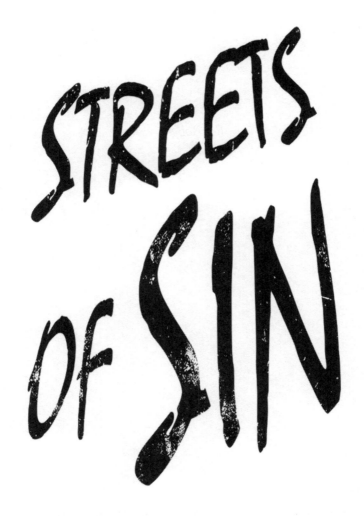

A DARK BIOGRAPHY OF
NOTTING HILL
FIONA RULE
FOREWORD BY JERRY WHITE

The
History
Press

For Robert

First published 2015

The History Press
The Mill, Brimscombe Port
Stroud, Gloucestershire, GL5 2QG
www.thehistorypress.co.uk

© Fiona Rule, 2015

The right of Fiona Rule to be identified as the Author
of this work has been asserted in accordance with the
Copyright, Designs and Patents Act 1988.

British Library Cataloguing in Publication Data.
A catalogue record for this book is available from the British Library.

ISBN 978 0 7509 6238 4

Typesetting and origination by The History Press
Printed and bound in Great Britain by TJ International Ltd

CONTENTS

FOREWORD
BY JERRY WHITE

Notting Hill! The very name holds magic for us, conjuring before our eyes those strikingly elegant terraces in white or coloured stucco at the ready-to-burst end of London's hyper-inflated property market. With super-rich property come the people to match. Here are the Russian oligarchs and worldwide billionaires, here are the Hollywood film stars and TV entertainers, the footballers, the celebrity WAGs and fashion models, even the brightest stars of British political life from across the party divide. It was a world unforgettably celebrated in a film of 1999 called – what else – *Notting Hill*.

The one thing all of these people must have, it seems, is money. And the other, perhaps, is a love of London, for in part Notting Hill crystallises some of the best that London has to offer its citizens and the world. It still has its council estates that continue to give the area a diverse mix of classes, with working people and the moderately rich rubbing shoulders in street and park and local shops. Just as important, Notting Hill bears the legacy of having been in at the birth of a multicultural metropolis in the years soon after the end of the Second World War. In many ways it was the most important centre in the country of the West Indian diaspora of the 1940s and '50s. For a generation it became the capital's showcase of Caribbean food, music and club life. This legacy has been kept joyously alive in the Notting Hill Carnival, staged here every August bank holiday since the mid-1960s, the largest street festival in Europe, second only to the Rio carnival worldwide, and drawing in between 1 and 2 million visitors each year. Both London and Notting Hill have become even more multiculturally diverse in the last thirty years or so and we can see that in the range of food on offer in Notting Hill's restaurants: Indian, Thai, Caribbean, Eritrean, Mexican, American, 'International', Italian, French, Spanish, Greek, 'Modern European', British – the list seems endless and probably is.

And yet. Scratch the surface, as anywhere, and there are problems. When a world-famous fashion model was reported in the week I am writing this to have had her home burgled, she was described by police as the 'latest victim of criminal gangs targeting wealthy celebrities in Notting Hill'. The easy conjunction of criminal gangs and Notting Hill would jar with many readers, but not with Fiona Rule. For it is this darker tradition of Notting Hill that she has brought to life in her new exploration of London's seamy side. We might think, and it's probably true, that anywhere has its darker side to be unearthed by a sharp-eyed investigator. But what she reveals about Notting Hill will surprise many. For Notting Hill's dark side is very dark, and runs very deep, indeed.

Even before what we think of as Notting Hill took shape in brick and slate on the open fields of North Kensington, the district was mired in filth and lawlessness. Part of it was known as 'The Piggeries' and for obvious reasons, the pig-keepers' lakes of liquid manure making this the most malodorous suburb in the whole metropolis. Nearby were 'The Potteries', where colonies of brick makers and potters dug up the local clay and baked it in kilns, their pungent odour and black smoke adding to the district's grime. The fields were dangerous to walk in alone at night, and violent robberies were commonplace. When building did get underway, from the 1860s in particular, the speed and cheapness with which much terraced housing was run up made part of this new suburb, though designed for a smart incoming middle class, notorious as 'Rotting Hill'.

The land on which the piggeries and potteries had held sway, and on which gipsy encampments were a prominent feature, were also eventually developed with housing, even cheaper and worse built and more badly drained than the more prosperous streets. This western part was christened Notting Dale. By the end of the nineteenth century it was one of the most desperately poor and unruly districts of London. Here, bizarrely, was what appeared to be an East End slum at its worst, transplanted to the new smart suburbs of the west. It became for journalists and social reformers in the 1890s and for twenty years after, 'the West-End Avernus', or hell-on-earth. Over 4,000 people were living here at the turn of the twentieth century. The infant mortality rate in Notting Dale was such that even as late as 1896, forty-three children out of every hundred born there would die before they reached their first birthday.

Notorious Notting Dale would remain intact until just before the Second World War; sufficient of it remained in 1958 to help mobilise the worst outbreak of anti-black rioting ever seen in this country, the 'Notting Hill Race Riots'. Close by, at 10 Rillington Place off St Mark's Road, one of the very darkest dramas in Notting Hill's secret past had been only recently played out. Here between 1949 and 1952, John Reginald Halliday Christie murdered five women and a baby, having killed at least two other women before moving there. He seems to have been a necrophiliac, murdering mainly for sexual gratification. Christie will forever remain the central exhibit in Notting Hill's chamber of horrors, as he rightly does in this book.

Christie apart, Fiona Rule has been able to populate Notting Hill's sinful saga with a memorable cast list of villains and victims. She has found confidence-tricksters, even slave traders, among the investors of Rotting Hill; there are nefarious doings, including murder, in the blackout and among the spivs of black market Notting Hill during the Second World War; we enter the world of the slum landlord Peter Rachman and meet some of his more famous contacts; we are shown the dreadful murders in the mid-1960s of young prostitutes working the streets of Notting Hill and elsewhere in west London by an unidentified man, so-called 'Jack the Stripper'; and we learn of much else previously hidden away in these overpopulated 'Streets of Sin'.

Through her painstaking investigation, Fiona Rule shows us one by one the skeletons hidden in Notting Hill's darkest cupboards. It's all a fascinating story because, as Rule memorably reveals, Notting Hill is that intriguing urban puzzle – a glitzy district with 'a past'.

Jerry White
May 2015

INTRODUCTION

Back in the early 1990s, I found myself working in the marketing department of a, sadly, now defunct London bookshop chain. A major part of my job was to attend book launches that were organised by publishers in all manner of interesting and enticing locations. My attendance at these events was supposed to be a fact-finding mission so that I could effectively promote the books in question. However, like virtually everyone else, I generally went for the free wine.

One evening, my boss, who hated these junkets with a passion, thrust a smartly printed invitation into my hand and said, 'There's a cook book launch in Notting Hill tonight. It's at the publisher's house and I promised her that one of us would go.' Clearly, the 'one of us' was going to be me.

As I sat on the Central Line train heading towards Notting Hill Gate, I realised that I was venturing into a part of London about which I knew virtually nothing. As a staunch north Londoner, my social life rarely took me further west than Marble Arch and the only thing I associated with Notting Hill was the annual carnival, which, according to the press, was so dangerous that no one in their right mind would want to go there. The train rumbled into the station, I alighted and made my way out into the sunlight. It was a glorious, late summer evening and the atmosphere as I stepped on to the broad, shop-lined thoroughfare exuded a calm that never permeated the endless hubbub of my West End workplace. I checked the address on the invitation and after consulting my A–Z, made my way towards Ladbroke Road.

On arriving at my destination, I apprehensively hovered around outside, hoping that some other guests might soon turn up so I wouldn't have to go in alone. As I scanned the street for possible candidates,

I noticed that the houses looked much the same architecturally as those in north London's inner suburbs. However, at the same time, they were also distinctly different. My old stomping grounds of Kentish Town and Islington had more than their fair share of Victorian stucco-fronted terraces, but the houses there were often rather careworn and looked their age. The properties on Ladbroke Road could have been built yesterday, such was the standard of decoration. Their frontages were painted in a tasteful range of creams, whites, blues and pale pinks; their gardens were pristine and their front doors glossy.

As I was taking in the scene, a couple arrived and made their way up the steps to the house. Seeing my chance to enter the party discreetly, I followed them. Once inside, the property's interior took my breath away. The great Victorian designer William Morris famously said, 'Have nothing in your houses that you do not know to be useful or believe to be beautiful', and the owners had followed his advice to the letter. As I made my way down the lofty hallway, I glimpsed the front sitting room – a sumptuous retreat furnished in opulent shades of chocolate and cream. Further down the hall, a small flight of stairs led to a kitchen fitted with carved oak cabinets and a terracotta tiled floor. Delicious aromas were emanating from a large range, where hostesses were producing trays of hors d'oeuvres which they efficiently slid on to serving plates before whisking them off into the garden, where most of the guests had assembled. Nervously accepting a glass of champagne from a smiling waitress, I made my way outside.

On entering the garden, I quickly realised that most of my fellow guests had, like me, arrived alone. Consequently, it was easy to strike up conversations without feeling like I was butting into a private clique. Most of the chat took the inevitable form of polite, mundane comments about the lovely house, the beautiful weather, the generosity of the host, etc., etc. However, one conversation made me prick up my ears. 'Of course, Christie lived just down the road from here,' a middle-aged man idly commented as I joined a small circle of people on the lawn.

'The murderer?' I asked.

'One and the same,' he replied, before rapidly moving on to another topic.

The party continued for another hour or so before I noticed some of the guests were preparing to leave. By this stage, the warm sunlight that had filled the garden was beginning to fade and it was getting distinctly chilly. I thanked the hostess, took my complimentary copy of the cookery book (which looked fiendishly complicated) and left the party.

Travelling home on the tube, I flicked through the book I'd been given and realised that my initial suspicions were correct. The recipes were terrifyingly sophisticated. I quickly shut it and my thoughts turned to the brief conversation about the murderer, Christie. At the time, I knew little of the sordid case, but I had seen the film *10 Rillington Place*, in which Notting Hill was presented as a dilapidated, poverty-stricken slum. The scenes I recalled bore absolutely no relation to the Notting Hill I had just witnessed at the party. How could one small area of London have changed so much in such a short space of time? I resolved to find out.

Once I began to research the story of Notting Hill, I quickly realised that the fine houses and neatly tended gardens now lining the district's thoroughfares are largely a modern phenomenon. Well within living memory, many of these properties were among the most rundown in the whole of London and the grinding poverty endured by their inhabitants created an environment in which unspeakable acts of exploitation, debauchery, and even murder, were committed on a frighteningly regular basis. By the end of the 1950s, so much shame and scandal had been heaped on the area that the *Daily Mirror* renamed it 'Rotting Hill'.

Originally intended to be west London's answer to Regent's Park, Notting Hill's fall from grace was fast, spectacular and almost permanent. It is only in the last few decades that the area has managed to wrest itself from its sordid past and finally become the upmarket residential enclave that the original landowner dreamed of creating back at the beginning of the 1800s. However, its inexorable climb out of the ghetto has come at a cost. This is the troubled story of Notting Hill, W11.

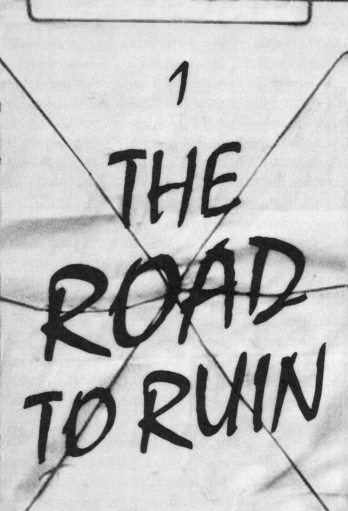

The evolution of Notting Hill from a tiny, rural community to a fully-fledged inner London suburb was fraught with scandal and disaster, borne by blind ambition and greed. Back in the mid-1700s, the estate formed part of a sparsely populated, agricultural landscape that was located a good half an hour's walk from the outer reaches of the metropolis. The land was the property of Richard Ladbroke – a hugely wealthy, but largely absent landlord who rarely visited his estate, preferring to divide his time between his mercantile business in the City and Tadworth Court, a sprawling country property near Banstead Downs Racecourse in Surrey.

Ladbroke's estate lay by the side of an ancient thoroughfare linking London to the market town of Uxbridge. Close by, a tollgate collected funds from travellers to keep the road's final stretch into the city navigable. Although long since vanished, the tollgate was responsible for giving the area the name by which it is known today – Notting Hill Gate.

The narrow ribbon of buildings that flanked the toll road in the mid-1700s were collectively known as Kensington Gravel Pits – a rather prosaic name given that the locality was renowned for its magnificent views and outstanding natural beauty. That said, the gravel beds were responsible for putting the area on the map. Used extensively in road building, gravel played an essential part in the development of eighteenth-century London and today, the natural resources from Kensington Gravel Pits still lie buried beneath the streets.

The eastern and western borders of Richard Ladbroke's estate were marked by two bumpy cart tracks leading north. The easternmost track led through a patchwork of meadows to a smallholding known as Portobello Farm. This ramshackle, L-shaped building had been constructed by a Mr Adams in 1740 and proudly named after a famous sea battle that had taken place the year before, where the British captured the Portobello naval base in Panama from the Spanish.

Although it was situated quite close to the Uxbridge Road, the farmhouse possessed a distinctly remote atmosphere. A narrow front garden bounded by a low brick wall led to a sun-bleached front porch. By the side of the house, a patch of scrubland where carts and carriages could be parked was bordered by a small thicket of trees and a dilapidated fence, which led round to the back of the property, enclosing a small garden. Outside the fenced perimeter, a footpath wound past an old pond into the fields beyond, while close by, huge haystacks – themselves the height of houses – stood like monoliths amid the bucolic landscape.

The western edge of Ladbroke's estate was bounded by the other country lane. This gravelly track, which led to a natural well used by the villagers, was known locally as Green's Lane in memory of the Green family, who had operated a market garden there during the first half of the 1700s. Green's Lane came to an abrupt end at the well and anyone wishing to travel further north would have to cross two large meadows before they came upon the next vestige of civilisation – Notting Barns Farm.

Owned by the wealthy Talbot family, this large and impressive edifice had long ago been the local manor house and was described by the topographer Thomas Faulkner in 1820 as 'an ancient brick building, surrounded by spacious barns and out-houses'. To the east of the farmhouse, a large pond lay by the side of a deeply rutted cart track leading to the village of Kensal Green, about 1 mile away.

Although Richard Ladbroke's land was surrounded by lucrative enterprises, such as the two farms and the gravel pits, none actually lay on the estate itself. Thus, he had to content himself with the comparatively small rents derived from a few houses along the Uxbridge Road and two smaller farms. One of these farms stood by the side of the toll road (on the site now occupied by the Mitre Tavern); the other – Notting Hill Farm – stood on the summit of Notting Hill. By 1800, this particular farm comprised a rather decrepit complex of dwellings, sheds, haylofts and barns that straddled a busy footpath to Kensal Green. Consequently, the Hall family, who operated the farm in the first decades of the 1800s, had to constantly contend with pedestrians and horses filing through their farmyard.

Neither Richard Ladbroke nor his son (also Richard) made any attempt to develop their Notting Hill estate, despite the fact that it lay only a couple of miles from the rapidly expanding borders of the City of Westminster. In 1794, Richard Ladbroke junior died childless and the estate passed to his cousin, Osbert Denton. Keen to preserve the family name, Richard had stipulated in his will that the Notting Hill estate had to be inherited by a Ladbroke. Thus, Osbert was compelled to change his surname.

This caveat applied again in 1818 when Osbert died, and the Ladbroke estate passed briefly to another cousin – Cary Weller – who, unfortunately, expired less than two years after receiving his inheritance. The estate then changed hands once again, this time to Cary's younger brother, James, who, in accordance with the will, changed his surname to Weller Ladbroke and set about putting his stamp on the Notting Hill estate. His ill-conceived plans would prove to have a devastating effect on the area and would ultimately throw the little community that surrounded it into turmoil.

James Weller Ladbroke was born around 1776 – the second son of the Reverend James Weller and Richard Ladbroke's aunt, Mary. As he was the youngest male in the family, neither James nor his parents ever considered that he would one day inherit the estate at Notting Hill and James was encouraged to go into the military, first joining the 47th Foot Regiment and then the 23rd Light Dragoons, with whom he served at Corunna and Talavera during the Peninsular War of 1808–14. In 1803, he married a distant cousin – Caroline, the daughter of Robert Napier Raikes, vicar of Longhope in Gloucestershire. The couple had one child – a daughter, whom they named Caroline – and lived in modest comfort at a country house named Hillyers, near Petworth in Sussex.

James Weller Ladbroke's army career was unremarkable and after retiring around 1815, he spent four uneventful years ensconced at Hillyers where he idled away the hours by running the local cricket club. The sudden death of his older brother, Cary, in 1819 changed his life totally and irrevocably.

Although he had never expected to become a major landowner, James Weller Ladbroke relished his new vocation and was utterly seduced by the possibilities that presented themselves. All thoughts of the cricket club faded into insignificance as he began laying plans to develop his newly acquired land into the most ambitious luxury housing estate ever seen in Britain.

Ladbroke's inspiration for his grand scheme was nothing less than regal. Back in 1811, the Prince Regent (later George IV) had entered into discussions with the fashionable architect John Nash, to create a palatial estate at the old royal hunting park in Marylebone. With a virtually unlimited budget at his disposal, Nash drew up a plan to rival the most opulent palaces across the globe. The huge, 500-acre park would be landscaped, and in the western section a long, curved boating lake would be created, across which the prince and his retinue could row to a series of little islands at its centre. Over on the east side of the park, a long, rectangular ornamental lake lined with avenues of trees would echo the gardens of the greatest palace of them all – Versailles. The palace building was envisaged at the centre of the park, standing amid neat formal gardens of box hedge and sweet-smelling roses. Around the perimeter of the park elegant, stucco-fronted mansions for the prince's inner circle would be built in the latest Regency style.

Work began on the 'Regent's Park' in 1818 – just one year before James Weller Ladbroke inherited his estate, and although much of Nash's original scheme never came to fruition, the development made a huge impression on him. Heady with ambition, Ladbroke resolved to build west London's answer to Regent's Park on his land in Notting Hill. The only problem was, he did not have the backing of the future king (nor any other nobility), who might have added the cachet needed to attract London's elite to an estate that at the time, was a long way out of the fashionable West End.

The fact that James Weller Ladbroke's land was in a rural backwater rather than a royal hunting park did nothing to dampen his enthusiasm for the project. Almost as soon as he inherited the estate, he set about finding an architect who was up to the monumental task in hand, but who would not charge the exorbitant fees of John Nash. The man he chose for the job was Thomas Allason.

Allason undoubtedly possessed considerable creative talent. A student of the great Gothic revival architect, William Atkinson, he had won the Royal Academy of Architects' silver medal in 1809, at the tender age of just 19. Five years later he travelled to Greece, and the classical architecture he found amid the ruins of the Parthenon inspired him greatly. From Greece, he travelled to Pola, a town on the Istrian Peninsula, where he produced a series of beautifully executed illustrations of the Roman ruins he saw there. These drawings were published in book form in 1819 and it is likely that this is how Thomas Allason came to the attention of James Weller Ladbroke.

Although he was undeniably a gifted architect, Allason's career failed to reach the dizzying heights of contemporaries such as John Nash and he was forced to earn a living as surveyor to the Alliance Fire Assurance Company. This rather mundane work, combined with a lack of prestigious private commissions, meant that his fees were well within the reach of men like James Weller Ladbroke and in 1823 he was commissioned to design the estate at Notting Hill.

Allason's plans were every bit as ambitious as his client had desired. Using Notting Hill's most prominent and attractive feature – the hill itself – as the centrepiece, he created a plan for a wide, straight avenue (today's Ladbroke Grove) that ran northwards from the Uxbridge Road, over the brow of the hill (straight through the old farmyard) and halfway down the other side.

An expansive circus – 1 mile in circumference – crowned the summit of the hill, bisected by the central avenue to create two enormous crescents. Allason proposed that both crescents would be lined with houses similar to those planned for Regent's Park, but standing in private grounds of up to 5 acres. The innermost portions of the crescents contained the most unique element of the development – large, communal gardens that Allason referred to as 'paddocks'. Barely visible from the road, these paddocks were only accessible from the houses that surrounded them. Original leases show that they were intended for the 'convenience and recreation of the tenants and occupiers', who could stroll and 'demean' themselves there. Servants were not admitted unless they were 'in actual attendance on the children or other members of the family'.

Allason's paddocks were a revolutionary idea that would eventually (in a scaled-down form) become a unique feature in this part of west London. Housing estates had been created around garden squares for years, but these open spaces were always at the front of the properties and usually separated from the houses by a roadway. The fact that the paddocks could be accessed directly from the residents' back doors was novel and their inherent privacy a boon, although one wonders why a householder with 5 acres at his disposal would want communal land beyond his garden.

To the east of the hill, another, triangular development with a pad-
dock at its centre was planned, while to the south, a road running parallel
with the Uxbridge Road formed the southern boundary of the estate.
This road was named Weller Street, in deference to the landowner.

While Thomas Allason was surveying the land in preparation for planning his great scheme, James Weller Ladbroke was attending to matters
that were more mundane but no less important. One of the caveats in his
uncle's will specified that any building leases issued on the land could
only have a duration of twenty-one years. With no funds to construct the
planned estate himself, Ladbroke had to rely on selling leases to developers. However, he knew that no builder would take on a twenty-one-year
contract as it was too risky. Thus, in 1821 he was compelled to force a
private Act through Parliament enabling him to issue ninety-nine-year
leases, which would be a much more attractive proposition to builders.

While Ladbroke was keen to start dishing out contracts, Thomas
Allason urged him to progress cautiously. Although London was
expanding rapidly by the 1820s, Notting Hill was still mainly farmland. The only developed area in the vicinity was the old village of
Kensington Gravel Pits, but even that comprised just a few private
dwellings, an ancient almshouse, a school and probably a couple of
beer houses and shops (although none are mentioned in contempo-
rary sources). Realising that luring builders out to this backwater of the
metropolis was not going to be easy, Allason suggested that a test site
should be developed, the majority of which he would build himself.

The land he earmarked for the trial lay on the northern edge of
the Uxbridge Road, on the eastern perimeter of the Ladbroke estate.
Here, Allason laid out a relatively short, L-shaped cul-de-sac, named
Linden Grove (today's Linden Gardens) and lined with modest cottages. Designed to appeal to professional families in search of a rural
idyll close to London, these cottages comprised a breakfast room,
a dining parlour and a kitchen on the ground floor, with three decent
sized bedrooms upstairs. Outside, the properties had a wash house
contained within a back yard which, in turn, led to reasonably large
private gardens. In a bid to recoup his building costs as quickly as possible, Allason recommended that the cottages be rented out at the very
competitive rate of just £40 per annum (rents on similar properties

closer to central London could top £70 at the time.) His strategy paid off and the Linden Grove cottages quickly attracted tenants.

As Thomas Allason had intended, the Linden Grove development acted as a showcase for the Ladbroke estate. Speculative developers could now see that properties at Notting Hill could be let quickly and, although they could not achieve high rents, the comparatively low cost of the building leases made up for this.

In the early years of the 1820s, the Ladbroke estate looked like it might live up to its owner's high expectations. With the test development complete, Ladbroke and Allason turned their attentions to their grand scheme at the top of the hill, and in 1823 they issued leases to two builders who could turn their dream of building London's most exclusive suburb into reality.

The first building plot to be snapped up (a strip of land fronting the Uxbridge Road at the western end of the estate) was leased to Ralph Adams, a brick and tile maker who had wholesale warehouses at St Chad's Row, Islington, and Maiden Lane in the City. Realising that it was only a matter of time before the rapidly expanding city reached Notting Hill, and impressed by Ladbroke and Allason's aspirational plans for the area, Adams also leased a large field by the side of Green's Lane where he set up brick kilns.

A corresponding strip of land along the Uxbridge Road at the eastern end of the estate was leased to just the type of property developer that Allason had hoped to attract with his Linden Grove experiment. Joshua Flesher Hanson was a house builder with a prestigious reputation. Over the past twenty years, he had been responsible for building some of the most impressive properties in England, including the elegant Regency Square in Brighton and Hyde Park Gate, one of the capital's most sought after addresses.

Now they had two developers on site, Ladbroke and Allason were impatient to begin realising their dream. As an incentive to complete the building work quickly, Adams' and Hanson's leases stipulated that the annual ground rent on each plot would amount to just £25 in the first year, but would rise steadily in the years thereafter, reaching a ceiling of £150 in the sixth year. This strategy worked and Adams and Hanson lost little time in starting work.

The first houses to be completed gave a tantalising glimpse of what was planned on the upper slopes of Notting Hill. By 1824, elegant, stucco-fronted terraces lined the north side of the Uxbridge Road; their pillared entrances leading through to gracious, airy rooms illuminated by large, sash windows. Behind the properties, gardens stretched northwards towards the rising slopes of the hill that lay beyond. These properties, some of which still exist today, were among the finest in London and, although enticing families out of the city still proved challenging, the lower rents and large amounts of outdoor space proved popular.

With the future of the development looking promising, Allason and Ladbroke were bemused when Joshua Flesher Hanson suddenly pulled out after completing just eight of the twenty houses he was contracted to build, selling the leases on the remaining plots of land to an architect named Robert Cantwell. It transpired that Hanson had been very shrewd indeed. Just twelve months later, Britain's economy was in turmoil and Ladbroke and Allason's grand designs lay in shreds.

The root of the misfortune lay in national economic circumstances that are not unfamiliar today. Back in the early 1820s, when James Weller Ladbroke was formulating his plans for the Notting Hill estate, Britain was in the midst of an economic boom. The country had recovered well from the fiscal ravages of the Napoleonic Wars (which ended in 1815). An unprecedented rise in large-scale engineering projects, such as canal and road building, led to the creation of thousands of new jobs and, as the population acquired more disposable income, manufacturing ran at record levels. In this optimistic and economically buoyant atmosphere, public confidence in financial investment was high and developers like Adams and Hanson had little trouble obtaining funding for their speculative building projects. Their investors got fast returns on their money and were hungry to make more.

During the same period, on the other side of the globe, several regions in Central and South America declared independence from Spain. The new countries that emerged presented commercial opportunities, and soon the British banks were lending money to investors keen to exploit their rich resources. By April 1822, a committee of city merchants, manufacturers and ship owners announced that 'since the establishment of Independent Governments in the countries of South America which were formerly under the dominion of Spain, an extensive trade has been carried on with them from this country, either directly, or through the medium of other places'.

In addition to trade, the British public were keen to loan funds to the newly established countries, expecting that they would receive an excellent return on their money. By 1824, proposals were circulating in the City for subscriptions to a huge loan for the 'United Provinces of Central America'. In return, the United Provinces began making offers that seemed almost too good to be true. In January 1825, they issued an official decree to encourage foreign settlers that stated, 'It is open to every foreigner to exercise any business he may think fit, mining included.'

On arrival, new settlers were advised to form townships, for which they obtained an agreement from a local magistrate. The regulations for the townships were as follows:

1   [Each] township must contain within it fifteen married couples
    at least.
2   Each married couple are to have a lot of land assigned to them.
3   A foreigner joining the township may have the same quantity
    of land, provided he marries within six years; and in the case of
    his marrying one of the native aborigines, or a woman of colour,
    a double portion of land.
4   Every settler may withdraw from the country when he pleases,
    and dispose of his property without hindrance or molestation.
5   Each new settlement is for twenty years free of all imposts whatever.
6   Exports and imports are to be free for twenty years.
7   No slaves to be admitted – the very act of introduction giving
    freedom to the slave.

Although many of the offers of a new life in the Americas were genuine, the market unsurprisingly acted as a magnet to con men, the most notorious of whom was an audacious Scottish adventurer named Gregor MacGregor.

In many ways, MacGregor was the perfect confidence trickster. Described by contemporaries as being strikingly handsome, his

self-assured nature and ability to tell a good story made it easy for
him to fool even the most cynical City traders. And like every hustler
before or since, he played on people's greed.

MacGregor first turned up in London in 1820 with his South
American wife, Josefa. He made a point of frequenting the coffee
shops and inns in the city, where he recounted an amazing story to
anyone who would listen. MacGregor claimed to have just returned
from Central America, where he had played a vital role in liberat-
ing several of the new republics from the clutches of the Spanish.
In gratitude for his efforts, King George of the Mosquito Coast had
apparently given him the territory of Poyais, a 12,500-square mile
principality, 40 miles up the Black River in the Bay of Honduras.

MacGregor – who had styled himself the *Cacique* (Chief) of
Poyais – waxed lyrical about his country, which reputably had acres
of fertile land, gold and silver mines, a well-established infrastructure,
friendly inhabitants (many of whom were descended from British
settlers in the 1730s) and even the beginnings of a democratic government. In truth, the land was an uninhabitable jungle.

The London merchants took to MacGregor immediately, and he
and his wife soon became the toast of the town. The lord mayor even
organised a special reception for them at the Guildhall. MacGregor
took full advantage of this, and after his sojourn in London he and his
wife travelled to Scotland, where he played the same scam. Soon, investors were queuing up to invest in Poyais and MacGregor began to draw
up deeds of sale for land there at the extremely reasonable price of 3s
3d per acre. This, of course, meant that anyone could invest in Poyais
and consequently, hundreds of poorly paid workers signed up to the
scheme, hoping that Poyais would change their lives forever.

In order for his con to work, MacGregor had to ensure that people
actually got on ships and went to Poyais. This was the most dangerous part of the deceit as he knew full well that, if anyone returned,
he would be exposed. Nevertheless, by the autumn of 1822, he had
arranged for two ships to take the new settlers to Poyais. The *Honduras
Packet* left the port of London with seventy pioneers on board in
September and, four months later, the *Kennersley Castle* departed
from Leith with another 200 hopeful settlers.

Many of the families on board the ships had ploughed their life savings into their emigration, so when they arrived at the Mosquito Coast they could not believe their eyes. Far from having any sort of township, the region was virtually deserted apart from a few fishermen who lived in dilapidated shacks. The settlers frantically searched the area for the farmland and gold mines described by MacGregor, but none were to be found. By the time they fled back to the *Honduras Packet*, the ship had sailed. The duped colonists were now stranded in hostile territory and had to fend for themselves – a difficult task, as most of their provisions had been lost when the boat carrying them overturned.

By the spring of 1823, worrying reports about Poyais were beginning to filter back to Britain. On 13 April, a merchant in Honduras sent a letter to Lloyd's with some very distressing news. He wrote:

> Five or six of the deluded creatures whom Gregor MacGregor sent to the Mosquito Shore as settlers to his Viceroyship of Poyais arrived here about 8 days ago. Out of the 55 who arrived at one time at the shore, 9 remain. Some put to sea to reach Belize, others up the river and have never been heard of, and others died miserably where they landed, which was absolutely among mangrove trees, which they had to cut down … General Codd [the Commander-in-Chief at Belize] intends sending immediately for the remnant of another load which were sent there lately. If he does not, they must perish from exposure, if not disease.

The merchant's letter was not the only report that found its way back to Britain. In the same month, a rescued settler in Belize wrote to his friend in Leith:

> We found the country very wild and nearly covered with wood. MacGregor had told us that there was a town where we were to be landed; but we saw neither town nor inhabitants, except a few fishermen. The heat and mosquitoes were insufferable. Every one was disappointed; and all wished to get away from the place. Six of us and a woman, wife of one of the party, determined to make our escape at all hazards; and as we knew that one of the boats, which had been

employed landing the stores, was lying about five miles from where
we were, we resolved to seize it, put it to sea, and endeavour to make
Belize, a British settlement, about 200 miles from the Black River.
At 12 at night, we secretly took away from the camp as many of our articles, and as much provision as we could manage. We crossed the river
in a canoe and travelled quickly, till we reached the boat. We jumped
in and pushed off with a fine breeze; but when we got out from land,
our boat filled with water; our provisions were all lost; and after suffering the most dreadful hardships for five days (during which time we
had not a drop of fresh water and only one biscuit, which we found
in the bottom of the boat), we were at length picked up by a small
vessel and taken to Port Mayhoe, a place belonging to the Spaniards,
and thence to Belize. The married man died on the boat before we
were picked up; we were obliged to throw his body overboard. We were
in a wretched condition when we arrived at Belize but were treated
with the greatest kindness and humanity by a Scottish gentleman there,
George Home Esq., who took us to his house and has kept us ever
since. We informed the Governor of the State of the settlers at Poyais
and that gentleman ordered a schooner to be got ready to ascertain the
fact. When the vessel arrived at Belize, it was found that nine of the
unhappy sufferers had died and the rest were all lying sick – not one
able to give a drink of water to another. As many as the schooner could
take were brought away. She made another trip and came off with the
remainder and the stores, which were sold to defray expenses. The sick
were put into the Hospital here and received every attention and assistance which could be given them; but they are dying in great numbers
from the effects of their former sufferings. Were MacGregor hanged,
it would not be an adequate punishment for the misery he has heaped
on so many unfortunate people.

By the time the letters from Belize and Honduras arrived in London,
the truth about Poyais had been exposed by sailors returning on
the ships. Concerned, the government dispatched a judge named
Marshall Bennett to the republic in order to establish the true state
of affairs in Poyais. Mr Bennett arrived at the township on 26 April.
He later told the inquiry committee that, 'Sickness and wretchedness

prevailed among the settlers to a very great extent, without the means of obtaining comforts suitable to their distressed state.' Some of the settlers begged Bennett to take them to Belize. He took sixty-six people on his ship and then went back for more.

The evacuation of Poyais exposed Gregor MacGregor's scam, but by then, the self-styled *Cacique* was long gone from British shores. He was later found in France, where amazingly, he was operating the same con. However, by this stage his notoriety was legendary and, although he tried to set up more schemes involving Poyais in the early 1830s, the public steered well clear. He eventually fled to Venezuela, where he died in 1845.

Back in London, news of the Poyais fraud made investors very wary of any schemes involving Latin America and the value of stocks and bonds began to fall dramatically as people bailed out of the market. This, in turn, created suspicion of other investments, particularly those overseas, and the market began to slide. Banks, which had been lending money at ridiculously low interest rates, began to panic as the stock market went into freefall. With pitifully low reserves, Britain's financial institutions were suddenly terribly exposed. The vaults of one bank – Pole Thornton – were literally left empty when one of their wealthy customers withdrew £30,000 without warning. Pole Thornton was not alone. By the middle of December 1825, numerous banks in London and the provinces were desperately scrambling to refill their coffers but, for many, it was too late. Some were saved from closure when the Bank of England began issuing emergency loans but, in total, seventy banks went into liquidation.

The financial crisis of 1825 had an effect that is all too familiar to us today. The banks that survived virtually stopped issuing loans for anything bar cast-iron investments, and as a consequence, the housing market collapsed. In the years following the banking crisis, building work at the Ladbroke estate ground to a halt and for the next decade very little development took place. By 1836, James Weller Ladbroke had failed to issue any new building leases for over two years. Disappointed and embittered, he must have wondered if his Notting Hill estate was really the golden egg he had once believed it to be. Then, just as Ladbroke was beginning to despair, a man named John Whyte appeared on the scene with an interesting proposition.

2

THE SLAVE OWNER AND THE RACECOURSE

Around the same time that James Weller Ladbroke had inherited his uncle's land at Notting Hill, John Whyte became heir to another, very different estate – three sugar plantations on the Caribbean island of Jamaica. The plantations, known as Cavebottom, Craighead and Windhill, had been purchased by Whyte's father, James, in the mid-1700s, and the family quickly became rich on the sugar, molasses and rum that they produced.

However, in taking on the lucrative plantations, they also became the owners of hundreds of slaves. A typical Jamaican sugar plantation in the early 1800s covered a massive 900 acres and was run on similar lines to an open prison. The plantation owner and his family lived in a grand, whitewashed mansion in one corner of the estate, having their every whim catered to by their unpaid domestic staff, while their enslaved workers lived at least ½ mile away in dilapidated sheds that contained only the most basic facilities. The slaves' lives were exhausting, their work was relentless and their situation hopeless. Children started work on the plantation from the age of 3 and were expected to continue working for the rest of their lives. Most never left the plantation, as every facility needed to run such an enterprise was on site – some estates even had their own hospitals.

By 1800, the number of slaves working on the Whytes' sugar plantations outnumbered the family by around fourteen to one. Given the desperate conditions endured by the slaves, uprisings were not uncommon and, thus, an air of paranoia was ever present in the plantation owners' grand houses. Terrified by the thought that they could be murdered in their beds if slaves were given the confidence and opportunity to resist their regime, Jamaican slave owners controlled their plantation workers using a chilling combination of force, fear and humiliation.

Around the same time as John Whyte's father settled in Jamaica, a Lincolnshire man named Thomas Thistlewood also arrived on the island. Unlike Whyte, Thistlewood did not possess the funds to purchase his own plantation, so instead he earned a good living as an overseer of enslaved workforces. Once he had saved sufficient money, he bought his own team of slaves, whom he rented out like farm machinery to other landowners.

Throughout his time in Jamaica, Thomas Thistlewood kept a diary. The journal was intended as simply a record of his day-to-day activities, which makes its contents even more shocking. Within its pages, Thistlewood revealed that Jamaica's white overlords shamefully and systematically abused their positions of authority on an almost daily basis. He and his colleagues behaved like wild animals, dragging terrified women, and even underage girls, to their beds whenever the mood took them. Thomas Thistlewood personally recorded over 3,000 sexual encounters with over 100 enslaved women during his time on the island. All of these encounters would today be considered rape.

Male slaves had different, though no less humiliating treatment, especially those who tried to abscond from the plantation. Thistlewood himself meted out a wide range of punishments, each one more appallingly sadistic than the last: He publicly flogged disobedient slaves and then smeared a mixture of pepper and lemon juice on to their bleeding wounds, while other transgressors were forced to kneel in front of the assembled workforce while overseers urinated into their eyes and mouth. However, Thistlewood's favourite reprimand was known as 'Derby's Dose', a repulsive punishment whereby one slave was forced to defecate into another slave's mouth, which was then forcibly tied shut for up to five hours.

Although James Whyte and his sons may have tacitly disapproved of punishments such as Derby's Dose, they would have considered it perfectly acceptable to rape and humiliate. However, while this utter disregard for their fellow man may have worked to their advantage in Jamaica, it proved to be John Whyte's undoing when he adopted the same attitude in Notting Hill.

Whyte and his two brothers inherited their sugar plantations as the age of slavery was in its death throes. By the mid-1820s the abolition movement was rapidly gaining momentum and, consequently, both plantations and slaves massively depreciated in value. In 1829, a beleaguered Jamaican slave owner (who preferred to remain nameless) complained to a local newspaper editor, 'Fifteen to twenty years ago, a good [enslaved] tradesman – mason, carpenter, saddler, etc. would have brought £180–£200: an able field Negro from

£140–£170 … a healthy infant £20–£25. During the last seven years, one quarter of the above would not have been offered.'

Much to the slave owners' disgust, tireless campaigning by abolitionists, like politician William Wilberforce and freed slave Olaudah Equiano, finally resulted in the abolition of slavery in Jamaica in 1834, just twelve years after the Whyte brothers had inherited their father's plantations. In order to make amends for what was effectively the destruction of their business, the plantation owners were handsomely compensated by the British Government.

In total, nearly £1 billion in modern currency was paid out to British slave owners in the West Indies. After receiving their settlement, the Whyte brothers sold off their land in Jamaica and closed down their London office in Mincing Lane. With the family business now totally defunct, John Whyte used some of his compensation money to buy Brace Cottage, an attractive villa on the slopes of Notting Hill, and paced its elegant rooms wondering what to do next.

Soon after he moved to the area, Whyte noticed that building work on James Weller Ladbroke's estate had ground to a halt. Cannily, he surmised that this sorry state of affairs must have caused a great deal of worry for Ladbroke, who had almost certainly spent a small fortune on architects and solicitors during the new estate's planning stages. He also realised that he could use James Ladbroke's bad fortune to his advantage.

In the early summer of 1836, Whyte arranged a meeting with James Weller Ladbroke and announced that he was prepared to take a twenty-one-year lease on the entire undeveloped portion of his land, if Ladbroke would allow him to create London's first racecourse on the site. Despairing at ever completing his estate and fondly remembering his family's long-held connection with Banstead Racecourse, James Weller Ladbroke shook hands on the deal.

With the land secured, John Whyte wasted no time. By the beginning of August 1836, the demolition of Notting Hill Farm was underway and a spectators' enclosure was erected at the summit of the hill, while the course itself was laid out on the slopes below. The site was well suited to horse racing for two reasons: firstly, the 360° hilltop vista gave spectators an unobstructed view of the runners and riders, and secondly, Whyte's racecourse, which he proudly named 'the Hippodrome', was far nearer to London than any other (Epsom Downs previously being the closest to the capital).

The construction of Whyte's Hippodrome was avidly documented by the press. On 17 May 1837 – just days before the first race meeting was due to be held – *The Times* carried a feature on the new race-course, stating:

> The design of the Hippodrome is, as its name almost implies, to pre-sent the inhabitants of the metropolis with a facility of pursuing any sort of equestrian exercise. In the centre of the ground is a hill appropriated to pedestrians, on which about 30,000 persons may stand; this is parted off by a circular railing, that they may enjoy the view of the sports and exercises around them, without running any risk of contact with the horses. Without this railing is a broad circle for gentlemen and ladies who ride on horseback, either for private exercise or for the sake of witnessing the sports in the outer circles. The next circle is a race-course, and beyond that is a further circle for the purpose of a steeple-chase, fitted with all the necessary obstacles of hedges and ditches, that the lovers of this hazardous diversion may enjoy those risks which are its peculiar characteristics.

Delighted with the press publicity, John Whyte made plans to ensure that the Hippodrome attracted the cream of London society to its first race meeting, which he had set for 3 June. He prowled the London clubs recruiting VIPs for the inaugural event and managed to secure fashionable patronage via the influential socialite Compte D'Orsay, and equestrian backing from Henry Scudamore-Stanhope, the 9th Earl of Chesterfield – a keen horseman. John Whyte's pub-licity campaign and the creation of the new racecourse had been brilliantly executed.

However, he had overlooked one crucial factor – the popular public footpath leading to Kensal Green ran right through the Hippodrome. The inhabitants of Notting Hill and Kensington Gravel Pits had been aware of the fact that their footpath ran straight through the new racecourse for some time. At first, they assumed that John

Whyte was unaware of the path's popularity and trusted that he would lay out the course in such a way as to avoid the ancient right of way. However, it soon became apparent that both the track and the spectators' enclosure stretched right across the footpath.

The villagers' appeals to John Whyte ended in frustration when it became clear that he could not care less about the inconvenience he was causing, so a delegation angrily made their way to Kensington Vestry (the forerunner of the local council), where they exasperatedly explained their plight to the chairman. Knowing full well that the footpath had been in use for longer than anyone could remember, the vestry wrote to Whyte, demanding he remove all obstacles immediately and fining him 40s for obstructing a public right of way. Their letter was totally ignored.

John Whyte's high-handed attitude towards the people of Notting Hill blighted the first race meeting at the Hippodrome. The publicity campaign he had unleashed in the gentlemen's clubs of Mayfair and the coffee bars of the city paid off handsomely, and on the morning of 3 June 1837 the Uxbridge Road was crowded with the shining coaches of some of London's wealthiest and most fashionable inhabitants. However, as the carriages neared the entrance to the Hippodrome, they were forced to run the gauntlet of a band of angry locals, volubly protesting about the unlawful obstruction of their footpath.

By this stage, it had become clear that John Whyte had absolutely no intention of opening up the right of way, regardless of how much money he was fined by the Kensington Vestry. To add insult to injury, he had made the footpath impassable by dumping all manner of detritus along its route. Thus, any villager wishing to assert his or her right to use it would be forced on to the racecourse and could thus be accused of trespassing. This incensed the locals, and the fiery dispute quickly turned into a class war, with the ordinary people of Notting Hill on one side and Whyte and his aristocratic cronies on the other.

A few days after the first race meeting, another delegation marched to Kensington Vestry and demanded that the authorities put more pressure on Whyte to open up the footpath, but – possibly due to pressure from the influential racecourse patrons – the chairman dithered.

This incensed the villagers even more. Mr Hanson, a local lawyer, demanded to know why a summons had not yet been issued to John Whyte and, after consultation with some sympathetic magistrates, Mr Griffiths, the parish surveyor, assembled a team of vestry staff, constables and local residents with the express intention of reclaiming the footpath once and for all.

On Saturday, 17 June, Griffiths and his men armed themselves with picks and shovels, marched to the Hippodrome entrance and proceeded to dig out the former course of the footpath, removing any obstacle that happened to be in their way. A furious John Whyte appeared on horseback and demanded that the gang stop what they were doing, but the men ignored him and calmly carried on with their work. Once the footpath had been re-dug, the men made their way to the top of the hill and gave three deafening cheers for their victory.

Sadly, the triumph proved to be short-lived. As soon as Mr Griffiths and his men had left the Hippodrome site, John Whyte began blocking the footpath again. However, their actions did force Kensington Vestry to reconsider the matter. On 22 June, the access rights to the footpath were argued at Kensington Petty Sessions. John Whyte did not bother to turn up, sending his lawyer, John Duncan, in his place. As Duncan spoke on behalf of his client, it quickly became clear that even if Whyte was breaching local by-laws, he still would not open the footpath and have his high-class race meetings sullied by the presence of the local hoi polloi. However, he *was* prepared to build a bridge over the racecourse so the locals could get across to Kensal Green while remaining a safe distance away from the lords and ladies.

Had Whyte offered this compromise from the outset, there was a strong possibility that the local people would have accepted it. However, by now, his staggering hubris had angered them so much that they rejected the offer out of hand. With both camps in a state of deadlock, the case was adjourned.

A few days after the court hearing, John Whyte appealed for a bill to be passed through Parliament allowing him to divert the footpath once and for all. Realising that if the bill was passed, Whyte would effectively win the dispute, the people of Notting Hill resorted to underhand tactics.

Knowing that a few race meetings were scheduled to take place at the Hippodrome in July, the protestors covertly recruited spies, who were instructed to attend the races and report back on any breaches of regulations they witnessed. The results were encouraging – the spies noted that, on each race day, numerous people set up unlicensed booths inside the Hippodrome from which they sold beer. They also spotted several prostitutes offering their services and, after talking to some of the racegoers, discovered that pickpockets were at large. Realising that the Hippodrome could now be portrayed as a den of vice, the protestors drew up a petition for its closure, which read:

1   [The Hippodrome should be closed] Because it is situate only two miles from the end of Oxford-street and collects immense crowds of the idle and dissolute, who have no honest means of subsistence and who live from day to day by robbery and pillage.

2   Because the frequency of these races keeps up a perpetual agitation and excitement and is totally unlike the meetings at Ascot or Epsom, which take place only in the spring and autumn.

3   Because it is a serious interruption to walking and travelling on the Uxbridge Road, the line of communication with Southall, Portman and Smithfield Markets, and thronged with droves of cattle, sheep, pigs, etc., with carts of hay straw, etc.

4   Because it affords a convenient 'plucking ground' for the gamblers of the metropolis to practise their tricks on the young and unwary.

5   Because it is a serious injury to the peace and safety of the surrounding inhabitants, by corrupting their children and servants and by rendering their workmen dissolute and idle.

6   Because it interrupts the business of the honest tradesman, by preventing a safe and easy access to their shops and by exposing them to numberless frauds and impositions.

7   Because it is a serious injury to the numerous and respectable
    establishments for young ladies in this neighbourhood who are thus
    prevented from taking their accustomed walks in the fields and in
    Kensington Gardens.

8   Because it is injurious to the neighbourhood by destroying the peace
    and privacy which are essential to a spot where so many invalids are
    sent for the benefit of the air.

9   Because it has greatly multiplied the beer shops and gin shops in
    the neighbourhood and diffused drunkenness and depravity and
    Sabbath-breaking to a frightful extent.

10 Because it occasions perpetual conflicts between the police and
    the people.

11 Because it is totally contrary in its influence and effects, to the
    public walks in the parks, etc. for the innocent recreation of the
    people, by tempting them to sports destructive of industry and
    virtue and by deluding them into scenes of gaming and debauchery.

This petition was distributed to the press, who quickly saw the commercial value of publicising this battle of 'the gentry versus the people'. Thus, by spring 1838 the local dispute had grown into a national news story and, to John Whyte's dismay, the papers backed the protestors. That March, *The Times* published a leader article on the dispute, stating:

Had the Hippodrome proved ... a place where manly, healthy and innocent sports might be more conveniently pursued than in riding-schools, tennis-courts, or fencing-rooms, it would have had our praise, not our censure; but now that after a sufficiently long trial it has been found to be, as it must always be while its races are kept up, a rendezvous for the lowest thieves and vagabonds of the metropolis, we do not see how any respectable man can continue to countenance it.

John Whyte replied to the accusations in the press by denouncing them as complete fabrications. In response, *The Times* challenged him to prove them wrong and demanded he invite one of their reporters to the next race meeting so he could see for himself what iniquitous delights lay behind the high fences surrounding the Hippodrome.

Whyte did not reply to their challenge, and instead concentrated on pushing his Bill to get the footpath diverted through Parliament. His efforts were unsuccessful and with satisfying irony, he was forced to alter the route of the racecourse. This he reluctantly did, raising money for the work by dividing the Hippodrome site into 5,000 individual parcels of land, for which he sold 'proprietorships' at £10 each.

By the closing months of 1838, the footpath had been reinstated, although the stunning views across the countryside were now obscured by ugly metal fencing, erected by the vindictive Hippodrome Committee. To drive their point home, the committee placed advertisements in the press stating:

> The HIPPODROME, Bayswater, near Hyde Park – RACES will take place here on Thursday the 26th and Saturday 28th July, when neither expense nor trouble will be spared by the proprietor to render these national sports worthy of the distinguished patronage they have hitherto received. A first rate band will be in attendance and the footpath is now secured by iron palisades so as to prevent the intrusion of improper characters among the company. Signed, the Earl of Chesterfield and Count D'Orsay.

However, despite the best efforts of John Whyte to keep the Hippodrome running in the face of adversity, his racecourse was ultimately doomed to failure.

His nemesis came in an unexpected form. As Whyte began to schedule his July meetings, he was dismayed to find that many jockeys and trainers turned down the offer to race. Further investigation revealed that this was not due to the bad publicity suffered by the Hippodrome. Rather, it was because they considered the course to be extremely dangerous. The heavy London clay baked hard in the summer sun and, during storms, the rain streamed down the hill on to the steeplechase course, creating a wet bog. Both terrains were considered hazardous for the horses and some jockeys were so appalled by the state of the course that they called for the Society for the Prevention of Cruelty to Animals to examine the racetrack.

The beleaguered John Whyte responded to their concerns by treating the course with tan, which he assured would give riders the sensation of 'riding on a Turkey carpet'. The jockeys remained unconvinced and continued with their boycott.

The Hippodrome struggled on for two more seasons, but its problems left John Whyte mentally exhausted and financially restricted. In 1840, he offloaded the lease to John Duncan, his faithful solicitor, and the last race at the Hippodrome was run on 4 June 1841.

Although the Hippodrome racecourse had been an unmitigated disaster for John Whyte, it had served its purpose for James Weller Ladbroke. During the racecourse's brief life the London property market had begun to recover and, by the time Whyte sold his interest in the Notting Hill land to solicitor John Duncan, James Weller Ladbroke was keen to start building again.

However, he had learned valuable lessons from his first foray into property development and this time he eschewed any fanciful ideas about creating a rival to Regent's Park. Instead, Ladbroke resolved to create an upmarket estate at the top of Notting Hill, with smaller, middle-class homes on its lower slopes. This was undoubtedly a sensible idea. However, Ladbroke once again showed his naivety by allowing the project to be driven by John Duncan – a man who may have been skilled in the profession of law, but knew precious little about property development.

By the time he took over John Whyte's lease, John Duncan was 35 and a partner in Roy, Blunt, Duncan & Johnstone – a thriving law practice with offices in Westminster and the City. His work brought him into contact with many, hugely wealthy clients, several of whom had made their fortunes from property development. Envious of their success, Duncan resolved to grab a slice of the lucrative real estate market for himself and, when he learned that John Whyte planned to sell the Hippodrome site, he saw his chance.

Taking a £6,000 loan from one of his clients, the Westminster Bank, he bought out Whyte. He took on the remaining years of the lease, along with a debt of £8,200 owed to a builder named William Chadwick, who had helped create the Hippodrome back in 1836 but had never got paid due to Whyte's trials and tribulations.

At this point, John Duncan made the first of many errors that would eventually lead to ruin. Firstly, he blithely agreed to pay the Westminster Bank loan back within six months – a ridiculously short amount of time. Secondly, he persuaded his business partner, Richard Roy, to underwrite the loan, thus giving him first charge on the estate. Thirdly, he signed over the eastern half of the Hippodrome to Jacob Connop, a developer with a very dubious reputation.

With the leases secured, Duncan and Connop met with James Weller Ladbroke to obtain building leases. Mindful that, this time, he wanted to make some serious profit, Ladbroke drove a hard bargain and insisted that the men agree to spend £100,000 (an astronomical sum at the time) over the following twenty years on development of the site. Connop agreed to build up to 350 houses on his land, while Duncan was obliged to erect up to 250 properties. As he had done with the previous developers, James Weller Ladbroke set the ground rents at a manageable level for the first five years, but warned that they would rise considerably each following year to induce swift completion of the work.

After securing the building leases, work on John Duncan's half of the estate began. At first, he concentrated his attention on the original road that Thomas Allason had proposed to run northwards from the Uxbridge Road, over the crest of the hill where Notting Hill Farm had once stood. Naming the new road Ladbroke Grove, Duncan leased twenty building plots to Mark Markwick, a speculator from Worthing, who contracted builder John Jay to construct in carcass a range of ten spacious houses at a cost of £1,000 each. The plan was to borrow more money once the carcasses were complete, but construction costs spiralled and, by the time John Jay had completed the fifth carcass, the entire budget had been spent.

Over on the eastern side of the Ladbroke estate the situation was even worse, as it quickly became apparent that Jacob Connop was nothing more than a con artist. As soon as he secured the building leases from James Weller Ladbroke, Connop released details of his proposed development to the press in a bid to attract funding.

The details of the estate were impressive. Connop announced that he planned to convert the western part of the racecourse into a stud farm, while to the east, he would build a series of 'Italian villages' – small, private estates of grand houses built in Italianate style, set around squares and the communal 'paddocks' suggested by Thomas Allason in the original plans. The elaborate proposals were well received by investors, but instead of ploughing the raised funds into the development, much of the money went straight into Jacob Connop's pocket.

Building work progressed at a snail's pace and by the closing months of 1843 the investors were impatiently demanding to see a return on their money. Rapidly running out of excuses, Jacob Connop fled London. He was eventually tracked down by the authorities in December 1844, hiding in lodgings belonging to one of the Knights of Windsor Castle. When constables tried to detain him, Connop protested that, according to an ancient law, he could not be arrested in property belonging to a knight. The constables disagreed and he was taken to Reading Gaol to await his appearance in the debtors' court.

Jacob Connop's court appearance was set for 18 January 1845. As the disgraced developer stood in the dock, the clerk gravely announced that he owed over £36,000 and that most of the debt had been incurred through the development at Notting Hill. The court declared Connop bankrupt and what remained of his assets were seized. Auctioneer Frederick Chinook was instructed to sell off the few properties on the Ladbroke estate that had actually been completed, and the stud farm was handed back to a despairing James Weller Ladbroke.

With his plans derailed once again, Ladbroke abandoned all hope of creating the Elysium he had once envisaged at Notting Hill. He died in 1847 at his home in Petworth, Sussex, having only seen a small portion of his doomed plans realised.

Interestingly, his last will and testament revealed his changing state of mind as the saga of the Notting Hill estate unfolded. When he first drew up his will, soon after inheriting the estate, Ladbroke had stipulated that his burial should be almost theatrical in its bombast. Pallbearers were to be dressed in white smock frocks, complete with black worsted stockings and black bands around their hats, as they solemnly conveyed the elaborate coffin to its final resting place. Shortly before he died, Ladbroke changed this request, stating that he should be buried 'in the plainest manner, as a perfect pauper'.

Following James Weller Ladbroke's death, the Notting Hill estate was inherited by his cousin, Felix. Not having been involved in the events of the previous twenty-five years, Felix Ladbroke had the energy and enthusiasm to resume development of the land.

By the time he died in November 1869, the majority of the estate was complete, but as the builders finished their work at the top of the hill, the land surrounding its lower slopes was rapidly becoming one of the worst slums in London. Ignored by the authorities, and inhabited by some of the city's most deprived citizens, a small shanty town at the base of the hill, originally no more than a handful of acres in size, slowly and silently spread across the surrounding landscape, paving the way for unimaginable horrors and hardships that prevailed well into the twentieth century.

3

THE SLOUGH OF LOATHSOME ABOMINATIONS

*E*ven before James Weller Ladbroke inherited the doomed estate at Notting Hill, a series of changes were taking place along the western edge of his land that would play a large part in its eventual downfall. The problems began during the early years of the 1800s, when a man named Arthur Lake arrived in the district looking for land to rent as business premises. Unfortunately, the trade in which Mr Lake was engaged was the most antisocial in London.

By the time he arrived in Notting Hill, Arthur Lake was proprietor of a successful firm that provided two essential services for the people of London – keeping their chimneys clear of soot and their latrines free from sewage. The latter task was performed by a group of workers known as 'night men', so named because they performed their onerous duties under cover of darkness. Their job was arguably the worst in the capital.

In the days before Joseph Bazalgette laid his revolutionary sewer system beneath the streets, Londoners' waste was collected in thousands of cesspits, which had to be cleared by hand. The wealthiest families had their own cesspit, which was usually situated in their back garden (although some were inside the house). However, the majority of properties, particularly those in more overcrowded districts, shared a cesspit with several of their neighbours. In the poorest areas, it was not uncommon for one pit to be used by ten or more households.

Arthur Lake and his men operated in the St Pancras district, where they were responsible for sixty large cesspits. The sheer amount of sewage deposited in these stinking holes kept the men busy every night of the year – a labour study conducted in the early 1840s revealed that Lake's contractors removed 360 cartloads of sewage annually.

The men worked in teams of four that comprised a 'hole man', a 'rope man' and two 'tub men', all of whom had specific tasks to perform. Each night, they would leave the yard on their rounds, armed with a list of cesspits that required emptying. On arrival at a property, they would first set about removing the flagstones that covered the pit. Often, particularly in poorer neighbourhoods, cesspits would not be emptied for weeks and thus, they could be full to overflowing when the night men finally arrived.

Once the cover had been lifted, the tub men would repeatedly dip buckets into the slurry and then carry them on poles to the cart,

where the revolting contents were tipped into a larger tub. This part
of the job had to be done with great care to prevent spillage, especially if the buckets had to be carried through the house. Once the
reachable contents had been emptied, the most noxious part of the
night men's job began. A ladder was lowered into the cesspit and
the hole man climbed down into the filth and began stirring it up.
Once it was loose enough to move, he shovelled it into the buckets,
which the rope man hauled up to the surface to be carried away by
the tub men.

Despite the awful nature of their job, the night men made the
most of the work, taking regular nips of gin from a bottle tradition-
ally left by the cesspit owner to help deaden their senses. During the
1840s, the journalist Henry Mayhew accompanied a team of night
men on their rounds and wrote about the experience in the *Morning
Chronicle* newspaper. His observations give a fascinating insight into
this most terrible of professions:

> Large horn lanterns (for the night was dark, though at intervals the
> stars shone brilliantly) were placed at the edges of the cesspool. Two
> poles also were temporarily fixed in the ground, to which lanterns
> were hung, but this is not always the case. The work went rapidly on,
> with little noise and no confusion.
>
> The scene was peculiar enough, the artificial light, shining into
> the dark, filthy-looking cavern or cesspool, threw the adjacent houses
> into a deep shade. All around was perfectly still, and there was not an
> incident to interrupt the labour, except that at one time the window
> of a neighbouring house was thrown up, a night-capped head was
> protruded and then down was banged the sash with an impatient
> curse. It appeared as if a gentleman's slumbers had been disturbed,
> though the nightmen laughed and declared it was a lady's voice!
> The smell, although the air was frosty, was for some time, perhaps
> ten minutes, literally sickening; after that period the chief sensation
> experienced was a slight headache; the unpleasantness of the odour
> still continuing, though without any sickening effect. The night-
> men, however, pronounced the stench 'nothing at all'; and one even
> declared it was refreshing!

In addition to clearing St Pancras' sewage, Arthur Lake also ran a team of chimney sweeps. Although the sweep's job was a little less noxious than the night man's, it was more dangerous, especially for the 'climbing boys' who had to crawl into flues, sometimes no more than 7in wide, in order to dislodge stubborn soot and other obstructions such as dead birds.

The use of children to sweep chimneys had been fraught with controversy for decades. As London became more overcrowded in the 1700s, houses – and their chimneys – got smaller, and reports surfaced of climbing boys becoming stuck in flues where they suffered terrible injuries or suffocated. Consequently, many climbing boys (and girls, for they too were occasionally used) became terrified of entering smaller chimneys for fear they would never get out again. Frustrated, their masters adopted barbarous tactics in order to force the frightened children up the flues. Often, a second child would be sent up behind them, charged with sticking pins in their feet to keep them moving. Some sweeps even lit straw in the hearth below, forcing the climbing boys to scramble quickly to get away from the heat and acrid smoke.

As if the claustrophobic nightmare of climbing into tiny chimneys was not enough, the climbing boys faced the additional danger of contracting 'chimney sweep's carcinoma' – a deadly skin cancer caused by carcinogens in the soot. Because clothes could easily become caught in the sharp angles of the flues, many climbing boys went up the chimneys naked. As a result, their bodies became covered with grazes, into which soot became embedded. Once under the skin, the soot caused horrendous sores on the boys' thighs, knees and elbows, but more worryingly, if it got embedded in the scrotum, the sores it produced could, once the child reached puberty, rapidly become cancerous. Few climbing boys who contracted chimney sweeps' carcinoma survived for more than a year.

Understandably, the horrendous conditions suffered by the climbing boys and girls meant that the sweep would rarely contemplate sending his own offspring up the chimneys. Instead, children as young as 5 were procured from the local workhouse or 'rented out' by impoverished families who, in their desperation for food, were forced to ignore the horror stories and hope their child would return to them unscathed. Unsurprisingly, the sweeps developed a fearsome reputa-tion – until the latter part of the 1800s, parents would deter children from wandering off on their own by warning, 'the sweeps will get you'.

The horrifying combination of the risk of death through suffo-cation or cancer, and the blatant exploitation of children from the poorest sector of society, finally prompted Jonas Hanway MP (who, incidentally, was also the man credited with introducing the umbrella to London's streets) to bring a Bill to Parliament calling for climbing boys to be banned. Unfortunately, only a watered down version of the Bill was actually passed and climbing boys and girls continued to be forced up London's chimneys until 1875, when the enforced registra-tion of sweeps finally meant that legal restrictions on their working practices could be effectively enforced.

Although the sad plight of his climbing boys would, perhaps, have caused concern among Arthur Lake's neighbours, and the rumbling of the night men's carts would undoubtedly have been an annoyance to anyone living nearby, neither of these were the catalyst for his move to Notting Hill. The real reason for his relocation lay in his back yard.

Since the late 1700s, Arthur Lake had operated his business from a site in John Street, behind Tottenham Court Road. At the time he moved into the premises, the location of the site had been perfect. The properties he served in St Pancras were just a short cart ride away and the resulting loads of soot and sewage could be stored in a large yard overlooking fields, from which it was sold to market gardeners and farmers who used the sewage as manure and the soot as a pes-ticide. The mess and stench emanating from the yard caused few problems as the adjacent land was unoccupied.

However, by the early 1800s, the inexorable spread of London had reached John Street. As ranges of tall town houses and shops sprang up around him, Arthur Lake found himself under increasing pressure to move his noxious yard somewhere less populous. Wary of moving too close to his coveted clients in St Pancras and unable to move north due to the proximity of the royal park at Marylebone, he was forced to look westwards. The site he chose lay by the side of Green's Lane, which of course ran along the western perimeter of the Ladbroke estate.

At first, Arthur Lake's new yard caused few problems in Notting Hill as his noxious sewage and soot carts joined the constant parade of builders' vehicles up and down the Uxbridge Road. However, as so often happens, the presence of his malodorous premises quickly attracted other unpleasant businesses to Green's Lane. The first to arrive was a man named Stephens, who was engaged in the unsavoury occupation of making bowstrings from catgut, a natural fibre found in the walls of animal intestines. Before long, the stench of Lake's sewage yard was enhanced by the stomach churning smell of Stephens' rotting offal. This choking atmosphere was made even worse when Stephens decided to diversify into pig keeping a few years later.

Stephens' decision to rear pigs proved catastrophic for Green's Lane and the area that surrounded it. On hearing of his activities, an entire community of pig keepers, who were about to be ousted from their previous settlement near Marble Arch by developers, moved to the lane in the 1820s and the fields adjoining James Weller Ladbroke's estate were filled with jerry-built sties to house the animals. The little rural cart track that led through the centre of this porcine ghetto rapidly descended into a morass of mud mixed with animal sewage. No doubt James Weller Ladbroke initially hoped that once his grand estate took off, the pig keepers would be driven out by pressure from developers, just as they had from Marble Arch. In the event, the opposite happened and, while Ladbroke's grand houses failed to materialise, more pig keepers kept arriving.

Green's Lane deteriorated even further when Ladbroke's builder, Ralph Adams, opened his brickfield there around 1826. The site was rapidly populated by a motley collection of labourers so unruly that, according to an elderly resident of Notting Hill, they made the pig keepers look respectable.

By the end of the 1820s, the little cart track on the lower slopes of Notting Hill had become so notorious that it was unofficially renamed 'Cut-throat Lane'. Few non-residents dared to go there, especially after dark. Indeed, a local woman who was interviewed in 1858 recalled:

> Once … I happened to be out late in the evening and had to go
> through Cut-throat Lane just as it was getting dark; I heard some
> people coming along, fighting and swearing and I was so frightened
> I got down into the bottom of one of the ruts, and there I stopped till
> they had gone.

In 1830, the hostile atmosphere of Cut-throat Lane attracted the
attention of a notorious showman named Samuel Wedgebury, who
decided to exploit its notorious reputation by opening a pit for animal
baiting and dogfights there. The pit was vociferously denounced by
several animal welfare groups, who volubly protested that Wedgebury
had only recently been released from prison having been found guilty
of organising illegal fights in another pit at Green Dragon Yard in
Holborn. However, the pig keepers and brickfield labourers welcomed its arrival, as it provided them with some exciting weekend
entertainment. Some even purchased vicious dogs to enter into the
fights and these snarling creatures served to make Cut-throat Lane
even more forbidding to the more genteel residents of Notting Hill.

By 1833, Green's Lane had become a sizeable shanty town of poorly
constructed shacks interspersed with stinking pig sties. In the centre of
the ghetto lay 'the Ocean', a field that had been so totally consumed
with slurry that it resembled a vast expanse of water. Close by, Ralph
Adams' muddy brickfield had grown so dominant that the whole
locality became known as 'the Potteries'. This name was to become synonymous with chronic want, and all the evils that poverty can bring.

In the summer of 1849, residents of the Potteries began to experience profuse diarrhoea and sickness. At first it was hoped that the illness
would pass, but as more people succumbed, it became clear that the
area was in the grip of a cholera epidemic. Today, it is universally understood that cholera is primarily spread by drinking water contaminated
with the faeces of an infected person. However, back in the mid-1800s,
it was thought that the disease was carried in bad smells that wafted
through the air. The fact that the epidemic had broken out in an area
full of pigsties compounded this theory, and blame for the epidemic
was laid squarely on the local pig keepers. Suddenly, the very livelihood
of the majority of the Potteries' residents was under threat.

In October 1849, while the slum was still in the grip of the epidemic, Mr C.M. Frost, medical officer for the district, visited the Potteries and was shocked at what he found. There were at least sixty families living in the shanty town whose living depended solely on pig keeping. Frost estimated that there were up to 900 pigs in the area at any one time and counted thirty-eight in just one tiny back yard.

Frustratingly, Frost also unwittingly uncovered the root of the cholera problem during his visit, but failed to recognise it as such. Buried in his report was a quick reference to the fact that the sole source of clean drinking water was an ancient well that stood some distance away from the settlement, in the middle of a field. With the benefit of modern knowledge, it seems highly likely that the local inhabitants would often resort to drinking dirty water, rather than trudge some distance to the well. However, believing the disease to be airborne, Frost ignored the remoteness of the water source and recommended to the local magistrates that all the pigs be removed from the area. In addition, he more helpfully recommended that the notorious Ocean be filled in and not allowed to get into the same state in the future.

Frost's recommendations infuriated the inhabitants of the Potteries. They pleaded with the magistrates that if they removed their pigs, they would simultaneously take away their sole means of income. With regard to the Ocean, they complained that they had applied to the sewer commissioners to improve the drainage and water supply but had repeatedly been ignored.

The residents' passionate argument put the magistrates in a difficult situation. On one hand they were convinced that the pigs were the cause of the cholera outbreak, but on the other, they realised that their removal would cause many families to fall into destitution. Unable to work out the best course of action, they ordered that the pigs should be removed, but only until the cholera epidemic had subsided. This ill-conceived compromise unsurprisingly had no effect whatsoever.

In 1850, shortly after becoming 'conductor' of a new, weekly magazine called *Household Words*, Charles Dickens – always a champion of London's poor – published an article on the Potteries. It made uncomfortable reading for the magistrates, who had hoped that their

order to temporarily remove the pigs would prompt the neighbourhood to drift back into obscurity. The article stated:

> In a neighbourhood studded thickly with elegant villas and man-
> sions, viz., Bayswater and Notting Hill, in the parish of Kensington,
> is a plague spot, scarcely equalled for its insalubrity by any other
> in London; it is called the Potteries. It comprises some seven or
> eight acres, with about two hundred and sixty houses (if the term
> can be applied to such hovels), and a population of nine hundred
> or one thousand. The occupation of the inhabitants is principally
> pig fattening. Many hundreds of pigs, ducks and fowls are kept in
> an incredible state of filth. Dogs abound, for the purpose of guard-
> ing the swine. The atmosphere is still further polluted by the process
> of fat boiling. In these hovels, discontent, dirt, filth and misery are
> unsurpassed by anything known even in Ireland. Water is supplied
> to only a small number of the houses. There are foul ditches, open
> sewers and defective drains, smelling most offensively, and generat-
> ing large quantities of poisonous gases … Nearly all the inhabitants
> look unhealthy; the women especially complain of sickness and want
> of appetite, their eyes are sunken and their skin shrivelled.

Three years after *Household Words* published their damning article
on the Potteries, Mr Frost, the medical officer, revisited the district,
accompanied by Dr Milroy of the Metropolitan Board of Health.
Nothing had changed, and Milroy described the area as:

> … one large slough of loathsome abominations – revolting alike to
> sight and smell, and most fatally pernicious to health.
>   At the time of my visit last week, the roads and streets were no
> better than long tracts of black putrescent slush, with pools of foul,
> stagnant water in different parts … To cross one side [of the road] to
> the other without getting ankle deep in stinking mire was impossible.

Although outsiders were appalled at what they found at the Potteries,
the inhabitants dared not complain lest the authorities should decide
to take away their pigs again. Not that the animals provided them with

anything approaching a decent standard of living. Rather, the human residents of the Potteries subsisted on a diet that was little better than that of their livestock.

A female resident of the slum, who spoke to social activist Mary Bayly in the late 1850s, told her:

> We most of us keep a horse, or a donkey and cart, and we go round early in the morning to the gentle-folks' houses, and collect the refuse from the kitchens. When we comes home, we sorts it out; the best of it we eats ourselves or sells it to a neighbour, the fat is all boiled down, and the rest we gives to the pigs.

The summer represented lean times for the people of the Potteries as the suppliers of their free food often went away. Bayly's interviewee told her, 'When the families goes out of town, the servants is put upon board wages and they scrimps and saves everything; we ain't wanted to call then 'cause there's not a scrap left for us.'

By the mid-1800s, the Potteries had become one of the most deprived and disease-ridden districts in London. While the average age of death in the metropolis was 37, in the Potteries, it was just 12 years. This statistic took into account the high rate of infant mortality in the district – a devastating effect of poverty that was witnessed in all its gut-wrenching horror by Mary Bayly.

Disgusted by the lack of care available for babies and young children in the Potteries, she set up a local Mothers' Society in the early 1850s. Members benefited from access to basic healthcare and could call on the society should they, or their children, become ill. This inevitably took Mary Bayly into some of the worst homes in the area. She later remembered one particularly harrowing experience that, to modern sensibilities, seems inconceivable:

> In a small bedroom on the top floor [of one of the cottages] I found one morning, that a woman and child had died [of cholera] in the night and another woman in the same room, though still alive, appeared in a dying state. I shudder when I think of that room; no pen can describe its horrors.

The room in which the women lay was partitioned off and consequently had no windows. In a desperate bid to get some ventilation
into the fetid atmosphere, Bayly frantically loosened some bricks
and pulled them out of the back wall, but her efforts were in vain.
The dying woman succumbed later that day.

The workers at Adams' brickfield (many of whom also lived in the
Potteries) fared little better than their pig-farming neighbours. In order
to make enough money to pay the weekly average of 7s rent on a hovel
in the neighbourhood, the men had to work up to sixteen hours a day,
seven days a week. One of the brick makers spoke to Mary Bayly about
his working conditions and made the following sad observation:

> You know, ma'am, when we working men look at all these fine houses
> and gardens about, and see all the fine furniture that goes into them,
> we know that it is all done by our labour, and that the great people
> couldn't do without us, any more than we could do without them. And
> it do seem to me, the world would be a good deal happier, and better
> too, than it is, if we felt that sort of thing to one another; felt, I mean,
> that we were all wanted, like, to make the world go on right.

Although the horrific conditions in the Potteries were well publicised,
it did not stop some foolhardy builders succumbing to the temptation
to develop the cheap land on Notting Hill's lower slopes. By 1850,
several new streets had been laid out to the north of Cut-throat Lane,
on the eastern edge of the brickfield.

This new development was designed to serve the lavish houses at
the top of the hill and comprised two types of property. The streets
nearest to the hill were lined with small but elegant homes, liberally
interspersed with shops. To the west of these distinctly middle-class
streets, a small cluster of terraced cottages were hastily thrown up.
These buildings, which were designed to house servants such as
grooms and gardeners, quickly became almost uninhabitable. Many
of them had been carelessly erected below the level of the road
and, thus, water drained towards them instead of away from them.
Consequently, the permanently clammy walls developed a thick
layer of black mould, while an ever-present smell of damp mingled

intermittently with the powerful aroma of raw sewage as it rushed down the slopes of the piggeries during wet weather.

As the Potteries ghetto festered, the homes and shops on its perimeter unsurprisingly failed to attract the middle-class families for which they had been built. Desperate to recoup their costs, the builders of these ill-conceived properties had no option but to carve them up and let them on a room-by-room basis to poor local inhabitants. Soon, the genteel, airy parlours became makeshift bedsits accommodating entire families forced to share facilities such as kitchens and WCs with many others.

This mass of entirely unsuitable housing stock was destined to blight the lower slopes of Notting Hill for generations and, as the authorities studiously ignored the problems, the situation grew pro-gressively worse. In 1864, the Hammersmith & City Railway opened a station in the fields to the north of Notting Hill. With the city now within easy reach, it was hoped that the middle-class houses at the bottom of the hill might at last be taken by the clerks and shopkeepers for whom they had been designed.

Sadly, it was not to be. The railway company offered cheap work-men's fares on the trains, and thus lured even more poorly paid artisans and labourers to the area along with more migrants who, like the pig farmers forty years previously, had been cast out of their previous homes by developers. By the end of the 1860s, the Potteries had spread eastwards around the foot of the hill and a new raft of poorly built ter-races had been thrown up to house displaced slum dwellers from the inner city rookeries of St Giles and a notorious den of iniquity known as Jennings' Buildings, off Kensington High Street. The once rural Green's Lane and its surrounds had now been swallowed up into the ever-expanding metropolis and, although Notting Barn and Portobello Farm still hinted at the area's pastoral heritage, they were now separated from Notting Hill by the iron tracks of the railway.

As urbanisation crept around the slopes of Notting Hill, Ralph Adams' old brickfield gradually shrank as more and more land was sold off to house builders. Keen to obscure the district's notoriety, they quickly renamed the area Notting Dale in a bid to attract a better class of resident. Ironically, the developers inadvertently succeeded where the authorities had failed. Ever since the arrival of the railway, the resident pig farmers had been finding it increasingly difficult to find land on which to keep their swine and, in 1878, they finally moved away to a site further west.

Eleven years later, Kensington Vestry purchased the notorious Ocean, which had contributed so much to the miserable existence of the inhabitants for decades. The site was subsequently drained and covered over to create Avondale Park, in memory of the recently deceased Duke of Clarence and Avondale.

Aptly, the duke after which the park was named also had a notorious past. Shortly before his death, Prince Eddie (as he was commonly known) was rumoured to have been involved in the Cleveland Street Scandal – an infamous case involving a homosexual brothel. Almost 100 years later, these rumours formed the central part of bestselling book, *The Final Solution* by Stephen Knight, which purported to solve the mystery of Jack the Ripper.

Although the pig keepers had moved on, the vestry's acquisition of the Ocean did little to relieve poverty in Notting Dale. In fact, as the nineteenth century drew to a close, conditions in the streets encircling the bottom of Notting Hill worsened. As industries moved out of the centre of London to the suburbs, unemployed labourers and other unskilled workers flooded into the area, as it was one of the few places they could afford to live. Soon, Notting Dale once again found itself the subject of a wave of critical reports.

On 24 January 1893, the *Daily News* published 'A West End Avernus' (or 'gateway to hell'), in which the anonymous reporter wrote of 'whole streets steeped to the lips in iniquity, veritable hotbeds of everything vile and abandoned, and hundreds, if not thousands, of people living under conditions of life that are a foul disgrace to our civilisation'.

The dilapidated cluster of terraces in which Mary Bayly had tended cholera victims in the 1850s had been turned into a seedy collection of common lodging houses and furnished rooms in which prostitutes wiled away their idle hours in the company of hawkers, thieves and professional beggars.

The writer Arthur H. Beavan visited Notting Dale while compiling his book, *Imperial London* (1901), and noted that, although the pigs had long since departed, the stench remained:

Even a casual passer-by cannot fail to be struck by the atmosphere of dirt and idleness that hovers over the place – crowds of loafing men, half-naked women, and unwashed children utterly indifferent to everything but the ease of the moment, with habits worse than those of the beast, and in such a state of filth that the policeman on his beat is often compelled to hold his handkerchief to his nose as he passes.

Embarrassed by the new batch of damning indictments, the Kensington Vestry was finally shamed into making a half-hearted attempt to improve living conditions in Notting Dale. They quickly dispatched their resident medical officer, Dr Dudfield, to the slum with the remit to shut down any houses he considered unfit for human habitation.

Dudfield did as he was instructed, in the process adding to the problem of overcrowding. With nowhere else to go, the residents of the houses he closed were forced to move into even more cramped accommodation in the surrounding streets. Dr Dudfield also conducted a three-year study into death rates in the district. The findings were chilling: 432 out of every 1,000 children born in Notting Dale died before they reached their first birthday. The figure for London as a whole was 161 in every 1,000.

Despite Dr Dudfield's shocking findings, the vestry remained largely indifferent to the myriad problems at Notting Dale. A committee set up to discuss ways in which to improve the dreadful slum came to the popular conclusion that the conditions were the direct result of the 'vicious proclivities and evil habits of the people themselves'. At the same time as the committee were discussing the area, the housing situation at Notting Dale worsened once again as hundreds of navvies employed to dig the subterranean tunnels of the Central London Railway flooded into the area looking for cheap lodgings.

Thankfully for the unfortunate residents of Notting Dale, their days of being governed by Kensington Vestry were numbered. Suspecting that the local inspectors were not acting in the best interests of the slum's destitute inhabitants, the London County Council sent their own inspector to the filthy ghetto. His report completely contradicted that of the vestry committee, stating, 'The condition of rooms such as those found in large numbers in Kensington can by no means be excused on the grounds of the uncleanly habits of the occupants.' A year later, in 1899, the vestry was closed and replaced by Kensington Borough Council.

The new overseers of Notting Dale launched their own enquiry into living conditions and promptly condemned vast swathes of the cheap terraces that had been thrown up in the middle of the century. Mary Bayly's despised slum was demolished and a new council-run estate was built in its place. Completed in 1906, the new estate offered at least some of the residents decent accommodation. However, the higher rents forced others out. They moved further east around the bottom of the hill, settling in more streets that had been optimistically built for middle-class families who never arrived.

As the Notting Dalers moved in, any families who could afford to moved out. Gradually, despite the best efforts of the council, the slum was encircling Notting Hill. In 1911, the district medical officer summed up the problem succinctly, when he explained:

> The housing problem becomes more and more perplexing. Landlords find themselves in a dilemma where the choice lies between receiving the lowest class of tenant and leaving their houses unoccupied. If they elect to take lodgers of doubtful character, their property is knocked about and the rent not paid. On the other hand, if no more than half the tenements in a lodging house are let to persons who pay regularly, and the rest of the house stands empty, legitimate returns on the capital outlay are eaten up by the cost of necessary repairs.

By the outbreak of the First World War, the once tiny slum by the side of Green's Lane had spread right around Notting Hill, from the west to the east, only stopped in its tracks by the wide thoroughfare of the old Uxbridge Road.

The eastern side of the hill had been subject to the greatest change in fortune. Elegant squares and terraces of stucco-fronted houses, originally intended for affluent families, were now home to up to seven households. These buildings were ill-equipped for multiple occupancy: they often had just one toilet and one water tap, both of which were located in the basement. The upper floors had no bathrooms or even sinks, so water had to be carried up and down in buckets that slopped over the stairs and corridors.

Realising that these houses were hopelessly lacking in facilities, the council trialled a conversion of some houses in shabby Powis Square in 1919, creating self-contained bedsits for single people. The project was a resounding success, but the experiment proved to be a one-off. Under pressure, the council issued a statement explaining that in order to create more bedsits like those in Powis Square, they would have to purchase considerable amounts of property from private landlords and 'there are many objections to the local authority of any area becoming property owners on a large scale'. In other words, they did not want the hassle.

While Kensington Borough Council tried to wash its hands of the housing problem, others saw opportunities in the outmoded terraces of Notting Hill. At first, those who took on the dilapidated estates did so with the residents' best interests at heart. In the 1920s many houses in the area were taken over by newly formed housing associations such as the Improved Tenements Association (now the Rowe Housing Trust). Others, such as the Kensington Housing Trust and the Wilsham Housing Trust, not only bought up old properties but also built new ones.

However, despite this, much of the vast slum remained in the hands of private landlords who saw little value in updating the crumbling edifices. During the 1920s the lower slopes of Notting Hill remained distinctly down-at-heel but, although there were problems with prostitution and thievery, the deadly epidemics that had been endured by Notting Dale in the Victorian period had gradually subsided.

During this interwar period, Portobello Market (which had existed since the late 1800s) became one of London's premier street markets when it merged with Bangor Street Rag Fair. Previously, the Rag Fair had supplied the impoverished residents of the Potteries with food, second-hand clothing and a means of disposing of stolen property. However, once it merged with the slightly more genteel market at Portobello Road, the stolen merchandise rapidly disappeared, although the 'rag' element remained.

The author Monica Dickens (who lived in Notting Hill, where her father Henry was a local councillor) recalled in her autobiography:

> Ever since memory, the Portobello Road market has happened on Saturday mornings. In those early days when we ran down for a packet of sherbet … it was still literally a flea market. All along the gutter rickety stalls and barrows were piled high with rags, torn jerseys, mismatched shoes, chipped china, bent tin trays, three legged furniture and malfunctioning appliances from the early days of electricity.

The market formed the epicentre of Notting Hill and was a place where all classes and cultures came together. Wealthier families from the smart stuccoed houses at the top of the hill rubbed shoulders with costermongers from tumbledown shacks in Notting Dale; raucous Irish labourers worked alongside black-hatted Eastern European Jews. It was rumoured that an Irish woman named Rosie, who ran a vegetable stall at Portobello Market, dealt with so many Jewish families that she became fluent in Yiddish.

In his memoirs, the *Daily Express* cartoonist Osbert Lancaster, who lived on Elgin Crescent, described the character of Notting Hill at this time:

> The vast stucco palaces of Kensington Park Road and the adjoining streets had long ago been converted into self-contained flats where an ever increasing stream of refugees from every part of the civilised world had found improvised homes, like the dark age troglodytes who sheltered in the galleries and boxes of the Coliseum. Long, long before the outbreak of war these classical facades had ceased to bear any relevance to the life that was lived behind them; the eminent KC's and the Masters of City companies had already given place to Viennese professors and Indian students and bed-sitter business girls.

Unfortunately, this congenial era was not set to last. By the mid-1930s the market had become the regular haunt of National Socialists, who climbed on to soapboxes where they spat fascist dogma at passers-by and cast all manner of aspersions on the Jewish stallholders. Despite the best attempts of local Labour groups to disrupt their hate-filled diatribes, the National Socialists created quite a following in Notting Hill, until the outbreak of the Second World War brought their activities to an abrupt halt.

RLD
BEST
SUNDAY
PAPER
4
BLACKOUT

*B*ritain's declaration of war on Germany on 3 September 1939 came as no great surprise to the people of Notting Hill. Most realised that dark days lay ahead if negotiations with Germany over their foreign policy broke down. In preparation for the coming storm, plans had been made to evacuate all children from the area to safe havens in the British countryside to protect them from the predicted Luftwaffe bombardment 'of a kind that no other city has ever had to endure'.

On 31 August Notting Hill families' worst fears became reality when the government issued the order to 'evacuate forthwith'. Over the following four days, nearly 3 million children and their guardians (mainly schoolteachers) were moved from areas of Britain under threat from enemy bombing to rural places of safety. At Notting Hill, parents bravely kissed their children goodbye and grimly watched them assemble in the school playground, where they had labels pinned to their jackets bearing their name, address and school. The children then left on coaches headed for Paddington Station where they boarded trains bound for the west of England. Most of them had no real idea of what was happening to them, apart from the fact that they were going on an adventure to the countryside. Neither the children nor their parents knew how long this adventure would last.

The arrival of the Notting Hill evacuees at their destinations caused quite a stir. Most of the locations to which they had been sent were considered 'safe' because they were remote and rural. Thus, the sudden influx of savvy London kids from a myriad of cultures came as quite a shock. Host families were allowed to choose their evacuees and, sadly, an innate sense of tribalism resulted in black and Asian children being the last to be selected – some remembered this rejection for the rest of their lives.

In the event, the mass evacuation was not a great success. Unsurprisingly, the children were enormously homesick and found country life unfamiliar and difficult. Relationships with the families with whom they were billeted were frequently strained and they were often shunned by the local children, who resented their presence.

That said, there were some benefits to country life. Michael Chalkley, who was billeted at a dairy farm in north Wales, became fascinated with the business of milk production and spent hours watching and learning about the process. Jewish children found, to their delight, that Saturday mornings were now entirely their own as synagogues were non-existent in the farming villages of the West Country. As an added bonus, they were also exempt from attending church on Sundays.

As the winter of 1939 closed in and the Luftwaffe failed to appear in the skies over London, many parents began to question why their children were hundreds of miles away. The separation was proving far more difficult to endure than many had predicted and, while the skies remained quiet, it seemed utterly pointless. As Christmas approached, countless families could bear it no longer and went to bring their children home. In London alone, thousands of evacuees had returned by the first weeks of 1940. However, although spring was uneventful on London's streets, the light evenings of summer brought forth a relentless stream of air raids designed to bring the capital to its knees. Notting Hill's close proximity to the West End meant that it was right at the centre of the action.

Although news reports of the raids were banned from being published in the press, detailed accounts of the bombings were written in the diaries of its people. Notting Hill's most diligent chronicler during this troubled period was Vere Hodgson. Vere was 38 when war broke out. She lived alone in rented rooms on Ladbroke Road and was employed as a welfare worker by the Greater World Association Trust at the Sanctuary in nearby Lansdowne Road.

During the war, the trust collected and distributed food and clothing to the city's most needy families, many of whom were to lose what little they owned in bombing raids. It was from her desk while on night-time fire watch at the Sanctuary that Vere wrote her wartime diaries. They were originally intended solely for her cousin Lucy, who had recently moved to Northern Rhodesia, but in time, Vere realised their social importance and published them in book form. There is no doubt that they make fascinating reading. Vere's 'keep calm and carry on' attitude exemplified the remarkable stoicism of Londoners, particularly during the Blitz. Moreover, her diary shows just how disruptive and unsettling the war was for ordinary people.

Due to the relentlessness of the bombing raids during the Blitz, Vere and her neighbours existed in a state of chronic exhaustion, often only managing to sleep in their own beds for an hour or two each night before being disturbed by 'Wailing Winnie', the air-raid siren. The unremitting fatigue was made worse by the constant anxiety of not knowing if the next bomb to fall 'had their name on it'. However, despite this, neither Vere nor her associates ever gave up hope, even in the darkest hours of the Blitz. It was this optimism that kept communities from collapsing during probably the most testing period in London's history.

Vere Hodgson's published diary began on Tuesday, 25 June 1940. That evening, she wrote:

> Last night at about 1 a.m. we had the first air raid of the war on London. My room is just opposite the police station so I got the full benefit of the sirens. It made me leap out of bed halfway across the room. I shook all over, but managed to get into my dressing gown and slippers, put my watch in my pocket, clutch my torch and gas mask and get downstairs first.

Many Londoners assumed that this raid was the start of the much anticipated 'Blitzkrieg' that Hitler had vowed to unleash on the city. However, it proved only to be a precursor. The real Blitz began some weeks later on 7 September and lasted for fifty-seven consecutive nights. During this time, Notting Hill was regularly bombarded. The Luftwaffe assisted the council's slum clearance at the old Potteries and the crumbling mews houses north of Bomore Road and Treadgold Street were all but destroyed in the Blitz. High-explosive bombs also flattened homes in nearby Sirdar Road and Portland Road. Even the old Ocean site was hit twice.

The top of the hill fared little better, with bombs falling on Ladbroke Square, Kensington Park Gardens, Lansdowne and Stanley Crescents, and Lansdowne Road. On Thursday, 26 September 1940, Vere Hodgson wrote:

> Worst night on record! I was aroused at 1.20 a.m. by the whole house shaking to its foundations and terrific explosions rending the air. Slept again but was roused by still more horrible sluicings through

the sky, with bangs, plonks and rumblings. Miss M came down from her room to say there was an incendiary in the garden. We ran to the window and could see one burning in the next garden – ours seemed to have gone out. Really awful to listen to the sounds in the sky. We felt no stone could be left standing on another … On investigation in the morning, we discovered a house in Lansdowne Rd., nine doors from us, was gone inside. The walls were standing but it was burnt-out inside. Walked to Clarendon Cross. Every pane of glass had gone, and several houses down. A pretty bad night! It does not bear enquiring into too much! There seems no end to it.

North of the Ladbroke estate, a parachute mine landed on St Stephen's Gardens, destroying several properties while high-explosive bombs wreaked havoc in St Quintin Avenue, Bassett Road and Oxford and Cambridge Gardens. The destruction in the latter two roads was recorded by Vere on 7 October 1940:

A very nasty one just came down. You could hear it swinging in the air for several seconds and then plonk. The house shook in its socket – though the bomb must have been a mile away. I was beginning to cheer up, but I feel we are in for it tonight.

Vere was right. She wrote two days later of the damage done during the raid:

Five houses were struck at the far end of Lansdowne Road. No wonder we felt it. Some people saved – others buried. All round Oxford and Cambridge Gardens, and Ladbroke Grove Station, houses and shops were down. Also Pembridge Place and Chepstow Villas. Mr Booker [the owner of a café that Vere frequented] told us the story of two men who were told by a policeman to take cover. They walked on and were terribly injured. First Aid parties had to turn out and face the bombs through their foolhardiness.

Like many other Londoners, Vere Hodgson had a morbid fascination with the local bombing raids. After hearing bombs fall on

Notting Hill during the night, she would often go out the following morning to investigate the damage. Perhaps the finding and recording of the bombs gave her a sense of control in what threatened to be a completely overwhelming situation.

On 14 and 15 October 1940 (after a sustained raid) she noted in her diary:

> I tried to trace our bombs, but happily, though many came down near us they nearly all fell in gardens or roads and not on property. Hearing there was an Oil Bomb in Stanley Gardens, I hurried there after lunch. Found the hole – plonk in the middle of the road – grease spread everywhere. Curtains flapping in the air from broken windows.

Vere's fire-watch duties at the Sanctuary meant that she was generally above ground during an air raid. However, she was in a minority. Once the sirens began to scream their warning, the majority of Notting Hill residents took shelter underground. Basements, church crypts and hastily constructed public bunkers dug under parks and garden squares were all used during the Blitz, but by far the most popular shelter in the area was Notting Hill Gate Station.

When the war first began, the government was loath to use tube stations as shelters. Genuine concerns about dangerous overcrowding on platforms, combined with the more fanciful notion that tube inhabitants would develop a 'bunker mentality' and refuse to come out, resulted in the authorities eschewing London Transport's subterranean labyrinth in favour of purpose-built shelters.

However, once the Blitz began, their attitude rapidly changed. During bombing raids, people's main fear – greater than being killed – was being buried alive. The shallow, government-built shelters offered real potential for this fear to be realised. On the other hand, the public considered tube stations to be perfect shelters as they were much deeper underground and the train line running through them offered an alternative escape route should the street exits become blocked. Thus, as the Blitz intensified, the tube became the Londoners' favourite sanctuary.

The popularity of the stations during air raids prompted the London Passenger Transport Board to equip some with basic catering equipment and run 'tube refreshment specials', supplying the makeshift subterranean cafés with food. At Notting Hill Gate, three large 10-gallon boilers were installed to heat up water, and refreshments were served every night between 7 and 9 p.m. The catering staff then slept on pneumatic mattresses in the station so they could rise at 5 a.m. to serve early morning tea.

Soon after the service began, *The Times* sent a 'special correspondent' into one of the stations serving refreshments to describe the scene. He wrote:

> Up and down the platforms, threading their way among the family groups pass young women pleasingly clad in green frocks, with bright red kerchiefs on their heads. Some carry giant teapots from which they serve tea at 1*d* a cup (or you may have cocoa for the same price). Others carry a tray of refreshments – buns and pieces of cake 1*d*; meat pies 1 and a half pence; bars of chocolate 2*d* and packets of biscuits 2*d* … For shelterers the rule is 'Bring your own cup or mug'. Milk is provided for children and babies' bottles are warmed.

Notting Hill Gate Station became so popular as a shelter that, by the end of November 1940, London Transport announced that season tickets would be issued. Under the new scheme, special folding bunks would be installed along the platforms, which would be allocated to regular 'shelterers' so they could get a better night's sleep. In addition, a medical centre was also opened in the station complete with a lady doctor and several nurses.

The refreshments at Notting Hill Gate Station were gratefully received by the area's residents, not least because since January 1940, food and drink had been strictly rationed. To modern appetites, the amount of food available per week seems pitifully small. For example, each adult was allowed 4oz of ham or bacon – the equivalent to one 'quarter-pounder' burger. In theory, an additional pound of red meat could also be consumed but beef and lamb were often in very short supply. Consequently, meals were bulked out with potatoes (which could be grown at home) and dripping from the cooked meats was saved and spread on toast.

Sugar was also strictly rationed – each adult was allowed just 8oz per week – along with tea (2oz) and cheese (2oz). Eggs and imported fruits were particularly scarce and provided inspiration for the title of Vere Hodgson's book, *Few Eggs and No Oranges*. The dearth of eggs gave rise to recipes using 'powdered egg', a heinous ingredient that was literally dehydrated egg ground into a powder. Although the government suggested that powdered egg could be used in exactly the same way as proper eggs, those forced to eat it vehemently begged to differ. In practice, it was only really useable in cakes – wartime diners agreed almost unanimously that dishes such as scrambled egg or omelette made with powdered egg were inedible.

While basic foodstuffs were officially rationed, luxury goods, such as cigarettes and alcohol, were permissible in any quantity, although they were expensive and often in very short supply. The dearth of reasonably priced alcohol caused much worry for London's pubs, bars and restaurants. Already severely compromised by the nightly blackouts and regular air raids, publicans and restaurateurs were desperate to find cheap booze and this gave rise to a hugely lucrative black market. Whisky was a particularly sought after commodity in the underground liquor trade and, by 1945, competition between various suppliers had erupted into gang warfare that spilled out on to the streets of Notting Hill.

On the morning of Thursday, 18 October, a taxicab was found abandoned near Notting Hill Gate Station. Minutes afterwards, the body of its driver was discovered in a fire brigade pump house on Lambeth Bridge. He had been shot through the head and, in a half-hearted attempt to conceal his identity, his registration badge had been ripped from his coat. Police quickly established that the dead man was Frank Everitt, a 56-year-old retired policeman who worked for the London General Cab Company of Brixton Road, but they remained baffled as to why he had been killed. The single gunshot to the head suggested that Mr Everitt had been executed by an experienced hit man, but why would anyone want to kill a taxi driver?

Less than two weeks later, on 1 November, the body of 39-year-old Reuben Martirosoff, otherwise known as 'Russian Robert', was found

on the back seat of his car on a muddy patch of Notting Hill waste-
land. Like Frank Everitt, he had been shot in the head. Damage to
the front of his car suggested it had recently hit something, and blood-
stains found nearby reinforced that theory. In the mud, propped up
against one of the rear wheels, lay a woman's hat.

The police were not altogether surprised to find the body of
Martirosoff. As part owner of a seedy West End drinking club, he had
come to their notice some months before during a covert investigation
into an Eastern European smuggling ring specialising in supplying
contraband liquor. Conversations with their underworld contacts
quickly led them to the Ilford home of Marian Grondkowski and
Henryk Malinowski, two deserters from the Polish Army who were
known to be involved with the smugglers. A subsequent search of
their rooms uncovered several items belonging to Reuben Martirosoff,
along with the revolver that had ended his life.

Grondkowski and Malinowski were duly arrested and taken into
custody, where each man initially swore it was the other who had
committed the murder. Eventually, Malinowski told police what had
really happened: After deserting from the army, he and Grondkowski
became involved in the supply of black market whisky to West End
clubs, where they met Reuben Martirosoff. At first, their venture
went very well but when police cracked down on smuggling at the
docks, the Poles' supply of whisky ran dry. Desperate for money, they
began to dabble in illegal currency dealing but this enterprise failed
to prosper.

By the autumn of 1945, Grondkowski and Malinowski were down
to their last few shillings so they decided to rob their old customer,
Rueben Martirosoff. Telling him they had just received a large con-
signment of whisky, the two Poles arranged to meet their victim at
a deserted bombsite at Notting Hill where they would hand over
the goods for cash. In the meantime, Frank Everitt – who was using
the taxi as cover for his real job as a private detective – got wind of
the whisky deal. The real reason why he was assassinated has never
been ascertained, but it seems likely that Everitt had been hired by
Martirosoff to check whether the Poles' offer was genuine. He was
shot before he could report his findings to his employer.

Having received no warnings from Everitt, Reuben Martirosoff kept his appointment with the Poles at Notting Hill. It was the last journey he was to make. As he was opening the boot of his car to get the money, either Grondkowski or Malinowski coldly shot him in the back of the head. They then bundled his body into the back seat, grabbed the money and made their escape, swerving through the bomb debris of battle-scarred Notting Hill towards their shabby rooms on the other side of the city.

Marian Grondkowski and Henryk Malinowski were brought to trial at the Old Bailey in February 1946. Although Martirosoff's money never came to light, his other possessions, found in the Poles' rooms along with the revolver, were enough to persuade the jury of their guilt. Both were found guilty of murder and sentenced to death. The owner of the hat found by Martirosoff's car was never found.

Although the murders of Frank Everitt and Reuben Martirosoff were shocking, they did not unnerve the people of Notting Hill as much as another series of terrifying wartime murders that had taken place three years before. On 17 February 1942, Vere Hodgson wrote in her diary:

> There seems to be a murderer about killing women in lonely flats – hope he does not settle on me as a likely subject. I walk up the middle of the road and swing my torch around. Dying for one's country is one thing but being murdered by a maniac for your handbag is a very poor ending to life.

Vere was commenting on recent newspaper reports that a serial killer was stalking the dark streets of west London during the nightly blackout. On 9 February 1942, the body of 42-year-old chemist's assistant, Evelyn Hamilton, was found in the corner of an empty air-raid shelter on Montagu Place near Marble Arch. She had been strangled.

Despite combing the murder site, the police found no clue to her assailant, although the pattern of bruises around Evelyn's neck suggested that her killer was left-handed. At first it seemed that the motive for her murder had been robbery, as her handbag containing £80 – a significant amount of money at the time – was missing. With very little to go on, police began making enquiries at Evelyn's place of work to try and establish where she had been going on the night of her murder. However, they had barely made a start when they received the news that another body had been discovered, this time in a seedy Soho bedsit on Wardour Street.

Evelyn Oatley, a 35-year-old prostitute who plied her trade in and around the seedier hotels and drinking clubs off Piccadilly, had presumably trusted her murderer enough to take him home. Once there, he had strangled her and then violently mutilated her body with a pair of curling tongs and a can opener, removing her uterus in the process. The tools of mutilation were found on the floor beside the bed but, although fingerprints were found on the can opener, they did not match any of the police's suspects. This time, even the motive was perplexing as it did not seem as though anything had been stolen.

While the police were still reeling from the horrific discovery of Evelyn Oatley's body, they received word that yet another woman had been murdered, this time in a dilapidated bedsit in Gosfield Street, just minutes from the previous murder site. They rushed over there to find the mutilated body of another prostitute – 43-year-old Margaret Lowe. Like the previous victim, it seemed that Margaret had willingly invited the murderer into her home. Fingerprints on a beer glass left on a table matched those found on the can opener. After drinking with her, her killer had calmly picked up one of her silk stockings, tied it around her neck and strangled her, before viciously lacerating her stomach with a knife.

Desperate to stop the maniac before he killed again, the police quickly called in their pathologist, Sir Bernard Spilsbury, to examine the bodies while they turned the sordid little flat upside down in a desperate hunt for clues to the killer's identity. They were still there when news arrived that a fourth victim had been discovered in a flat in Sussex Gardens, Paddington.

Doris Jouannet, otherwise known as Doris Robson, was a 32-year-old who, like the other women, worked as a prostitute when times were hard. She lived at Sussex Gardens, a well-known red-light district, with a man who claimed to be her husband but may well have been her pimp. In any case, he had been out when Doris brought home the man who would strangle her and then mutilate her remains.

By the time the police found the body of Doris Jouannet, the press had got wind of the story. Soon the words 'Blackout Ripper' were scrawled across every sandwich board in town, alluding to the fact that his modus operandi and choices of victim were chillingly similar to those of Jack the Ripper, who had stalked the streets of London eighty years before. On reading the newspaper reports, the police dourly noted the appalling similarities between the two sets of murders but vowed that, this time, they would catch the killer. Their chance came on 14 February, when a young woman named Greta Haywood staggered into a West End police station, where she tearfully explained that she had just been violently assaulted by an airman.

After questioning her further, the police discovered that Greta had been dining at the Universal Brasserie in Piccadilly when a good-looking young airman had begun to chat her up. After plying her with a few drinks, he asked, 'Are you a naughty girl? Can you take me somewhere?' Greta refused, but did allow him to walk her home. They strolled away from the hustle and bustle of Piccadilly and turned into the quieter backstreets of Mayfair. Once the crowds had dwindled away, the airman gently leaned over to give what Greta first assumed to be a goodnight kiss.

However, she soon found herself being pushed into a dark doorway where, trembling with sudden rage, her companion placed his hands around her neck and began to strangle her. Greta lost consciousness and slumped to the floor. Her fate would have been sealed had a worried passer-by not seen her fall and run over to ask if she was alright. Shocked out of his murderous reverie by the man's cries the airman fled, leaving Greta gasping for breath while her rescuer shouted for a policeman. By the time help arrived, the airman was long gone, but this time he had left a clue: a gas mask that he had been carrying, which bore a distinctive serial number.

Amazingly, his close escape and the knowledge that he had left behind incriminating evidence did not deter the airman from his depraved mission. Just minutes after assaulting Greta Haywood, he returned to Piccadilly and hastily picked up a prostitute known variously as 'Mrs Mulcahy' and 'Kathleen King'. The pair left the West End and headed back to Mrs Mulcahy's flat in Southwick Street, near Paddington Station. Once his victim had lowered her guard, the airman prepared to strangle her, but rattled by his previous encounter he omitted to notice that Mrs Mulcahy was still wearing a heavy pair of boots.

Fighting for her life, the feisty woman managed to land several sharp kicks on his shins and, as her distracted attacker loosened his grip, she screamed for help. Her cries brought other residents in the house running to her door, but they were too late. The airman had once again fled, this time leaving his belt behind.

By the time news of the assault on Mrs Mulcahy reached the police, they were on the killer's trail. A serial number found on the gas mask revealed that it had been issued to an RAF cadet named Gordon Cummins, who was billeted at nearby St John's Wood. They rushed to the barracks, where a search of his possessions revealed cigarette cases belonging to Evelyn Oatley and Margaret Lowe, and a pen engraved with the name 'Doris Jouannet'. The police had their man.

Gordon Cummins was finally apprehended on 16 February and charged with four counts of murder. After various legal wranglings, his trial finally began at the Old Bailey on 27 April. The man who emerged at the trial surprised both jury and observers alike. Cummins was a well-mannered Yorkshireman whose casual boasts of a noble ancestry were not doubted by his colleagues, who good-naturedly nicknamed him 'the Count'. He had been a member of the RAF for some time and held down a responsible position as an aircraft mechanic. He had no criminal record nor any history of violence.

Cummins pleaded 'not guilty' to the charges against him but, after a one-day trial, it took the jury just thirty-five minutes to find him guilty of the murder of his second victim, Evelyn Oatley. This was enough for the judge to pronounce the death sentence and, on 25 June, while air-raid sirens wailed outside the high walls of Wandsworth Prison, Gordon Cummins was hanged. Just what precipitated his reckless and wanton killing spree was never established.

Ironically, while the female residents of war-torn Notting Hill worried about the shocking crimes of Gordon Cummins, little did they realise that there was already another serial killer in their midst, who quite possibly was listening to their anxious chatter in the cafés of

Ladbroke Grove. Like Cummins, this killer had a pathological hatred of women, but unlike the airman, his murderous career was to last a decade and ultimately have a far greater impact on Notting Hill, exposing to the world just how lawless the area's bomb-ravaged streets were.

*I*n 1971, the director Richard Fleischer released *10 Rillington Place*, a feature film starring Richard Attenborough and John Hurt, which told the shocking story of serial killer John Reginald Christie. The film was a hit, and the titular address instantly became Notting Hill's most notorious location. Since then, much has been written about Christie and his crimes, but much less is known about his relationship with Notting Hill and the house in which many of his crimes were committed.

In many ways, Rillington Place represented all that was wrong with Notting Hill in the first half of the twentieth century. Built by speculative developers in the mid-1800s, it never housed the middle-class families for which it had been designed and by the end of the century had become a dilapidated slum. However, in the 1940s and early 1950s this unremarkable little street became the venue for scenes of deprivation and depravity that still shock us today.

This is the story of Rillington Place – in particular, No. 10 – and the people who lived there.

Nowadays, anyone lucky enough to find a vacant piece of land in London on which they can build property is guaranteed to make a great deal of money. However, this was not always the case. As we have seen, by the 1860s James Weller Ladbroke's land at Notting Hill was becoming seriously overdeveloped and the spacious houses being built were proving to be totally inappropriate for the type of people living in them. The problems being faced on the Ladbroke estate meant that most experienced developers steered clear of Notting Hill, leaving any new building leases to be snapped up at supposedly bargain prices by less canny speculators, who, as we have seen, were woefully inept at property development.

In the early 1860s, the Hammersmith & City Railway purchased a field at the foot of Notting Hill on which to build their new station. This field lay just outside the Ladbroke estate and was owned by a retired army man named Matthew Chitty Downes St Quintin who, like James Weller Ladbroke, was a largely absent landlord. St Quintin's Notting Hill land formed part of a vast portfolio of estates that were dotted across the English countryside. These holdings were overseen from the family seat of Scampston Hall – a sprawling Regency pile near the village of Rillington in North Yorkshire.

On the face of it, Matthew St Quintin was a man in a highly privi-leged position. However, in truth, he was extremely unhappy with the role that had been thrust upon him. Having inherited the family lands at the tender age of 5, as he got older he gradually came to realise that he had been handed a poisoned chalice. Scampston Hall cost a fortune to run and the family land had been mismanaged for generations. With no aptitude nor interest in property management, Matthew St Quintin literally ran away from the problem and joined the army.

The decades that followed were probably the happiest of his life, as he was able to temporarily forget about his responsibili-ties. However, when he retired from service in his mid-40s, he was forced to return to Scampston Hall. Faced with failing estates and a mountain of debt, Matthew St Quintin suffered a mental breakdown. He began selling off his cursed land (much of which had been in the family for generations) at ridiculously low prices to anyone who was prepared to take it off his hands.

It was clear that Matthew St Quintin wanted to completely rid himself of his inheritance and the commitments that came with it. In 1850, when he was 50 years old, he made another step away from his aristocratic roots when he married Amy Cherry, the daughter of a middle-class Paddington merchant. It ultimately fell to Amy to save what was left of the St Quintin fortune and in doing so, bring about the creation of Rillington Place.

Realising that her husband was mentally ill, Amy St Quintin began to keep a diary that recorded his behaviour. According to her entries, Matthew's moods swung between 'paranoid and excit-able' and 'passive and childlike'. These descriptions suggest that he was suffering from bipolar disorder – otherwise known as 'manic depression' – a condition that can be successfully treated today with medication and psychotherapy.

However, the Victorians had virtually no understanding of mental illness and their ignorance often led them to make quite brutal diagnoses. In Matthew St Quintin's case, his doctor came to the conclusion that he was an 'imbecile' and unable to make decisions for himself. As a result, Amy and a board of trustees took control of his fortune, finally freeing the unhappy landlord from his chains of obligation. Unfortunately, no records exist to reveal how this release affected his mood but, hopefully, the remaining years of Matthew St Quintin's life were happy ones.

In the meantime, Amy and the trustees noted the arrival of the railway on their land in Notting Hill with interest. Convinced that this would precipitate a housing boom in the area, they quickly set about preparing the estate for sale. An elegant residential plan was laid out across the fields and meadows comprising spacious properties designed to appeal to well-paid City clerks who could commute into work on the new railway.

However, a few of the streets on the St Quintin estate blueprint were not so desirable. Close to the looming shadow of the Hammersmith & City Railway, the family's surveyors laid out a short cul-de-sac that ran between St Mark's Road and an industrial site that had been let for some years to James Bartle, an iron founder. This unremarkable road was named Rillington Place, in recognition of the village adjacent to Scampston Hall, and was designed to house families who could not quite stretch to the airy villas that lined the neighbouring streets. In time, it was destined to become the most notorious address in Britain.

The subsequent development of the St Quintin estate did not progress quite as well as had been hoped. The first houses to be built on the land – pairs of semi-detached villas with south-facing gardens, fronting a wide avenue known as Lancaster Road – failed to attract the affluent city workers for whom they had been designed and many stood empty while the anxious developers searched for tenants.

By the time the building plots on the Rillington Place site went up for sale in 1868, it was rapidly becoming clear that no builder was going to make a fortune from the St Quintin's land. Consequently, the leases were bought by several novice developers who were prepared to ignore the financial risks. One such man was John Saunders Hinton, a 21-year-old carpenter who was ambitious to the point of being foolhardy.

The son of a farmer, Hinton had moved to the capital while still a teenager and had found plenty of employment at the numerous building sites that surrounded the outskirts of mid-nineteenth-century London. Work was plentiful, pay was good, and by 1867 he had raised sufficient funds to marry Annie Traies, the daughter of a Kensington tin plate worker. The couple settled close to Annie's childhood home and two years later, with his wife expecting their first child, John Hinton decided to make the risky move into speculative property development. Using a combination of savings and borrowed finances, he purchased building leases on several plots of land at Rillington Place and began construction.

Like most mid-nineteenth-century streets, Rillington Place was built to a predetermined plan. In some respects, John Hinton had chosen wisely, as the terraces of narrow townhouses that lined the street were among the smallest and cheapest to build in the whole of Notting Hill. Designed to deceive, their 17ft frontages were a 'mug's eyeful' with elegantly moulded pediments above the first-floor windows and solid, hardwood front doors flanked by classical pillars.

However, once inside, it became clear that the least amount of money possible had been spent on their construction. The internal layout comprised two rather cramped rooms on each of the three floors of the house, accessed by a narrow staircase. A brick-built extension to the main building ran halfway up the back of the houses, providing a small bathroom (running water and WC not included) on a mezzanine between the ground and first floors and a tiny kitchen on the ground floor. Beyond the kitchen, a low outbuilding contained a wash house with a copper boiler and an outside WC – the only toilet.

The completed Rillington Place was a narrow cul-de-sac lined with ten houses on each side – Nos 1–10 lay on the southern side, 11–20 on the northern. On their completion, the properties' annual rental value was £28 each. Number 10 – the future house of horrors – lay at the end of the southern terrace, wedged against a high brick wall that would soon shield Rillington Place from the noisome activities of the Western Iron Works – a noisy, smoky foundry built by James Bartle in 1888 to manufacture coach panels and cast-iron street furniture, most notably manhole covers (some of which are still in use today).

The acrid smoke that constantly billowed out of the enormous foundry chimney ensured that No. 10 and its immediate neighbours quickly became coated in a thick layer of soot. During working hours, the residents of 10 Rillington Place could sit in their little back garden and watch the travelling crane ponderously make its way back and forth along the foundry's southern wall carrying huge hunks of iron ready for smelting.

Although the quality of construction left a lot to be desired, the facilities in the houses on Rillington Place would have been adequate ... if each property had been home to just one family. However, as soon as the little cul-de-sac was completed it became clear that, despite the presence of the new station, Rillington Place and the adjacent streets were considered too remote by city commuters. The endless stream of horror stories emanating from the nearby Potteries did nothing to help sales, either. Consequently, some of the houses, including No. 10, failed to attract tenants for over a year after they had been completed.

This spelled disaster for John Hinton, who desperately needed to let his properties so he could pay his contractors and creditors. Anxious not to miss any potential tenants, he and his wife, Annie, moved into No. 14 Rillington Place in order to keep a close eye on the market; but few newcomers could be enticed to the mean little street, especially as deals could be done on larger houses nearby that represented much better value for money. As angry subcontractors demanded payment for their work, John Hinton became overwhelmed by debt.

By June 1869, Annie was six months pregnant and almost certainly exhausted by their worrying predicament. She left Rillington Place to stay with family in Wiltshire and in September gave birth to a daughter, whom she named Laura. In the meantime, her husband's financial situation hit rock bottom. With his reputation as a developer in tatters and with his creditors losing patience, he decided to simply run away. Early in 1870 he secretly boarded a ship bound for the United States, leaving his wife, child and irate business associates behind forever.

John Hinton's decision to flee may have been immensely irresponsible but it certainly wasn't risky. Back in the 1800s it was very easy to disappear. Formal registration of citizens was in its infancy (before 1837, even birth certificates did not exist), no identification was required to board a ship and entry to the USA from Britain could be easily obtained. Once safely across the Atlantic, John Hinton used his carpentry skills to work his way south from the eastern seaboard,

eventually settling in Texas, where he freely used his real name, safe
in the knowledge that the possibility of bumping into anyone he knew
from London was virtually non-existent.

Back in Britain, Annie Hinton despaired of ever finding her errant
husband and eventually gave him up for dead. She remarried in 1878
to John Cottrell, another carpenter, and moved to the sleepy market
town of Tiverton in Devon. In the meantime, her first husband added
bigamy to his list of misdemeanours when he married Sarah Bird in
Texas in 1881. They went on to have five children: Jesse (born 1882),
Pearl (1883), Robert (1885), Marshall (1888) and Edna (1899). It is
unlikely that Hinton's new family ever had any idea that he had
another wife and child living back in England.

Soon after John Hinton's hasty departure from Rillington Place,
the remaining leaseholders realised that there was no option but
to offer the terraces of empty houses on multiple occupancy lets.
This meant that the already scant facilities in the shoddily built
homes would be stretched to breaking point, but at least there would
be some return on their investment. This new letting arrangement
worked, and by the spring of 1871 all the houses were occupied.

Number 10 fared better than most and was let to one single family.
Lewis Bill, a widowed house agent in his mid-40s (who was probably instrumental in finding tenants for the other properties on the
street), lived there with his sister, Augusta, and three sons until 1876.
Following his departure the house was again let to one household –
the Barnfather family.

Richard Barnfather, a gas fitter from Soho, moved into No. 10 with
his wife, Elizabeth, and their four children. The preponderance of
new homes being built in Notting Hill at the time meant that he was
rarely out of work, but the family supplemented their income by subletting the two top-floor rooms of their home to lodgers, the first of
whom was William Rouse, a cellar man in one of North Kensington's
many public houses.

Once the properties in Rillington Place had been successfully
let, they briefly began to steadily rise in value. On 11 May 1878,
the *London Standard* announced that Messrs Newbon and Harding
had been instructed to sell the leases to Nos 9 and 10 Rillington

Place, which were currently being let at £35 per year – a 25 per cent increase on their original rental yield. The new landlord saw no reason to change his tenants, and the Barnfather family continued to live at No. 10 until the mid-1880s, when Thomas Dawson moved into the upstairs rooms, subletting the ground floor to a man named Henry Dale.

Unfortunately, during Dawson and Dale's time in the house, the London property market went into a steep decline precipitated by overdevelopment on the outskirts of the city. The value of the houses in Rillington Place began to fall rapidly. By 1891, when auctioneers Pettitt & Son & Byrne were instructed to sell Nos 12, 13, 16, 17, 18 and 20, each house was producing an annual rental of just £24 – a decrease of over 30 per cent on rents achieved thirteen years previously.

By this period No. 10, which had successfully evaded the rigours of multiple tenancy for many years, finally succumbed and was divided up into three makeshift apartments. Josiah Rogers, a timber yard porter, his wife, Helen, and their three children rented the two reception rooms on the ground floor; the first floor was occupied by plasterer William Yeates, his wife, Abigail, and their two young children; while the top floor was home to dressmaker, Elizabeth Cockayne, and her four children.

This little house, which had been designed to accommodate one family comprising two parents and a maximum of six or seven children, now groaned under the strain of housing fourteen individuals. Its tribulations were typical of Notting Hill's property. Privacy was impossible, and cooking, washing and toilet facilities were stretched to their limits. The small cast-iron cooking range and ceramic sink in the tiny kitchen at the back of the house had to be shared by all occupants, as did the wash house behind it and the adjoining single WC. If tenants wished to cook in their own rooms, they had to resort to balancing pots and pans on the fireplace.

There was no water piped to the upper floors and so this had to be collected from the kitchen. Calls of nature were answered using a chamber pot. There is no evidence that the property possessed a bath, although the small room on the mezzanine between the ground and first floors had been built to house one. Instead, the tenants would either bathe in a portable tin bath (which took an interminable time to fill with hot water) or make the trip to Kensington Public Baths (which stood on the corner of Lancaster and Clarendon Roads) to wash.

The only amenities that were conveniently located for residents of Rillington Place were St Mark's School, which stood opposite the entrance to the cul-de-sac, and a multitude of warm and welcoming pubs. The Kensington Park Hotel was five minutes' walk away on the corner of Ladbroke Grove and Lancaster Road; and the Elgin lay a little further south down Ladbroke Grove, on the corner of Cornwall Road (today's Westbourne Park Road). Both these pubs are still trading today. Over to the west, the Beehive stood at the junction of Talbot Grove and Walmer Road, while nearby, the Roundhouse stood at the junction of Walmer and Lancaster Roads. Both of these watering holes were demolished in the 1960s to make way for Kensington Sports Centre.

The fortunes of Rillington Place continued to wane for the remaining years of the 1800s. In the 1890s the philanthropist Charles Booth sent a researcher to the street as part of his monumental survey into the 'Life and Labour of the People in London'. The findings of the survey were illustrated on a map of the city, where every street was given a colour code. Yellow represented the wealthiest streets, while black highlighted the alleys and courts occupied by the 'vicious and semi-criminal' underclass. Booth coloured Rillington Place purple on the map, thus classifying the residents as 'Mixed. Some comfortable, others poor', and describing the road (which was rather presciently entered in his notebook as 'Killington Place') as inhabited by 'respectable working class. 3 st [storey] houses. Some poor.'

The colour code of the map was expanded upon further in Booth's full account of his survey. The wealthier residents of 'purple' roads such as Rillington Place were defined as having 'Regular standard earnings, 22s to 30s per week for regular work. Fairly comfortable. As a rule, the wives do not work but the children do: the boys commonly following the father; the girls taking local trades or going out to service.' Their less prosperous neighbours were described as:

Factory, dock and warehouse labourers, carmen, messengers and porters. Of the whole section none can be said to rise above poverty, nor are many to be classed as very poor. As a general rule they have a hard struggle to make ends meet but they are, as a body, decent steady men, paying their way and bringing up their children respectably.

The poorest residents in Rillington Place were described thus:

Intermittent earning. 18 to 20 shillings per week for a moderate family. The victims of competition and on them falls with particular severity the weight of recurrent depressions of trade. Labourers, poorer artisans and street sellers. This irregularity of employment may show itself in the week or year: stevedores and waterside porters may secure only one or two days' work in a week, whereas labourers in the building trades may get only eight or nine months in a year.

The chronic state of want suffered by some of the families in Rillington Place persuaded at least one resident to turn to crime. In March 1880, William Brooks, a coach builder living at No. 6, appeared at Bow Street Police Court along with four accomplices accused of running an illegal betting shop on Betterton Street near Drury Lane. According to the prosecution, the men had apparently selected the venue because of its proximity to the homes of artisans and labourers, 'in order that they might be tempted to assemble there during their dinner hour and squander away their small earnings'. However, although Sergeant Savew of the Met's E-Division produced betting books and cards he had found at the property, William Brooks' involvement in the gambling den could not be proved and he escaped with a warning.

Rillington Place found itself in the press again in December 1884, when the body of a man was discovered at Chiswick. The *Pall Mall Gazette* reported:

As police sergeant Timons was walking along the Chiswick Mall this morning about three o'clock, he found the dead body of a respectably dressed man lying face down in the mud on the foreshore of the

Thames. Dr Murdoch was called and expressed the opinion that the
man had been dead only two hours. The body, which was removed
to the Chiswick mortuary to await an inquest, is that of a man aged
68, five feet eight inches in height, stout with fresh complexion, bald
on the top of head with whiskers turning grey, wearing a black over-
coat and dark mackintosh, vest and trousers. In one of the pockets
was found an envelope addressed, 'Mrs Reynolds, Rillington Place,
St Marks Road, Notting Hill.'

Neither the identity of the body nor the intended recipient of the
letter were revealed in subsequent press reports. However, the note
was probably written to Mrs Emma Reynolds, the wife of a cab proprietor, who lived at 5 Rillington Place in the early 1880s.

In 1895, Nos 9 and 10 Rillington Place were put up for sale again.
Auctioneer Leopold Farmer placed a series of advertisements in the
London Standard promoting the sale, which was due to take place
at the London Mart on Friday, 31 May at 2 p.m. The annual rental
value of these two properties was £28 – slightly higher than that of the
neighbouring houses auctioned in 1891 – and they were snapped up
by Arthur Partridge, a railwayman who lived with his wife and sons at
11 Rillington Place.

Arthur Partridge was an interesting character. Born in Bisley,
Gloucestershire, in 1858, he joined the Great Western Railway after
leaving school and worked on the Bristol–London line, employed variously as a ticket collector, an inspector and a passenger guard. In 1880,
he married Catherine Frances Morgan, a widow ten years his senior.

For the first decade of their marriage, Arthur and Catherine (known to
all as 'Fanny') lived in and around Upton-upon-Severn in Worcestershire,
where they raised four children: Sydney George (born 1882), Fanny
(1884) and twins, Frederick Arthur and Joseph Percy (1887). The family
moved to London (probably due to Arthur's job) in the early 1890s.

At first they rented rooms at 126 St Clements Road, before moving
into No. 11 Rillington Place in 1893. Quite how Arthur Partridge
managed to purchase 9 and 10 Rillington Place on his railwayman's wages (which could not have amounted to much more than
30s per week) is perplexing. That said, the family were evidently

ambitious – during the First World War, Arthur's son, Joseph (who was known by his middle name of Percy), was mentioned in dispatches no less than seven times for 'valuable service rendered' to Allied troops in France. His gallantry was recognised after the conflict ended, when he was awarded the CBE, the CMG (the Most Distinguished Order of St Michael & St George) and the French Legion of Honour. He went on to become a highly respected senior member of civilian staff at New Scotland Yard – a remarkable achievement for the son of a railwayman during an era obsessed by class.

Although Arthur Partridge's finances remain shrouded in mystery, what is known for certain is that he lived at 11 Rillington Place until 1903. After that, he and Fanny moved to the quieter surroundings of Acton, but held on to the lease for Nos 9 and 10, letting the houses out on increasingly short terms to a transient population of tradesmen chasing work opportunities across the capital.

During the first decade of the twentieth century, 10 Rillington Place operated almost as a lodging house, such was the turnover of tenants. However, in around 1910, the top floor of the house was taken by Thomas Aldridge, a 66-year-old bricklayer's labourer, his wife, Alice, and daughter, Violet. The Aldridges remained at 10 Rillington Place for over twenty years and brought some much needed stability to the house.

Shortly before the outbreak of the First World War, Thomas and Alice Aldridge were joined by a man who was also destined to have a long association with 10 Rillington Place. Charles Kitchener, a 37-year-old railway plate layer, moved into the house with his wife, Sarah, and his three sons – Herbert (11), Leonard (6) and baby Arthur – in 1913.

Although it was teetering on the brink of becoming a full-blown slum, in some ways Rillington Place was a good place to raise children. In addition to the free school opposite, the fact that the road was a cul-de-sac meant that it became a playground in the warmer months. Lamp posts were festooned with ropes to make swings; goalposts were chalked on the high brick wall obscuring the iron works; and the kerb became seating for a toys' banquet.

The Kitchener family were initially content as they raised their children at 10 Rillington Place. However, in 1926, their lives began to unravel. For reasons undisclosed, Sarah Kitchener abandoned her marital home taking 16-year-old Arthur with her and, as the two older boys had already moved out, Charles was left alone. Around the same time, Thomas Aldridge died. His widow, Alice, remained in their old rooms, while the ground floor was taken by a couple named Edward and Winifred Smith. For the first time in decades 10 Rillington Place was not overcrowded, but the battering the house had taken was beginning to tell.

In 1937, Arthur Partridge died and 10 Rillington Place passed to his sons, along with the predicament of what to do with the house. The property was outdated and in a very poor state of repair. The Partridges realised they could achieve a much better rent if they gave the house a complete overhaul, but their lease had just twenty-seven years left to run. What was the point of spending money on improving a house that would soon revert back to the freeholder? Concluding that 10 Rillington Place was not worth the investment, Arthur Partridge's sons gave the house a quick lick of paint and put it up for sale.

It was purchased by a Mr G.W. Davies, who also did nothing to improve the dilapidated house. Instead, he continued to let each floor to separate households on relatively cheap terms. Charles Kitchener remained in his tatty rooms on the first floor above the Smiths' accommodation, while Alice Aldridge had recently passed away and so Mr Davies advertised her rooms to let. They were quickly taken by a middle-aged couple from Yorkshire named John and Ethel Christie.

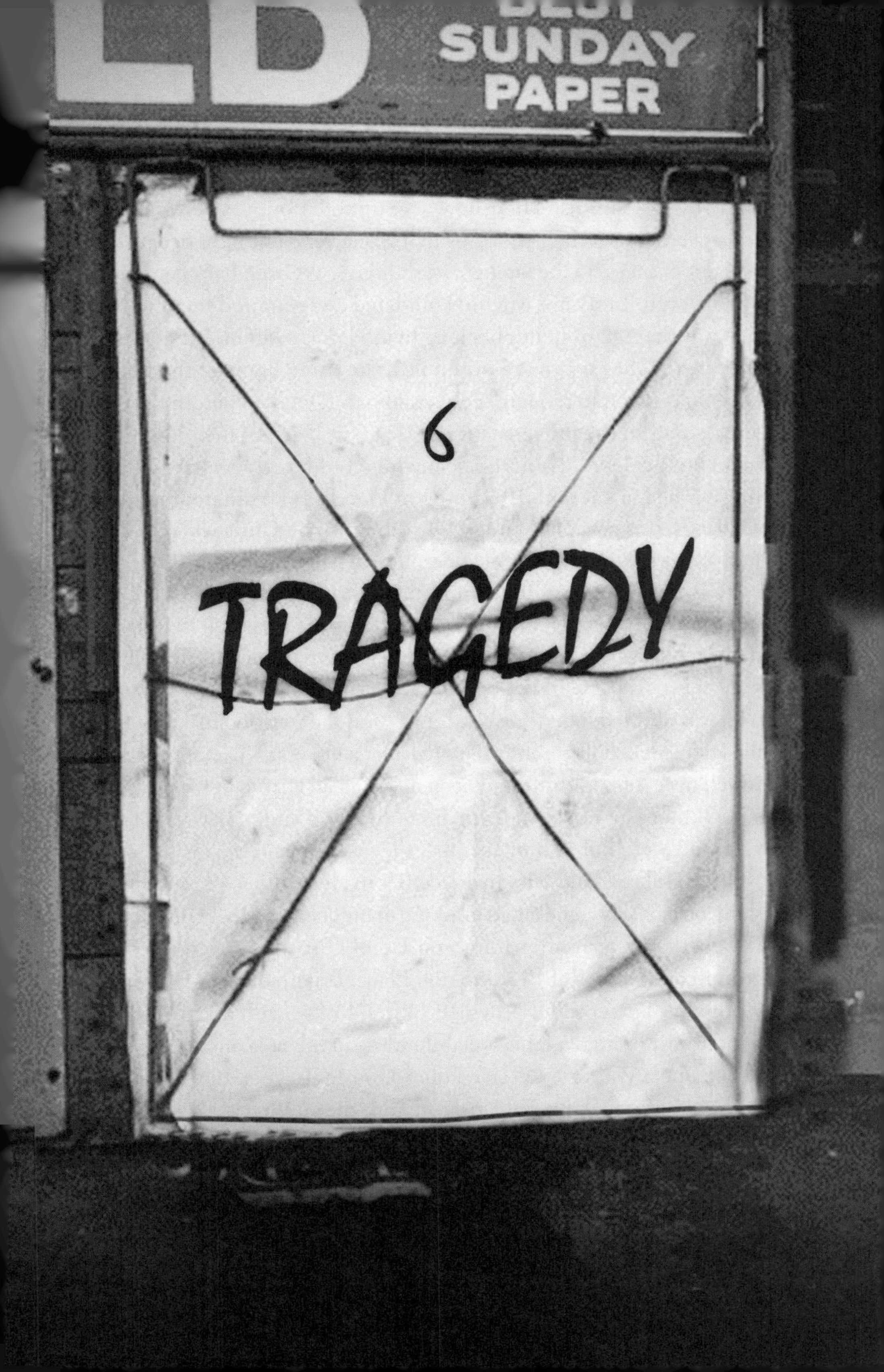
SUNDAY
PAPER
6
TRAGEDY

Just over a year after they had arrived at 10 Rillington Place, John and Ethel Christie moved from the cramped rooms at the top of the house to the ground floor, which had just been vacated by the Smiths. Their new accommodation was certainly an improvement on their previous living quarters, not least because it had direct access to the kitchen, wash house, WC and back garden.

However, it was still woefully outdated and required them to live in a way that seems quite shocking to modern sensibilities. Although they were let to separate households, the three floors of the house bore no relation to modern, converted flats. Detailed descriptions of later events in the property suggest that few, if any of the rooms had locks on the doors. Thus, the occupants could freely roam wherever they wished. That said, 10 Rillington Place was no different to most houses in this part of Notting Hill and, thus, the Christies were content to pay 12s a week in rent and settled in with minimal fuss.

To their neighbours, John and Ethel Christie seemed to be a mild, unremarkable couple, although John Christie's very well-mannered demeanour suggested that they had perhaps seen better days financially. For her part, Ethel Christie appeared to be a quiet, unpretentious woman who was devoted to her husband. Little did the neighbours know that the couple had only recently reunited after a ten-year separation, during which time John Christie had been detained at 'His Majesty's pleasure' several times for crimes ranging from theft to assault. However, if the Christies were not as they seemed, they were by no means the only Notting Hill residents who had secrets – in an area that was virtually a slum, no landlord could afford to ask too many questions about his tenants.

Less than a year after John and Ethel Christie moved into the ground floor rooms at 10 Rillington Place, Britain declared war with Germany. The conflict provided John Christie with an irresistible opportunity to increase his social standing in the area and he applied to become a Wartime Reserve Police Constable. Incredibly, nobody bothered to check his background and, despite having a criminal record, he was accepted and posted to Harrow Road Police Station, a short bus ride away from his home. Although no one knew it at the time, Christie's brief police career would be of great benefit to him long after the war was over.

Back at Rillington Place, the top floor of the property was briefly let to Stanley and Kathleen Clowes after the Christies moved downstairs. The Clowes moved out during the war and the rooms were subsequently let to one Henry Williams, who remained at the house until 1948. On his departure, Mr Davies, the landlord, let the vacated rooms to a young man named Timothy Evans and his wife Beryl – a couple whose names were destined to be indelibly linked to 10 Rillington Place.

Timothy Evans was born in November 1924 in Merthyr Vale, a mining village on the banks of the River Taff in Glamorgan. His parents, Daniel and Thomasina Evans (*née* Lynch), had been married for three years and already had one child – a daughter named Eleanor. However, by the time Timothy was born, Daniel had deserted his family for reasons that have never been explained. Consequently, Thomasina was left to bring up her two children alone, until around 1927 when she met a local man named Penry Probert with whom she would have two more children.

Although he never officially adopted Eleanor and Timothy, Penry Probert treated both of them as his own and the family appear to have spent the next ten years happily, although Timothy's education was constantly interrupted due to illness. His long stays in hospital (after a cut in one of his toes refused to heal) meant that he missed the crucial early stages of education and, as a result, could barely read by the time he reached adulthood.

In the mid-1930s, the Evans/Probert family moved to Notting Hill, probably because Penry Probert felt that the city offered better job prospects. Timothy initially went with them, but quickly returned to Wales where he lived with his maternal grandmother while he finished his erratic education. Unsurprisingly, he gave up on school at the first opportunity, and at the age of 14 moved back to London where he was employed first as a 'van boy' with a local firm, before securing a job as a driver with the Air Ministry.

Now back in Notting Hill and with wages to spend, Timothy spent the next few years of his life getting acquainted with the many pubs in the area. When not drinking with friends or colleagues, he also enjoyed going to the pictures, watching football matches and gambling at London's dog tracks. Unfortunately, the latter places in particular were the haunt of the capital's criminal underworld, and by the time he had reached his early 20s, Timothy Evans was mixing with rather dubious company. His family later reluctantly admitted that he was also an inveterate liar, especially if he felt it could benefit him financially. To their relief, in January 1947, Timothy met Beryl Thorley – a local girl, whom they hoped would be a stabilising influence in his life.

Beryl was just 18 years old when she met Timothy Evans at a dance. Although he was poorly educated, rather scrawny and just 5ft 5in tall, he was not a bad-looking chap and Beryl found him affable enough and enjoyed their dates. However, very soon after (or perhaps just before) the couple started going out together, Beryl's mother died and her grief-stricken father withdrew to the seaside town of Brighton, leaving Beryl and her brother, Basil, in London. Although she had regular employment as a telephonist, Beryl would have found it very difficult to survive in the capital as a single girl and her financial situation almost certainly influenced her decision to marry Timothy Evans just nine months after they had first met.

Initially, the newlyweds lived with Timothy's mother and stepfather at their lodgings in St Mark's Road, Notting Hill, but from the outset they were understandably keen to find their own home. Their search became more pressing in early 1948 when Beryl found out she was pregnant. Now desperate for somewhere to live, Timothy and Beryl heard that two top floor rooms had just become available at 10 Rillington Place. Liking the fact that the address was just a short walk away from Timothy's mother, they decided to take the rooms at 12s a week.

As Beryl's pregnancy progressed, Timothy began to take his responsibilities more seriously. He secured himself a new job as a driver with local firm, Lancaster Food Products, and although he remained a regular patron of the nearby pubs – the Kensington Park Hotel being a particular favourite – much of his spare time was spent at 10 Rillington Place. The Evans' seem to have got on reasonably well with their neighbours, the Christies, and despite the large age gap between the two couples, they became, in the words of John Christie, 'friendly acquaintances'.

Charles Kitchener, however, was not so polite. In fact, he suspected that both John Christie and Timothy Evans stole items from his rooms when he was out. As both men had convictions for theft, Mr Kitchener may well have been right.

Beryl Evans gave birth to a baby girl on 10 October 1948 at Queen Charlotte's Hospital, Hammersmith. She and Timothy named her Geraldine and both were utterly devoted to her. However, once she was discharged from hospital, Beryl became depressed. The relentless demands of motherhood, combined with a chronic lack of money and long periods alone with Geraldine in the gloomy atmosphere of Rillington Place, felt unbearable. After discussing her problems with her mother-in-law, who agreed to look after the baby, she returned to work.

Beryl's new job was intended to make her life better, but in the event it had the reverse effect. Timothy had not been happy about the arrangement from the outset, probably feeling that her place was at home with Geraldine. When Beryl became friendly with a male colleague, her husband's limited patience ran out. He went to her workplace and created such a scene that Beryl was promptly sacked.

With no job and no references, Beryl Evans now had little choice but to return to the stifling, housebound existence she had tried so hard to escape. Her frustration was made worse by her husband's frequent visits to the Kensington Park Hotel, and the couple began to have furious rows. Things finally came to a head in August 1949 when Beryl suspected that Timothy had slept with their mutual friend, Lucy Endecott, who was staying with them at the time. Disgusted at her husband's betrayal, but unable to walk away from the marriage because she had no means to care for Geraldine, Beryl was trapped. To make matters worse, she was also pregnant again.

Had she been faced with the same situation today, Beryl would, of course, have several options available to her, including the prospect of terminating the pregnancy. However, in 1949, abortion was illegal unless the mother's life was in danger. A termination could be performed by a so-called 'backstreet abortionist' but this was expensive and extremely risky. After confiding in her friend, Mrs Lawrence, who lived at 8 Rillington Place, Beryl bought a syringe and began douching herself to try and induce a miscarriage but she just succeeded in making herself ill. By October, she saw no other option but to tell Timothy she was pregnant, hoping that he might agree to pay for an abortion. Unsurprisingly, he refused.

On realising that her last hope of ending the pregnancy had been extinguished, Beryl reluctantly resigned herself to the fact that she would soon have another mouth to feed, but privately she may have resolved to get out of her troubled marriage. Her brother Basil visited her on 4 November 1949 (by which time Beryl was about three months pregnant) and she told him she was hoping to take Geraldine on holiday. In fact, she was probably planning to go to her father's house in Brighton and not return.

It transpired that Basil Thorley would never see his sister again. The last time anyone saw Beryl Evans alive was on Wednesday, 8 November. That morning, builders were at 10 Rillington Place making various repairs to the shabby property. Frederick Jones, one of the labourers, was working outside the house at around 10 a.m. when Beryl and another young woman came out with Geraldine. Seeing the baby, he warned them that he was going to put a ladder on the stairs later that morning. 'I'll get by that alright', Beryl replied, as she put Geraldine into her pram.

Some time that same morning, Ethel Christie also bumped into Beryl, who informed her that she was expecting an acquaintance named Joan Vincent to call round later that day but that she did not want to see her as Joan had previously caused some trouble between her and Timothy. Ethel resisted the temptation to question Beryl further and went back into her rooms, where John Christie was resting, having been signed off from work with a bad back.

As Beryl had feared, Joan Vincent did call at 10 Rillington Place later that day, having walked round to the house during her lunch hour. Despite knowing Beryl was trying to avoid her, one of the Christies must have let her in, as Mr Kitchener – the only other resident – was in hospital. Joan made her way up to the second floor and, as she reached the top of the stairs, she called Beryl. On receiving no answer, she tried the door handle but felt that someone was on the other side pressing against the door to stop her opening it. Joan quickly gave up and hurried out of the house feeling distinctly uneasy.

Although Joan Vincent had been unnerved by her visit to 10 Rillington Place, neither she nor anyone else was perturbed enough to make any further enquiries about Beryl. In fairness, at the time there seemed no reason to be worried.

Timothy Evans returned home that evening and then went to work as usual the following morning. As he left the house, he met Frederick Willis, one of the contractor's plasterers, and asked him when he expected the work on the house to be finished. Willis told him it would be completed by Friday. That evening, Evans stopped off at his mother's house and told her that she would not need to babysit for him that night (as previously arranged) because Beryl had taken Geraldine down to Brighton to visit her father.

Neither Mrs Probert nor anyone else had any reason to think this was suspicious, as Beryl herself had discussed going on holiday. Indeed, the first sign that something wasn't right came two days later when, on Friday, 11 November, Timothy Evans announced to his boss, Emanuel Adler, that he was handing in his notice. Surprised at his sudden resignation and perhaps aware of his recent marital problems, Adler asked after Beryl. Evans told him she had gone to Bristol.

After collecting his wages, Timothy Evans made his way to Robert Hookway's second-hand furniture shop on the Portobello Road where he told the owner that he had some furniture he would like to sell. Mr Hookway accompanied him to Rillington Place and, after assessing the value of the pieces, offered £40 for the lot but warned that he could not collect it until the following Monday. His offer was accepted and he left 10 Rillington Place as the builders were packing up their tools and loading them into their van. By the time night fell, the house was silent.

Although he did not realise it at the time, Robert Hookway's announcement that he could not pick up the furniture until after the weekend probably kept Timothy Evans in Notting Hill two days longer than he had originally planned. He bided his time by visiting his mother, telling her that Beryl had been in touch and now might stay in Brighton for Christmas (even though it was only early November). He spent the rest of the weekend in various local pubs, during which time he met Albert Rollings, a rag and bone man, who he arranged to meet at 10 Rillington Place the following morning as he had some old clothes to sell.

The next day, Rollings knocked on the door at the appointed hour to be greeted by Evans, who took him upstairs to show him the clothes he wanted to sell. The rag and bone man noted with some concern that the clothes had been ripped up, but made no comment. While sorting through the clothing, he found a baby's rattle and asked Timothy if he wanted to sell it. Evans replied that he did not, as he needed to keep it for his daughter. Saying no more, Rollings quickly paid Evans for the clothes and left the house.

Robert Hookway's furniture van finally arrived at 10 Rillington Place at around 3 p.m. on Monday afternoon. Once the furniture had been loaded, Timothy Evans packed a suitcase and, leaving his rooms empty, save for Geraldine's clothes, rattle, chair and pram, walked out of 10 Rillington Place. He then made his way to the Royalty Cinema on Ladbroke Road where he met Basil Thorley. His brother-in-law could not help but notice the suitcase and asked where he was going. Evans replied that he had received a telegram from Beryl, telling him to meet her in Bristol. He then made his way to Paddington Station and caught the 12.55 a.m. train to Swansea.

At this point in the story, Timothy Evans' behaviour made absolutely no sense. Why had he told some people that Beryl had gone to Brighton and others that she was in Bristol? Why had he resigned from a job that he badly needed, sold all his possessions apart from Geraldine's things and then boarded a train to Wales? Most worryingly, where were his wife and daughter?

Evans' aunt and uncle – Mr and Mrs Lynch – were just stirring at their Merthyr Vale home on the morning of Tuesday, 15 November, when they heard a knock at the door. Standing on the doorstep was their nephew, who explained that his boss's car had broken down nearby and he needed to stay with them for a few days while it was being fixed. Mr and Mrs Lynch did not query this, but once Timothy had got settled, they did ask after Beryl and Geraldine. He told them they were in Brighton with Beryl's father and would not be home until after Christmas.

Evans stayed with his aunt and uncle for the rest of the week, during which time neither his boss nor the repaired car materialised. The Lynches suspected that the story was a figment of their nephew's fertile imagination and that, in reality, Beryl had thrown him out. They were quite relieved when, on the morning of Monday, 21 November, Timothy announced that he was going back to London.

Evans arrived in the capital in the late afternoon and made his way straight to 10 Rillington Place, where he immediately sought out John Christie. During later interviews, Christie offered no explanation as to why Evans had been so keen to see him. However, Timothy Evans gave a very plausible reason for his return to the house: 'He [Christie] asked me what I was doing back in London and I told him I had come up to find out about my daughter; and he told me my daughter was perfectly all right … That was the only reason why I came back to London.'

Evans' conversation with Christie suggested two crucial facts. Firstly, that he believed Geraldine to be very much alive, and secondly, that his erstwhile neighbour knew of her whereabouts. The conversation also goes some way to explain why the only items Evans left in his rooms belonged to Geraldine.

After paying his mother a visit, Timothy Evans took the train back to Wales, arriving in Merthyr Vale on Wednesday, 23 November. Mrs Lynch naturally asked him if he had seen Beryl and Geraldine in London. He told her he had, but went on to say that Beryl had walked out on him and the baby. Although this confirmed Mrs Lynch's previous suspicions, it did not explain where Geraldine was. Evans told his aunt that he had taken her to 'some people in Newport' who had agreed to take care of her. Although Mrs Lynch did not question him further, this revelation must have worried her greatly. She would have been even more worried if she had known that, on the following Monday, Timothy Evans sold his wife's wedding ring at a Merthyr Tydfil jeweller's shop.

By this stage, Timothy Evans' family suspected that something was terribly wrong. There had been no word from Beryl for over two weeks, and the latest revelation about Geraldine being in Newport seemed too fantastical to be true.

On Tuesday, 29 November, Timothy's half-sister, Mary Probert, decided to make her own enquiries as to the whereabouts of her niece and sister-in-law. She made her way over to Rillington Place and cautiously knocked on the door of No. 10. At first there was no answer, but then Mary noticed that Ethel Christie was peering round her living room curtain and gestured for her to come to the door. Once inside the hall, Mary asked Ethel about Beryl and Geraldine and was told that they had gone to Brighton. Perhaps irritated that she had been disturbed – or worried about Mary's questions – Ethel Christie went on to tell her that 'Beryl was not as nice as we thought she was', and that she had once caught her coming in smelling strongly of drink, having left Geraldine alone in the house.

Mary took great exception to this accusation and told Mrs Christie she was making things up. At this point, John Christie appeared. He snapped at her, telling her that she had no idea what her brother was really like and that he had known him from his days as a police officer. Although this may have been true, Mary was more concerned that Christie seemed determined not to let her any further into the house.

On the same day as Mary's altercation with the Christies, Mrs Probert received a visit from bailiffs who informed her that Timothy owed money on furniture bought on hire purchase and that, as guarantor for the loan, she was ultimately responsible for the repayments. This was the final straw for Evans' long-suffering mother and she wrote a furious letter to the Lynches telling them what had happened and warning:

If you are mug enough to keep him for nothing that will be your fault … I have done my best for him and Beryl – what thanks did I get? His name stinks up here. Everywhere I go people [are] asking [for] money he owes them. I am ashamed to say he is my son.

On receiving the letter the next day, Mrs Lynch sat Timothy down and read it to him. Although he vehemently denied that he owed anyone money, she could see that the letter had greatly upset him. Later that day, she decided to go shopping in Merthyr Tydfil.

Timothy accompanied her and while she was busy buying provisions, he walked round to the police station where he told DC Gwynfryn Howell Evans, 'I want to give myself up. I have disposed of my wife.' Shocked, the policeman asked him what he meant. 'I put her down the drain,' Evans replied.

Following his devastating revelation, Timothy Evans was instructed by the police to make a formal statement. In it, he claimed that Beryl had been desperate to have an abortion and that he had met a man in a café who had given him pills which would apparently do the job. His wife had taken these pills and shortly afterwards had died. Evans had then panicked and put her body down a drain in Rillington Place. While making his statement, he mentioned baby Geraldine and the police asked him where she was. He replied that he had given her to his neighbour, John Christie, who had arranged for her to be looked after.

Naturally, the Merthyr Tydfil police were sceptical about Evans' story, but they did telephone Scotland Yard who, in turn, contacted the police at Notting Hill. Officers were duly sent over to Rillington Place where they found a drain at the end of the road, outside the entrance to No. 10. After a great deal of effort, they finally managed to lift the heavy, wrought-iron manhole cover and shone a torch into the murky water. There was nothing there.

Following the fruitless search, word was sent back to Merthyr Tydfil that the drain was empty. On being informed of this, Timothy Evans admitted that, although his wife was dead, he had lied about the circumstances. 'I said that to protect a man called Christie,' he told them. 'I will tell you the truth now.'

The version of events that Timothy Evans now recounted to the police is best told in his own words. His statement read:

> As I was coming home from work one night, that would be a week before my wife died, Reg Christie [his middle name was Reginald], who lived on the ground floor below us approached me and said, 'I'd like to have a chat with you about your wife taking these tablets. I know what she's taking them for – she's trying to get rid of the baby. If you or your wife had come to me in the first place I could have done it for you without any risk.' I turned around and said,

'Well, I didn't think you knew anything about medical stuff.' So he told me that he was training to be a doctor before the war. Then he started showing me books and things on medical. I was just as wise because I couldn't understand one word of it because I couldn't read. Then he told me the stuff he used, one out of every ten would die with it. I told him I wasn't interested so I said goodnight to him and I went upstairs. When I got in, my wife started talking to me about it. She said she had been speaking to Mr Christie and asked me if he had spoken to me. I said 'yes' and told her what he had spoken to me about. I turned round and told her that I told him I didn't want nothing to do with it and I told her she wasn't to have anything to do with it either. She turned around and told me to mind my own business and that she intended to get rid of it and that she trusted Mr Christie.

On the Monday evening, that was 7 November, when I came home from work, my wife said that Mr Christie had made the arrangements for first thing Tuesday morning. I didn't argue with her, I just washed and changed and went to the KPH (Kensington Park Hotel) until 10 o'clock. I came home and had supper and went to bed. She wanted to start an argument but I just took no notice. Just after six I got up the following morning to go to work. My wife got up with me. I had a cup of tea and a smoke and she told me, 'On your way down tell Mr Christie that everything is alright. If you don't tell him I'll go down and tell him myself.' So as I went down the stairs he came out to meet me and I said, 'Everything is alright.' Then I went to work.

When I came home in the evening he was waiting for me at the bottom of the staircase. He said, 'Go on upstairs, I'll come behind you.' When I lit the gas in the kitchen he said, 'It's bad news. It didn't work.' I asked him where was she? He said, 'Laying on the bed in the bedroom.' Then I asked him where was the baby? So he said, 'The baby's in the cot.' So I went in the bedroom I lit the gas then I saw the curtains had been drawn. I looked at my wife … I could see she was dead and that she had been bleeding from the mouth and nose and that she had been bleeding from the bottom part. She had a black skirt on and a check blouse and kind of a light blue jacket on. Christie was in the kitchen. I went over and picked my baby up. I wrapped the baby in a blanket and took her in the kitchen.

In the meanwhile Mr Christie had lit the fire in the kitchen. He said
'I'll speak to you after you feed the baby.' So I made the baby some
tea and boiled an egg for her, then I changed the baby and put her
to sit in front of the fire. Then I asked him how long my wife had
been dead. He said, 'Since about 3 o'clock.' Then he told me that
my wife's stomach was septic poisoned. He said, 'another day and she
would have to have gone to hospital.' I asked him what he had done
but he wouldn't tell me. He then told me to stop in the kitchen and
he closed the door and went out. He came back about a quarter of an
hour later and told me he had forced the door of Mr Kitchener's flat
and had put my wife's body in there. I asked him what he intended
to do and he said, 'I'll dispose of it down one of the drains.' He then
said, 'You'd better go to bed and leave the rest to me.' He said, 'Get
up and go to work in the morning as usual' and that he'd see about
getting someone to look after my baby. I told him it was foolish to try
and dispose of the body and he said, 'Well that's the only thing I can
do or otherwise I'll get into trouble with the Police.'

Dazed and traumatised, Timothy Evans went to bed and the next morning obediently set off for work as instructed, leaving Geraldine in the
care of John Christie. When he arrived home that evening, he claimed
that Christie told him he had contacted a couple he knew in East Acton
and they had agreed to take his baby. Evans apparently believed him
but did not ask who these people were, or even where exactly they lived.

The next morning, while he was giving Geraldine her feed, Christie
appeared and told him that the couple would be arriving that morning. Evans once again compliantly went off to work. On returning
in the evening, he was concerned to see that, although there was no
sign of Geraldine, her pram and clothes were still in the flat. Christie
explained that they would be collected later and warned Evans, 'Now
the best thing you can do is to sell your furniture and get out of London.'

Evans' revised statement was forwarded to London and DI James
Black was put in charge of the investigation. He quickly dispatched
a team of officers to Rillington Place and instructed them to perform a more thorough search of the drains near the house. All were
empty. They also looked in the garden for signs of disturbed earth but

found nothing remotely suspicious. Inside the house, the Evans' old rooms were searched. The only vaguely incriminating things found were some newspaper cuttings on the murder of Stanley Setty, a used car dealer with gangland connections, who had been murdered in October 1949. Evans admitted the cuttings were his, but never explained why he had kept them. It was also never established why a man who professed in his statement to be almost illiterate had taken a keen interest in a series of newspaper reports.

Geraldine's pram, chair and clothes were found in the Christies' rooms, which prompted DI Black to take the couple to Notting Hill Police Station for questioning. Ethel Christie told police that the last time she saw Beryl was on 8 November and vigorously denied that she or her husband had been involved in a botched abortion. John Christie also refuted the allegation, and indignantly told the police, 'I cannot understand why Evans should make any accusation against me as I have really been very good to him in lots of ways.' He did not elaborate on what those acts of kindness involved.

By Thursday, 1 December, the police investigation had still failed to uncover any clues to the whereabouts of Beryl or Geraldine and Chief Inspector George Jennings took charge of the case. DI Black was sent to Merthyr Tydfil with the instruction to bring Timothy Evans back to London. In the meantime, Jennings and his men went through 10 Rillington Place with a fine-tooth comb.

Once again, their efforts yielded nothing in the house, and so Jennings turned his attention to the outbuildings. On entering the wash house, he noticed that, although the room had only recently been renovated (the builders had re-plastered the ceiling just weeks before), it was unusable due to a large stack of timber that had been placed in front of the sink. When Jennings and his men began to remove the wood, they quickly revealed what, at first, looked like an old bundle of clothes wrapped in a blanket and an old, green table-cloth. However, when they tried to move it, they realised that it was too heavy to contain only fabric. Jennings and his men dragged the bundle out into the yard adjoining the wash house and proceeded to unwrap it. Inside, they found the remains of Beryl Evans. A few feet away, hidden behind more timber, was the little body of Geraldine.

The police swiftly conveyed the two bodies to Kensington mortuary, where they were examined by police pathologist, Dr Robert Teare. Despite standing only 5ft 2in tall and weighing just 7½ stone, Beryl had apparently put up a brave fight before succumbing to her murderer. Dr Teare noted that there were swellings above her lips and right eye consistent with punches. She also had abrasions to her neck that suggested she had desperately tried to pull away the ligature with which she was strangled. Geraldine's brief life had also been ended by strangulation – a man's tie was still knotted around her neck.

Timothy Evans arrived back at Notting Hill Police Station at 9.45 p.m. on Friday, 2 December. Later that evening, Chief Inspector Jennings gravely showed him Beryl and Geraldine's clothing and told him that he had reason to believe that he was responsible for their deaths. Evans stared blankly at the evidence before uttering one word – 'yes'.

By 11.15 p.m. that same evening, the police had obtained a confession from Timothy Evans in which he claimed to have killed Beryl during a row over money. He then strangled Geraldine with his tie after becoming exasperated with her relentless crying. He was duly moved to Brixton Prison to await trial, but when his distraught mother visited him there on 4 December, he told her, 'I did not touch her Mum, Christie did it. I didn't even know the baby was dead until the police brought me to Notting Hill. Christie told me the baby was in East Acton. Don't trust Jennings, Mum, he's a swine.'

While Timothy Evans was languishing in Brixton Prison, the police interviewed the builders who had been working at 10 Rillington Place when Beryl and Geraldine disappeared. On being asked whether he had seen anything suspicious in the wash house, Frederick Willis – the workman who had warned Beryl about the ladder – told the officers that he had finished plastering the ceiling on 9 November and afterwards had been constantly in and out of the tiny room until he left the house on 11 November. During that time, he had not noticed anything irregular. His workmate, Frederick Jones, agreed and stated, 'After completing the work on Friday afternoon, 11 November, I personally swept out the wash house and also cleaned out the copper [washing boiler] which was in it. There was definitely nothing whatever in the wash house or the copper.'

The two workmen's statements conflicted with Evans' confession. During his interview with the police, he had claimed to have put Beryl and Geraldine's bodies in the wash house before the workmen had left the house. Realising that the statements did not fit their perceived version of events, the police called Jones and Willis in for additional questioning. The two men dutifully downed tools and went to the station where they were kept waiting for a considerable amount of time – a fact that annoyed both of them as they knew their wages would be docked.

When they were finally taken into the interview rooms, Willis (who perhaps wanted to get it over and done with as quickly as possible) agreed that there was a possibility that something was hidden under the sink while he was still at the house. However, his colleague Jones stuck to his original story. Both men later told their boss that they had felt under pressure to change their statements.

On Thursday, 15 December, the case against Timothy Evans was heard at West London Magistrates' Court. John and Ethel Christie were both called as witnesses and in a new revelation, they claimed to have heard strange noises emanating from the upper floors of 10 Rillington Place on the night of 8 November. Evans was remanded in custody until 22 December, when he was formerly committed for trial at the Old Bailey. Astonishingly, the principal witness for the prosecution was to be John Christie – the man whom Evans claimed had actually committed the murders.

Timothy Evans' trial finally commenced on Wednesday, 11 January 1950, presided over by Mr Justice Lewis. Senior counsel for the prosecution was Christmas Humphreys QC, who shrewdly opted to proceed with the indictment that Evans had murdered baby Geraldine, thus removing any argument of provocation that might have otherwise been offered by his defence lawyers. The judge did, however, rule that evidence concerning Beryl's murder could be used in court as it was relevant to the case. If found guilty of Geraldine's murder, Timothy Evans faced the death penalty.

Unsurprisingly, the main thrust of the prosecution's argument was that Evans had himself admitted to murdering Geraldine and her mother. They wasted no time in introducing their star witness, and responding to Christmas Humphreys' careful questioning, John Christie related that, on the night Beryl and Geraldine disappeared, he had heard a 'very loud thud' upstairs, which he took to be something heavy being moved. He also explained to the packed courtroom how Evans had hastily sold his furniture and left the house soon after his wife and child had vanished.

Throughout the questioning of his witness, Christmas Humphreys took care to present John Christie in a very sympathetic light, making much of the fact that he had been a policeman in the Second World War. Christie was only too happy to play the role of upright citizen, although he was no stranger to the courtroom dock himself. However, inwardly, the strain of the court case – and the burden of withholding some terrible secrets of his own – was already beginning to tell. During his appearances in the witness box, he could barely speak in more than a whisper (an effect of a mustard gas attack in the First World War, explained Christmas Humphreys) and during the course of the trial he would visit his doctor complaining of stress-related symptoms on several occasions.

While the prosecution spent much of the first day of Timothy Evans' trial presenting John Christie as a responsible and credible witness, the defence team used the second day to deconstruct this misleading image. Malcolm Morris QC (Evans' defence counsel) sensationally opened his interrogation by bluntly stating:

> Mr Christie, I have got to suggest to you, and I don't want there to be any misapprehension about it, that you are responsible for the death of Mrs Evans and the little girl; or, if that is not so, at least that you know very much more about those deaths than you have said.

'That is a lie', Christie answered.

Morris then made it absolutely clear to the court that the seemingly meek, respectable man standing in the witness box had, in fact, served time in prison on a number of occasions. He also told the court that Christie told Timothy Evans that he could perform abortions and that he had used this to gain access to Beryl. Once he had gained the Evans' trust, he had satiated his own depraved desires and then passed Beryl's murder off as a botched abortion. He had then pitilessly murdered Geraldine and hidden her body, telling her confused and grief-stricken father that she had been taken away by people who would care for her. Christie, of course, repudiated the startling accusations.

The Geraldine Evans murder trial ended on Friday, 13 January 1950. Despite John Christie's criminal record and Malcolm Morris's best efforts to portray him as the villain, the jury could not ignore two major facts. Firstly, John Christie – the mild-mannered, sickly man in the witness box – had no motive for killing Beryl or Geraldine. Secondly, Timothy Evans had previously admitted to murdering his wife and daughter. The fact that he had done so in a misguided attempt to protect their real killer seemed utterly implausible. In the end it took them just forty minutes to reach a verdict, finding Evans guilty of murdering his baby daughter. On receiving the decision, Mr Justice Lewis grimly turned to Evans and asked him, 'Timothy John Evans, you stand convicted of murder. Have you anything to say why the Court shall not give you judgement of death according to law?'

'No, sir,' were the only words Timothy Evans uttered as sobs rang out from the back of the crowded courtroom. The tears were being shed by John Christie.

Following the conclusion of the trial, Timothy Evans was moved to Pentonville Prison to await execution while his defence team frantically lodged an appeal against his sentence, arguing that 'the whole case was built wholly around the evidence of one witness, Mr Christie, who had previous convictions, one being for malicious wounding, therefore how could his evidence be taken except for what it is worth?' The appeal was not successful.

As he waited to learn the date on which he was to die, Timothy Evans spent his final days protesting his innocence to anyone who would listen to him. His protestations were so frequently uttered that one of his visitors, Dr Patrick Quinn, felt that they seemed 'rehearsed'. However, Father Joseph Francis, through whom Evans received spiritual counselling, later told his grief-stricken mother that he 'was not the sort of person to be a murderer'.

All the visitors to the condemned cell (including his mother and sisters) agreed that, although he maintained he was innocent, Timothy Evans also seemed resigned to his fate. His detractors have taken this as a sign of his guilt, reasoning that, had he truly been the victim of a massive miscarriage of justice, he would have been angry and bitter about his predicament. However, there is also the possibility that, with his wife and beloved daughter dead, he had simply given up hope.

Timothy John Evans was hanged at Pentonville Prison on 9 March 1950. At the time, his execution barely warranted a mention in the press.

Meanwhile, back in Notting Hill, life at 10 Rillington Place was never to be the same. Charles Kitchener, who had lived in the house since the Great War, understandably decided to move elsewhere. His landlord, Mr Davies, resolved to rid himself of the cursed property and in April 1950 sold it to a man named Jack Hawkins.

Mr Hawkins was a mysterious character about whom virtually nothing is known. A man bearing the same name lived in nearby Southam Street in the late 1940s, but there is nothing to suggest that he and the house purchaser were one and the same. The only known fact concerning Jack Hawkins is that he rapidly let and then sold 10 Rillington Place on to Charles Brown, an ex-boxer and nightclub bouncer of dubious reputation.

Originally hailing from the West Indies, Charles Brown had arrived in London shortly after the end of the Second World War and, by early 1950, was working on the door of the Sunset Club – a nightclub of somewhat louche repute at 50 Carnaby Street, on the edge of Soho. The owner of the club was Gus Leslie – a fellow West Indian expat, who was one of post-war Soho's most enigmatic and intriguing characters.

Gus had moved to London in 1947 and initially found work in the kitchens of various West End hotels, where he probably first became acquainted with Charles Brown. He soon became involved with the Soho nightclub scene, and in the first weeks of 1950, he opened his own establishment – the Sunset Club. At the time, Soho had a distinctly edgy reputation and Leslie played on this by turning the Sunset into a jazz club where West End revellers could come to party until the early hours. Pianist and steel band musician Russ Henderson later recalled, 'Soho was *the* place in those days, particularly the Sunset Club in Carnaby Street, where jazz played till seven in the morning. That was where the musicians went when the other clubs closed.'

Although London – and especially Notting Hill – would descend into racially motivated violence in the latter part of the decade, the early 1950s saw little cultural tension. Russ Henderson recalled both white and black jazz bands playing together at the Sunset Club and noted, 'racially, it was totally mixed. There was no such thing as a black clientele then.'

The success of the Sunset Club, combined with a burgeoning 'housing business', allowed Gus Leslie to live a flamboyant lifestyle. From his headquarters in Brixton, which he shared with his glamorous Scandinavian girlfriend, Johanna (whom he married in 1952), he oversaw his property empire, touring his investments in his luxury car, dressed in a Savile Row suit.

However, his playboy image belied the fact that he was also one of Britain's first campaigners for racial equality. In 1955, he set up the Racial Brotherhood – an organisation that promoted understanding and respect between white and black cultures. From its inception, the Racial Brotherhood attracted support from influential quarters. Archbishop of Canterbury Dr Geoffrey Fisher was its patron, and the speaker at its inaugural meeting was the eminent Jamaican statesman, Norman Manley.

Given that his doorman's wages would barely have kept a roof over his own head, it seems likely that Charles Brown's purchase of 10 Rillington Place, however cheap, was funded at least in part by his employer, Gus Leslie, who, as a property investor himself, would have known a bargain when he saw one. Brown became the official owner of the property in August 1950, by which time the only tenants in the house were John and Ethel Christie.

Knowing full well that the property's notoriety would put off many prospective tenants, Brown wisely maximised the rental yield by letting the rest of the house on a room by room basis to fellow West Indians who were prepared to ignore the property's recent history in return for cheap lodgings. His strategy worked very well, not least because Notting Hill was rapidly becoming a popular destination for young West Indians lured to England to fill the post-war labour shortage.

However, the reason for Notting Hill's popularity was not its proximity to the West End or its good transport links. In truth, it was becoming one of the few areas of the capital in which an unofficial colour bar was not in operation. Even so, many of the black newcomers were made to feel distinctly unwelcome by the locals. John and Ethel Christie were no exception, and from the outset were at loggerheads with their new landlord. From Charles Brown's point of view, the Christies were renting two rooms and had (unofficial) sole use of the kitchen but were paying just 12s 9d per week. In contrast, he could rent the other rooms in the house for £2 per week each.

Of course, the obvious plan of action would have been to raise the Christies' rent but, as long-term tenants, the amount they paid was controlled by law. Frustrated, Brown installed the rowdiest newcomers he could find in the upstairs rooms hoping that the Christies might move out. However, since the Evans trial, John Christie had barely done a day's work and so simply could not afford to move elsewhere. The situation caused a good deal of tension. By the closing weeks of 1950, relations between the Christies and their neighbours upstairs had got so bad that John Christie called in the local sanitary inspector, claiming that the habits of the other tenants were so filthy that they should be evicted. The sanitary inspector found no evidence to substantiate this offensive claim.

Aware that the atmosphere in 10 Rillington Place might descend into violence, Charles Brown installed his newly arrived associate, Beresford Brown (who was almost certainly a relative), in the house to keep an eye on proceedings.

Throughout 1951 and 1952, both John and Ethel Christie repeatedly complained about their new neighbours, and both talked to their respective doctors about the inevitable stress the situation was causing them. In the summer of 1952, they tried unsuccessfully to obtain council accommodation and even contemplated moving back to the north. In the meantime, Beresford Brown and his fellow lodgers upstairs did their best to ignore the Christies' constant protests and were no doubt relieved when, a couple of weeks before Christmas 1952, they found out that Ethel Christie had gone away to visit her sister, who had suddenly been taken ill. Their hopes were raised even further, when a few days later, Robert Hookway's van arrived to take away the majority of the Christies' furniture.

However, although he must have been living in virtually empty rooms, John Christie remained at 10 Rillington Place. Given their frosty relationship, the tenants upstairs thought it best not to ask what was happening, but Beresford's girlfriend, Lena Stewart (who was at home a lot with her new baby), noticed that Christie repeatedly disinfected the ground floor of the house, even though she had never noticed vermin there. She later recalled:

> He was sprinkling disinfectant all over the passage that leads from the front door ... He disinfected the back yard. I saw him pouring it down the drains. I also saw him put it outside under the window of his front room where I used to put my pram. He told me one morning that somebody had thrown dirty water down the drain. He never spoke to me as to why he disinfected the front passage or outside the front room window. He generally did the disinfecting between 8.30 and 9 a.m., when everybody had left the house to go to work.

John Christie remained at 10 Rillington Place over Christmas 1952 and into the New Year. However, on 13 March 1953, a local woman named Mary Reilly was out shopping in Ladbroke Grove when she passed a noticeboard advertising flats to let. She and her husband were looking for a new place to live and so Mrs Reilly stopped to have a closer look. While she was reading the cards, a man came up to her, introduced himself as John Christie and told her that he had a very nice ground floor flat to let at 10 Rillington Place.

The Reillys duly went round to have a look, liked what they saw and, thinking that Christie was the landlord, paid him a deposit of £7 13s. He told them that they could move in on 20 March, which they duly did, but their arrival did not escape the notice of Beresford Brown. That evening, Charles Brown appeared at their door and asked them what on earth they were doing in Mr Christie's flat. As the Reillys were unceremoniously ordered out of the premises, they realised that the nice Mr Christie had not only conned them out of over £7, but to add insult to injury had absconded with one of their suitcases, which Mrs Reilly had unwittingly lent him.

Soon after the Reillys' departure, Beresford Brown decided that it would make sense for him, Lena and their baby to move into the Christies' old rooms. He began cleaning them up, noticing that, despite John Christie's obsessive disinfecting, they were absolutely filthy.

He eventually got round to the ancient kitchen on 24 March. This was in a worse state than the other rooms and was appallingly badly equipped. A gas cooker had been wedged into a tiny space between the old (and probably defunct) cast-iron range and a dingy cupboard under the stairs. The space around it was so limited that the cooker door could only be fully opened if the kitchen door was shut.

Opposite the cooker, against the wall facing the back yard, stood a rickety but functional table and beyond that, in the corner, was an old sink. By the side of the sink, on the wall that divided the kitchen from the notorious wash house where the bodies of Beryl and Geraldine had been found, was a rudely constructed shelf, next to which was an old cupboard door that had been papered over.

Thinking this would be a good spot to install a radio, Beresford Brown knocked at the wall in an attempt to find the best place to fix some brackets and noticed that the part immediately above the old door seemed to be hollow. Intrigued, he decided to investigate and went to get a torch. Once back in the kitchen, Brown reached up and tore the corner of the paper away. As he had suspected, there was nothing behind it, so he took his torch and shone it through the hole. As the light illuminated the aperture, to his intense horror, he saw the back of a human body. Reeling in shock, he called his neighbour, Ivan Williams, and the two men ran to the nearest phone box to call the police.

On receiving Beresford Brown's frantic message, the police at Notting Hill must have jumped to the dreadful conclusion that Timothy Evans had killed more people than they had originally suspected at 10 Rillington Place. However, once they arrived at the squalid house, it rapidly became clear that the corpse in the wall had definitely not been there for over three years. They also discovered that the body was not alone. Two more were hidden behind it, crudely tied up and partially buried beneath a mixture of earth and ashes.

Highly unnerved by what they had found in the kitchen and not wanting to contemplate what the dreadful discovery meant, the police began to search the rest of the ground floor accompanied by their pathologist, Francis Camps. On entering the Christies' old living room, Dr Camps noticed that the floorboards seemed loose. With a growing sense of dread, he began to pull them up and found, buried under earth and rubble, the body of Ethel Christie. A search of the garden revealed the skeletal remains of two more women. The femur of one had been used to prop up the garden fence.

Following the terrible discoveries at 10 Rillington Place, the police launched a manhunt for the last occupant of the ground floor – John Christie. For several days, they were led on a wild-goose chase as numerous alleged sightings failed to secure an arrest. However, on 31 March, PC Thomas Ledger was on his beat in Putney when he noticed an unkempt man leaning over the embankment at the foot of Putney Bridge. As he drew closer, he realised that the figure bore a close resemblance to the circulated description of John Christie. PC Ledger calmly asked the man what he was doing there. He then asked him to remove his hat and, satisfied that he had found the most wanted man in Britain, took him to Putney Police Station. On arriving at the station, Christie was searched. Having lived virtually as a vagrant over the past week, he had little possessions about him. However, one item he had kept was a newspaper cutting from 1949 reporting Timothy Evans' arrest.

John Christie appeared at West London Magistrates' Court on 1 April 1953, charged with the murder of his wife. He registered a plea of not guilty, claiming that Ethel had died on 14 December from a respiratory attack brought on by the stress of living at 10 Rillington Place. Two weeks later, he was charged with the murders of the three women found in the kitchen cupboard, who had since been identified as Rita Nelson, Kathleen Maloney and Hectorina Maclennan. All three women had been strangled.

Christie was committed for trial, and while in prison he also admitted to killing the two women whose skeletons had been found in the back garden. In doing so, he also finally provided identification for these two victims, naming them as Ruth Fuerst and Muriel Eady.

The trial concerning the murder of Ethel Christie began at the Old Bailey on 22 June 1953, presided over by Mr Justice Finnemore. Sir Lionel Heald QC was counsel for the prosecution, while Derek Curtis-Bennett QC was faced with the unenviable task of representing John Christie, who continued with his plea of not guilty. Over the following four days the shocked courtroom sat in stunned silence as they listened to the sordid details of Christie's depraved career, which had cost the lives of at least six women (Christie claimed that he did not know how many women he had actually killed).

Christie's first known victim was Ruth Fuerst, an Austrian girl of Jewish/Christian parentage. Born in around 1922, Ruth had fled her homeland in 1938 to escape the wave of anti-Semitism that was sweeping across the country. She arrived in England in the summer of 1939 and quickly found work as a chambermaid at a hotel. Ruth's ambition was to qualify as a nurse and, to her delight, she was accepted on a training course. However, her studies were quickly curtailed by the outbreak of war.

After being forced to spend the first year of the conflict in an Isle of Man alien internment camp, she returned to London in late 1941, where she initially found work at the Mayfair Hotel. However, just a few months after arriving back in the capital, Ruth discovered she was pregnant and was promptly dismissed. Her daughter, Christina, was born in October 1942 but had to be put up for adoption as Ruth had no means to provide for her. Alone in a foreign – and sometimes hostile – city, and grieving for her baby daughter, she scratched a living by taking on any work she could find. If no jobs were available, she may have been forced to prostitute herself. Although there is only circumstantial evidence that Ruth sometimes walked the streets, it would explain how she had the misfortune to meet John Christie.

During Christie's wartime stint as a policeman, his colleagues became suspicious of his relationship with the prostitutes that plied their trade on the Harrow Road. Some got the distinct impression that he turned a blind eye to their activities in return for sexual favours. In addition, Christie himself claimed that he had first met Ruth while on his beat.

Whatever the circumstances of their meeting, Christie and Ruth became well acquainted during the spring and early summer of 1943. Christie later claimed that she fell 'madly in love' with him and the pair met up for romantic trysts whenever Ethel went to visit her relatives in Yorkshire. However, Christie constructed fantasies around many elements of his sordid life, so his claims about Ruth's feelings for him were probably false. Whatever the case, Ruth Fuerst did trust him enough to follow him into his bedroom at 10 Rillington Place in August 1943, where he produced a length of rope, tied it around her neck and strangled her.

The reason why Christie decided to kill Ruth is unknown. He later claimed that while they were in the bedroom a telegram arrived announcing Ethel's imminent return, and it has been suggested that this caused him to panic – but surely anyone else would have simply told Ruth that she would have to leave? The only known facts surrounding Ruth's brutal murder are that after he had killed her, Christie temporarily hid her body under the floorboards of his living room before moving it to the wash house and then a shallow grave in the back garden.

Apart from her daughter (who had been adopted), Ruth Fuerst had no relatives in England and her peripatetic existence during the months before her death meant that nobody was unduly concerned about her sudden disappearance. Her landlady and a refugee charity both reported her missing, but neither took the matter any further.

Around four months after murdering Ruth, Christie resigned from his duties as a special constable and went to work in the dispatch department of Ultra Electric's factory at Park Royal. While employed there he met Muriel Eady, a 32-year-old woman who worked on the assembly line. This time, Christie used a very different technique to gain her trust. He began inviting her for tea at Rillington Place, making sure to always invite a male colleague as well, whom Ethel probably assumed was Muriel's boyfriend. His strategy worked up to a point, but persuading Muriel to come to the house alone was a different matter. Poor Ruth Fuerst had been alone and desperate for money. In contrast, Muriel had family and a steady job so needed neither company nor cash.

However, by the end of September 1944, an opportunity presented itself. During one of their numerous chats, Christie discovered that Muriel was constantly afflicted by catarrh. Combining a rudimentary knowledge of first aid with a pack of lies, he persuaded her that he had developed a special inhalant for just such an ailment. Willing to explore any potential remedy, Muriel arranged to meet him at 10 Rillington Place on Saturday, 7 October, in order to try it out. When she arrived at the house she found Christie alone, but any apprehension she may have felt was quickly allayed when he told her that Ethel had just popped out and would be back shortly.

Muriel followed Christie into the kitchen where, placed on the rickety table was a glass jar filled with liquid from which two rubber tubes protruded. The first led to the jar's contents (a harmless concoction of water, perfume and Friar's Balsam); the other was connected to a gas pipe – a fact that Muriel seemingly did not notice. Christie instructed her to relax and deeply inhale the mixture, which she did, apparently unaware of the strong smell of gas that must have permeated the air. As her lungs filled with the deadly fumes, she lost consciousness. Christie then took her into the bedroom where he raped and strangled her before moving her body to the wash house. He then dug another grave and buried her close to Ruth.

Amazingly, Muriel Eady's friends and family made little fuss over her sudden disappearance, assuming that she had been killed by one of the numerous V2 rockets that were falling across the capital in the autumn of 1944.

To the best of anyone's knowledge, Christie halted his murderous activities for several years after killing Muriel. Indeed, his next 'official' victim was his wife. However, long before Ethel was killed, Beryl Evans arrived at Rillington Place. In many ways, she fitted Christie's victim profile perfectly – as his neighbour, she knew and trusted him, she was experiencing a crisis that clouded her judgement and her unplanned pregnancy gave Christie the chance to 'help' her.

Notably, following the murder of her and Geraldine, their bodies temporarily disappeared. Although many believed that Timothy Evans had hidden them in Charles Kitchener's rooms while he was in hospital, this was a risky strategy as there were builders working in the house at the time. Might Beryl and Geraldine have been under Christie's floorboards? In addition, the bodies were eventually found in the wash house – the place where Christie had previously hidden Ruth and Muriel before burying them in the back garden. It began to seem like there had been the most terrible miscarriage of justice.

While Timothy Evans' family followed Christie's trial in utter disbelief, the awful details of his other victims were revealed. Unsurprisingly, he stuck to his story about Ethel choking to death, as he was on trial for her murder. However, when it was made clear to him that his wife had been strangled, he claimed that he had taken a stocking and throttled her as he could not bear to see her fighting for breath. Afterwards, he had dragged her lifeless body into the living room and, after having the presence of mind to remove her valuable wedding ring, he buried her under the floorboards.

Throughout the trial, Christie's motive for killing Ethel remained a complete mystery. One can only assume that either she had known about one (or all) of his previous murders and had threatened to break her silence, or she had just discovered something about her husband's depraved activities. The latter seems more likely. Ethel Christie was close to her family and had the opportunity to escape to safety before she went to the police if she had long since known about her husband's crimes.

The court turned to the circumstances under which the three women in the kitchen had met their deaths. Kathleen Maloney (26) had led a lonely and often destitute existence. With no known family and five children to support, she regularly resorted to casual prostitution or modelling for amateur soft porn photographers in order to make ends meet. Shortly before Ethel's murder, Kathleen and her friend, Maureen Riggs, had posed for (and apparently with) Christie during a seedy photography shoot and so when the pair saw him in a pub the following January, they were happy to chat to him, especially as he was buying the drinks. It was to be the last evening that Maureen would spend with her friend. Kathleen left the pub with Christie before closing time and went back to 10 Rillington Place. Once there, he gassed her and then raped and strangled her before hiding her body in the kitchen cupboard.

Rita Nelson (25) was Christie's next victim. A native of Northern Ireland, she had arrived in London in 1952 in search of work but had quickly fallen into the same trap as Kathleen Maloney, preferring to walk the streets rather than sleep on them. On 12 January 1953, Rita visited a doctor who confirmed she was twenty-four weeks' pregnant and referred her to the Samaritan Hospital for Women. The next day, she was dismissed from her temporary job as a kitchen maid in a Notting Hill pub. Soon afterwards, she ran into John Christie.

The only account that exists of Rita's last hours is that related by Christie himself, and therefore it is almost certainly untrue. According to him, she accosted him in Ladbroke Grove asking him for £1 to 'take him round the corner'. When he refused, she demanded 30s and warned that she would scream that he had attacked her if he did not pay up. Christie then claimed:

> I walked away, as I am so well known round there, and she obviously would have created a scene. She came along. She wouldn't go and came right to the door, still demanding 30s. When I opened the door, she forced her way in. I went into the kitchen and she was still on about this 30s. I tried to get her out and she picked up a frying pan to hit me. I closed with her and there was a struggle and she fell back on the chair. It was a deck chair. There was a piece of rope hanging from the chair. I don't remember what happened, but I must have gone haywire.
>
> The next thing I remember was she was lying still in the chair with the rope round her neck. I don't remember taking it off. It couldn't have been tight. I left her there and went into the front room. After that I had a cup of tea and went to bed. I got up in the morning and went into the kitchen and washed and shaved. She was still in the chair. I believe I made some tea.

He then put Rita's body in the kitchen cupboard.

Throughout his trial, John Christie took great pains to portray himself as a victim and his account of what happened with Rita Nelson is a typical example of this. A far more likely version of events is that he already knew her and was also aware that few people would notice if she disappeared.

He was far less careful in the selection of his final victim.

Hectorina Maclennan, 27, first met John Christie in early March 1953 when, in circumstances that were chillingly similar to those concerning Mary Reilly, he told her that he had a flat to let in Rillington Place. Hectorina agreed to come and have a look but brought her boyfriend, Alexander Baker, with her. At the time, Baker noted that his presence seemed to irritate Christie, but he could not work out why. He and Hectorina wanted time to consider the flat and so, despite Christie's offer to put them up for a few days while they decided, they opted to return to their previous lodgings. However, once there, they found they had been locked out and so reluctantly returned to 10 Rillington Place.

Hectorina and Alexander stayed in the rooms with Christie for three days. On 6 March, they decided to go to Hammersmith labour exchange to look for work but, after registering, Hectorina told her boyfriend that she had to go back to Rillington Place to meet someone; she did not say who. Baker agreed to meet up with her later in the day, but when she failed to arrive he returned to Rillington Place and asked Christie if he had seen her. He said he had not, but realising that Baker was very worried he agreed to help him search for her. As the two men left the house, little did Alexander Baker realise that Hectorina's body was already in the kitchen cupboard.

John Christie must have possessed some impressive powers of persuasion. While out on the wild-goose chase with Alexander Baker, he somehow managed to convince him not to bother reporting Hectorina's sudden disappearance and, thus, her murder was not discovered until Beresford Brown accidentally uncovered her remains.

The trial of John Christie lasted four days. Despite his defence team arguing that no sane man could have acted in such a depraved manner, it took the jury just over one hour to find him guilty of first-degree murder. He received the death sentence and did not appeal.

The shocking revelations of the trial also raised troubling doubts over Timothy Evans' conviction, with counsel for the prosecution, Sir Lionel Heald QC, rhetorically asking what the chances were of two murderers living in the same house, at the same time. As a result, an enquiry into the Evans trial was launched and while he awaited his

execution in Pentonville Prison, Christie was once again asked if he
had murdered Beryl and/or Geraldine Evans. His answer was mad-
deningly ambiguous:

> It is not a case of whether I am prepared to [say I killed them] or not.
> I just cannot unless I was telling some lie or other about them. It [his
> memory] is still fogged, but if someone said: 'Well it's obvious you
> did, and there is enough proof about it', then I accept that I did.

In the event, the enquiry could not get over the fact that, although he
had later retracted his confession, Timothy Evans had admitted to
the killings, and ultimately advised that his conviction should stand.
The result devastated the Evans family. Knowing that time was running
out, Timothy's mother wrote to Christie on 2 July 1953 pleading with
him to confess to the murders of her grandchild and daughter-in-law.
It had no effect. Christie's last conversation regarding the Evans' murders
occurred on 13 July, when Dennis Hague, an old army friend, visited
him in prison. Hague looked him in the eye and asked him straight out
if he had killed Beryl and Geraldine. Christie replied, 'I don't know,
I can't remember', then gave Hague a cryptic look and blinked.

The Evans family's wish to get a confession out of Christie was never
fulfilled. He was hanged at 9 a.m. on 15 July 1953. His executioner,
Albert Pierrepoint, wrote of the murderer's last minutes in his memoirs,
recalling that as soon as he entered the condemned cell, Christie's:

> … face seemed to melt. It was more than terror. I think it was not that
> he was afraid of the act of execution. He had lived with and gloated
> upon corpses. But I knew in that moment that John Reginald Christie
> would have given anything in his power to postpone the moment of
> detail. My assistant and I had his skimpy wrists pinioned before he
> knew fully what was happening, and then he rose to his feet, a little
> taller than I was, so that I had to reach up to remove his spectacles.
> In that instant I met his eyes and quite slowly pulled off his glasses,
> laying them carefully upon the scrubbed bone table beside me.
> This was his last moment to speak. He blinked bewilderingly, screw-
> ing up his eyes. Then he focused them on the door that stood open

between the condemned cell and the execution chamber … Faltering pitifully, his movements were not so much a walk, as a drifting forward, his legs stumbling. I thought he was going to faint.

In the end, Albert Pierrepoint 'hanged John Reginald Christie, the monster of Rillington Place, in less time than it took the ash to fall off a cigar'.

Christie's death removed the Evans family's last chance of ever finding out what really happened at 10 Rillington Place on 8 November 1949. Everyone who had been in the house that night was now dead. Despite this, they vowed to continue their fight to clear Timothy's name and in 1965, an independent enquiry into the deaths of Beryl and Geraldine was launched, headed by Mr Justice Brabin. The enquiry took two months to conduct and was a frustrating affair, given the lack of witnesses.

Eventually, Brabin came to the official conclusion that Timothy Evans had probably killed his wife during an argument over money, but that Christie had probably killed Geraldine. However, his motive for killing a defenceless baby was never established and Brabin himself asked, 'can one accept that to this small house in their turn there came two men, each to become a killer, each a strangler, each strangling women, always by a ligature … some claim that to suggest that this coincidence could come about is to stretch credulity too far'.

As a result of Brabin's findings, Timothy Evans – who had been hanged for the murder of Geraldine, not Beryl – was given a posthumous pardon, much good did it do him. The fact remained, however, that had he been tried for the murder of Beryl, the verdict would have been upheld.

As for 10 Rillington Place, Charles Brown put the notorious house on the market as soon as the police had finished their searches of the property. However, on 27 July the *Daily Mirror* reported under the headline 'Christie House – No Takers':

Nobody wants to buy 10 Rillington Place, the Notting Hill home of strangler John Christie. The house, which is still empty, was put up for sale several weeks ago but so far the landlord, Mr Charles Brown, has received no offer which he would consider acceptable. What does Mr Brown consider a reasonable offer? He said yesterday, 'Oh, about £1,000, maybe less. No one is going to get the house for nothing.'

Unable to rid himself of the cursed property, Brown managed to find a few brave tenants who were prepared to live in the upper floors of the house and turned the ground floor into an after-hours drinking den known as the Celebrity Club. This new establishment was not well received by the other residents of Rillington Place, who were already being plagued by ghoulish sightseers wanting to catch a glimpse of the 'house of horrors'. A year after Christie's execution, they succeeded in persuading the council to rename the street 'Ruston Close' in an attempt to stop the tourists, and as the years passed things gradually returned to normal (although it is not known whether Charles Brown ever managed to sell No. 10).

Due to the dilapidated state of the street and its inherent notoriety, none of its landlords saw any value in extending their tenure and by 1970 the last of the original building leases had expired. Thus, Rillington Place reverted back to the St Quintin estate who wisely decided to erase all trace of it. The demolition crews arrived that autumn, shortly after the sordid events at 10 Rillington Place had been chronicled in Richard Fleischer's eponymous film. Parts of the movie were filmed on location and apparently Richard Attenborough's portrayal of Christie was so accurate that it prompted one resident to comment that it was like seeing him 'risen from the grave'.

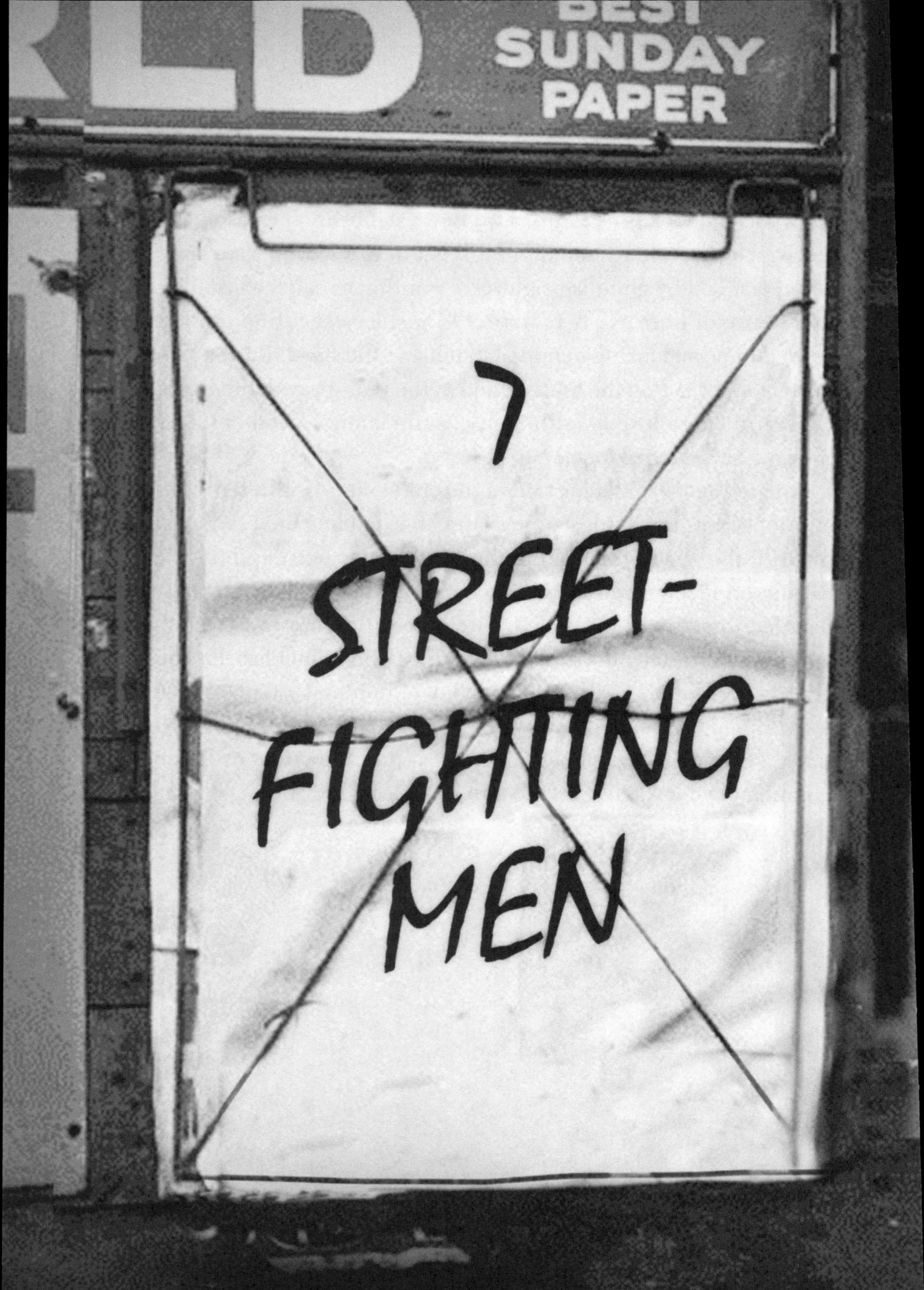
RLD
BEST
SUNDAY
PAPER
7
STREET-
FIGHTING
MEN

Today West Indians have common citizenship and
common cause with us and they have come over to help us.

Ministry of Information, 1944

**** off you coppers. We will deal with these black ****s.

Notting Hill resident, 1957

B y the mid-1950s, the people of Notting Hill, still reeling from the horrors exposed in the trial of John Christie, were facing a new crisis that would ultimately lead to destruction, division and chaos as one neighbour turned against another. Soon, Beresford Brown – the man who had exposed Christie's abhorrent crimes – and his fellow West Indians would be fighting for survival, as they became targets for white gangs, jaded and frustrated by a life devoid of prospects in one of the most deprived areas of the city.

The animosity of their white neighbours came as a complete shock to Notting Hill's newly arrived West Indian community. Many of them had spent time in Britain during the war, where they helped fill a massive labour shortage caused by the wholesale mobilisation of the armed forces and the commandeering of factories to manufacture munitions. By 1944, around 10,000 West Indian men and women were also working as pilots and ground crew for the RAF and thousands more had enlisted in the newly enlarged Merchant Navy. Their help was greatly appreciated by the British, and consequently, they were welcomed into communities with warmth and enthusiasm.

Most of the West Indians who came to Britain during the Second World War had no intention of staying permanently, and so once the conflict came to an end they boarded ships and made their way back to their homelands. It was a journey many of them would live to regret.

Poverty had posed a chronic and serious problem throughout the Caribbean for generations. Although by the 1940s slavery in the West Indies had been outlawed for over a century, the region was still struggling to overcome its effects. The sheer number of people transported to the islands to work on plantations while the slave system was in full force had made it impossible to economically sustain the population after emancipation and the collapse of the sugar trade.

At first, many West Indians had migrated to South America where they found work on civil engineering projects such as the construction of the railways and the Panama Canal. When these projects came to an end, they turned their attention to the USA, but the massive recession sparked by the Wall Street Crash in 1929 put paid to finding employment in America. By the eve of the Second World War, frustration and anger at the endless destitution in the West Indies had caused riots to break out in Jamaica – one of the worst affected islands – and thus, many people from the Caribbean were only too pleased to take the long voyage to Britain to help with the ensuing war effort. During their time there, memories of their impoverished homelands began to fade as they grew accustomed to a more comfortable standard of living. However, this only served to make readjusting to the hardships of life in the West Indies all the more difficult once the conflict was over.

After the war many repatriated West Indians dreamed of returning to Britain. Consequently, when a Jamaican newspaper carried an advertisement offering 300 places on the merchant ship *Empire Windrush* for those wishing to emigrate to the 'mother country', the shipping line was swamped with applications. By the time the ship departed on 24 May 1948, all the places had been taken and another 192 Jamaicans made the journey without berths, living and sleeping on the deck. Their departure sparked an exodus from the West Indies – between 1948 and 1962 nearly 100,000 people migrated from the Caribbean to Britain.

The *Empire Windrush* docked at Tilbury on 21 June and its passengers disembarked to face a future filled with uncertainty. Many had made no accommodation arrangements and, after arriving in London, 230 of them were forced to sleep in an old air-raid shelter on Clapham Common while they searched for employment and more comfortable lodgings. Work proved relatively easy to find. Within just three weeks, most of the *Empire Windrush*'s passengers were employed and before long, more ships bringing scores of eager young West Indians began arriving at Britain's ports. However, although work was plentiful, their co-workers were often unfriendly and suspicious.

The inhospitable welcome perplexed many of the West Indians, particularly those who had spent happy times in London during the war. However, certain factions of the white population saw them as a threat. The vast majority of West Indians who arrived in the capital after the war were young, ambitious and single. Consequently, they were hardworking, unencumbered by family obligations and prepared to take on low wage jobs to get their careers off the ground. While these attributes were welcomed by prospective employers, their existing employees had a very different opinion. In a misguided attempt to protect the interests of their members, the Transport & General Workers Union announced that the West Indian workforce 'constitutes a very grave threat to labour and social standards in this country'.

Many Londoners blamed the maladministration of the West Indies by successive governments for the sudden influx of migrants, but still deeply resented their presence. In a letter to the *West London Observer*, Mr Boyer of Talbot Road, Notting Hill, wrote, 'The coloured peoples have been betrayed by the false promises of politicians. But is that any reason why Britain should become a haven for exploited colonials?'

In the same newspaper, C. Barrow of Biscay Road, Hammersmith, agreed, 'Why should white citizens of this country be made to bear the burden of the politicians' past neglect?' Thankfully, other readers were more considered in their opinion on immigration. Mrs R. Brown, of Masbro' Buildings, W14, pointed out, 'I am sure that many of your readers have suffered directly and indirectly from Hitler's racial discrimination; countless men and women gave their lives that fascism might never again raise its ugly head here, or anywhere else in the world.'

Another part of life that proved challenging for the West Indian migrants was the search for somewhere to live. As they hopefully knocked on the doors of London's numerous lodging houses, many were confused to find that, even though vacancies were advertised on cards in the windows, no rooms were available. The reason behind this curious state of affairs became clear a few weeks later when an additional line was added to the vacancy cards – 'No Coloureds'.

In Kensington, a landlady interviewed by a television crew explained, 'I've got nothing against them [the West Indians] myself, but if I give them a room, all my other tenants will leave.' Soon it became painfully apparent to the West Indians that the only lodgings that would admit them were located in the most deprived areas of the city where no one else wanted to live. One such area was Brixton; another was Notting Hill. However, even there, they faced exploitation. Many landlords quickly realised that they could charge exorbitant rents to West Indian tenants because they were desperate. Those who could not afford to pay these inflated sums resorted to sharing the rooms and were then accused of 'taking over' by their angry neighbours.

The anxieties felt by Londoners – particularly those in Notting Hill and its surrounds – over the sudden influx of West Indians was fully exploited by right-wing extremists. Oswald Mosley's Union Movement spouted their hate-filled doctrine on Portobello Road, and walls across the district were daubed with the slogan 'Keep Britain White'. The National Labour Party also began campaigning in the area, producing leaflets that demanded a ban on 'coloured immigration', and announced their intention to contest selected wards in Notting Hill and Brixton at the next council elections. Their secretary, John Bean, explained the party's aims to a reporter from *The Times*: 'As a family man, I am against violence of any sort. We are not unfriendly to coloured people. We are for friendship – but no mixing. We shall agitate continually until coloured immigration is stopped.'

The fear of 'mixing' black and white cultures seemed to be at the heart of many people's prejudice. The Brentford & Chiswick Labour Women's Section held a conference to discuss whether they should attempt to restrict mixed marriages by law. John Edgecombe, an Antiguan who arrived in London in the early 1950s, later recalled:

For a white woman to go out with a black man she would totally alienate herself from the rest of white society. She would get lots of stick, like being called 'nigger-lover' by her neighbours. I'm not exaggerating. When Nelly [his white girlfriend] and I went out for a drink together, we always got funny looks. On many occasions we were even refused service. Imagine what it is like to ask for a pint of beer only to be told, 'No, we are not serving you.'

By the middle of the 1950s, the racial divisions in Notting Hill had become so tense that *The Times* newspaper dispatched one of their journalists to the area in an attempt to discover the root of the problem. They wrote:

> The great majority of the white inhabitants [of Notting Hill] have nothing against coloured people as such … and there are signs to prove it … On the other hand, racial feeling is not confined to gangs of youths who cause trouble in the evenings … your Correspondent found a group of men in a public house singing 'Old Man River' and 'Bye Bye Blackbird' and punctuating the songs with vicious anti-Negro slogans. The men said their motto was 'Keep Britain White' … Not all the whites resent coloured people. Few think that violence is justified. But there are some, especially of the men, who go around saying violent things. Quite young children repeat them: 'Whose side are you on?' A young boy asked me, 'We think all niggers should be shot.'

One group who seized on the anti-black feeling that prevailed in Notting Hill in the mid-1950s were white, working-class boys. These youths, who had grown up in a city being ravaged by war, were no strangers to violence and destruction. Like their fathers before them, they formed themselves into teenage gangs and in a misguided quest for excitement and a sense of belonging, they ferociously protected the dilapidated streets in which they lived.

By 1950, the Notting Hill gangs had become part of a violent national subculture known as the 'Cosh Boys'. Their ominous nickname had been acquired in 1948 when the *Daily Express* ran an article about escaped borstal boys attacking a tram passenger under the headline 'Cosh Boys Given Penal Servitude'. Soon, the phrase 'Cosh Boys' was being used to describe any group of young troublemakers and the youths involved were only too happy to live up to their violent reputation. The carrying of coshes became so widespread that the police began to randomly search groups of young men and confiscate the weapons. In order to get around this, the youths took to tying coins into a handkerchief, which did as good a job as a cosh but could be easily undone if a police search looked imminent.

By 1953, the Cosh Boys had become so notorious that a film was even made about them. Featuring a young Joan Collins, *Cosh Boy* told the story of Roy, a 16-year-old London gang leader, who vicariously satisfied his craving for violence and crime by bullying his weaker-willed associates. Although the film is tame by modern standards, it caused a great deal of controversy when it was first released, particularly as it drew uncomfortable parallels with the true story of 16-year-old Christopher Craig who, in November 1952, persuaded Derek Bentley – a 19-year-old epileptic with learning difficulties – to take part in a robbery he was planning in Croydon.

While the robbery was in progress, Craig and Bentley were discovered and in a panic Craig shot two policemen, injuring one and killing the other. At the ensuing trial, the police claimed that the 16-year-old had fired the fatal shot after they heard Bentley urge him to 'let him have it, Chris'. These words signed Derek Bentley's death warrant. The judge ruled that he had mentally aided the murder and he was sentenced to hang. Due to his age, Christopher Craig escaped with a ten-year gaol sentence. *Cosh Boy* was released shortly after Bentley's execution in January 1953 and was one of the first films to be awarded an X certificate.

As with any teenage subculture, the Cosh Boys quickly evolved. By the time their eponymous film was released, they had begun to adopt a flamboyant mode of dress that had first been popular with the roguish 'mashers' of the early 1900s. The fashion had originally made a comeback in 1949 when wartime clothes rationing ceased. Desperate to recoup the financial losses suffered during the conflict, Savile Row tailors cannily began to promote Edwardian-style masher suits to their wealthy clientele as they comprised very long jackets (requiring much more material than other styles) worn over waistcoats made from the most expensive silk, which could be sold at a very tidy profit. Savile Row's marketing worked and by 1950, the revamped Edwardian fashions had been adopted by many affluent young men. The ostentatious suits quickly caught the eye of the Cosh Boys, who asked their own tailors to copy the look.

The Cosh Boys' version of the Edwardian masher suit featured slim 'stovepipe' trousers to give a more broad-shouldered silhouette.

They customised the look further by wearing bootlace ties like their Hollywood Western heroes, John Wayne and Gary Cooper. American film stars were also responsible for the boys' adoption of a slicked back 'DA' hairstyle (so called because the back resembled a 'Duck's Arse'). A colourful waistcoat and a pair of Brothel Creepers – shoes with thick, rubber wedge soles, completed the dramatic effect.

The Cosh Boys' eye-catching outfits gave rise to them being collectively renamed 'Edwardians', which in turn corrupted into 'Teddy Boys' or simply 'Teds'. Interestingly, the 'Teddy Boy' nickname was not new. Back in the first years of the 1900s, the term had been used to describe members of the Territorial Army; the chorus of a popular song called 'Bravo Territorials' ran:

> When called to fight or die
> They will give us cause to cry
> Gallant Teddy Boys, bravo!

It was ironic that a name originally used to describe brave and disciplined young men ultimately became synonymous with feckless and indolent street gangs.

Like its predecessor, the Teddy Boy subculture quickly found itself linked to crime and violence. In September 1953, 16-year-old Ronald Coleman, otherwise known as 'Ronnie-the-Masher', appeared in court charged with the murder of rival gang member, John Beckley. The *Daily Express* noted:

> He [Coleman] preened. He was fond of his own good looks; he believed that clothes made not only the man but the leader of men. And for clothes, this Clapham shop assistant chose the style of the 'mashers', or men-about-town of Edwardian days. He wore a grey Edwardian jacket with stovepipe trousers, and he arranged for a quiff of hair to fall forward. Then he went across Clapham Common as Ronnie-the-Masher – ready to challenge comment and spoiling for a fight. He did not believe altogether in individual combat, because individuals often meet their match. He believed in the effectiveness of numbers. He recruited followers – mostly older than himself.

Some of his followers – four of them were jailed yesterday – dressed
like him ... Together they looked for trouble on the Common or in
milk bars, in pin-table saloons, and in cinemas.

Although the press were quick to seize on the Teddy Boys as the
embodiment of all that was bad about Britain's youth, it should be
stressed that, like the myriad subcultures that followed (punk rockers
being a prime example), the Teddy Boy fashion was widely adopted
by all types of teenagers, good and bad.

In 1954, the *Picture Post* visited the Mecca Ballroom in
Tottenham – a favourite haunt of Teddy Boys – and found the patrons
to be hard-working, fun-loving teenagers who would rather chat up
girls than fight rival gangs. A year later, the writer and broadcaster
James Hemming wrote in the *West London Observer*, 'Teddy Boys
are not always tough [but] they feel they must impress themselves on
the world, by being different.' Nevertheless, the Teds remained social
pariahs among the chattering classes.

Over in Notting Hill and its surrounds, the street gangs were early
adopters of the Teddy Boy look, which in itself sometimes led to violence. In July 1955, 22-year-old Cyril Murphy was arrested after he
and a friend were involved in a savage gang fight outside the cinema
on Hammersmith Broadway. At his subsequent court appearance,
he explained that the fight had started when members of the rival
gang taunted him over his DA haircut:

My hair is not the same as theirs and they started laughing. I asked
what they were laughing about and they were then joined by three
other youths. They started on us and I called two of my mates out of
the milk bar. There were only four of us against six of them.

When no fights were in the offing, the Teds did themselves no favours
at all by resorting to general delinquency in order to pass the time.
In 1954, the *West London Observer* reported that 'a gang of boys wearing Edwardian clothes' overturned a car parked in Princes Place,
Notting Hill, and then proceeded to throw some discarded scaffold-
ing boards into the basement of a nearby house. In another incident,

which took place in March 1956, the patrons of a Teddy Boy club in West Kensington infuriated their neighbours by throwing bottles and buckets of water at passers-by.

Although the Teds' antics were often antisocial and destructive, at first they were rarely sinister. However, in 1955 an incident occurred that turned out to be a precursor for much more troubling behaviour. On 5 March, William Butler, a West Indian man who had recently arrived in Britain, was walking through Shepherd's Bush Market when he was set upon by two Teddy Boys. The youths punched and kicked him to the ground and then picked up a nearby stool, which they used to viciously beat him around the head before running off, leaving Mr Butler bleeding and semi-conscious. Although the market was packed with shoppers and stallholders, nobody did a thing to stop the boys and they were never apprehended.

Over the following months, the west London Teddy Boys' territorial instincts became increasingly irritated by the large numbers of West Indian immigrants in their midst, particularly in Notting Hill. Their resentment was wholeheartedly encouraged and cynically exploited by the National Labour Party, who made sure they received copies of the *Black & White News* – a paper produced by the Britons' Publishing Society, an anti-immigration organisation who used their sixpenny rag to propagate vicious rumours about Notting Hill's new black community, under inflammatory headlines such as 'Blacks Milk Assistance Board' and 'Blacks Seek White Women'. Inside each issue of the newspaper was a declaration against 'the permanent settlement of coloured people in Britain', which readers were encouraged to sign and send to their MP.

The divisive efforts of the National Labour Party and the *Black & White News* were terrifyingly effective. When *The Times* dispatched a reporter to the streets of Notting Hill to record the inhabitants' views on immigration, he found that many whites repeated the lies and rumours they had read:

> There are three main causes of resentment against coloured inhabitants of the district. They are alleged to do no work and to collect a rich sum from the Assistance Board. They are said to be able to find

housing when white residents cannot. And they are charged with all kinds of misbehaviour, especially sexual. Talking to housewives at their garden gates, menfolk in saloon bars and teenagers in corner cafés, your Correspondent had no doubt that these charges are universally believed to have some substance in them. At least a dozen men claimed for example that they had seen a coloured man 'just off the boat', collecting £5 as a week's National Assistance ... Several men told your Correspondent that their wives had been accosted by coloured men and many told the story of a young white girl who is said to have been raped by one. Several houses in the troubled district are generally believed by local people to be brothels.

The existence of brothels in Notting Hill was by no means a new phenomenon, and there is no documentary evidence to confirm that any of them were owned by West Indians. However, the mere fact that black men were seen to be working in or patronising these dubious establishments was sufficiently damning. Ernest Ickle, a black journalist and cricket commentator who had lived in Britain since 1937, interviewed white residents of Notting Hill in the late 1950s and found that many of them firmly believed the myth that many West Indian men lived off prostitution.

A youth, who preferred not to give Ickle his name, told him that Notting Hill had 'the worst' of the West Indian migrants 'because they've got girls on the game'. A café owner, who also remained nameless, explained, 'I don't think that coloured people *shouldn't* live here, but I would certainly say that there is a large element who should be taken out because they're living on women.' Mr Bramley, the owner of a local pub, agreed, 'A lot of the houses around here are run as brothels, which is altogether wrong,' he told Ickle.

Had the white population been given the opportunity to mix with their new West Indian neighbours, they would have found that many of their fears were unjustified. However, by the mid-1950s an unofficial apartheid existed on the streets of Notting Hill. The authorities did virtually nothing to ease the tension and consequently the situation became so grave that the West Indies Commission felt compelled to write to the Secretary of State for Colonies complaining,

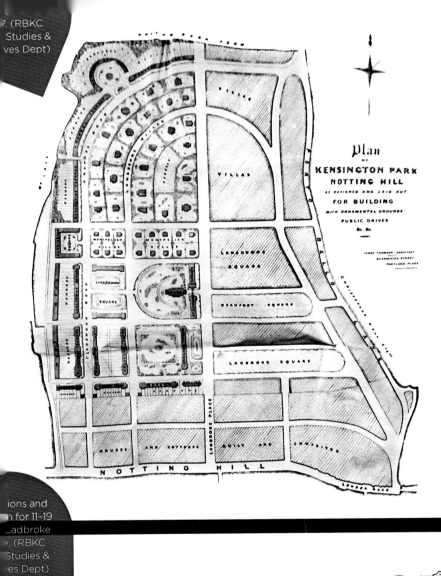

Plan
of
KENSINGTON PARK
NOTTING HILL
AS DESIGNED AND LAID OUT
FOR BUILDING
WITH ORNAMENTAL GROUNDS
PUBLIC DRIVES
&c &c

JAMES THOMSON ARCHITECT
DEVONSHIRE STREET
PORTLAND PLACE

11   19

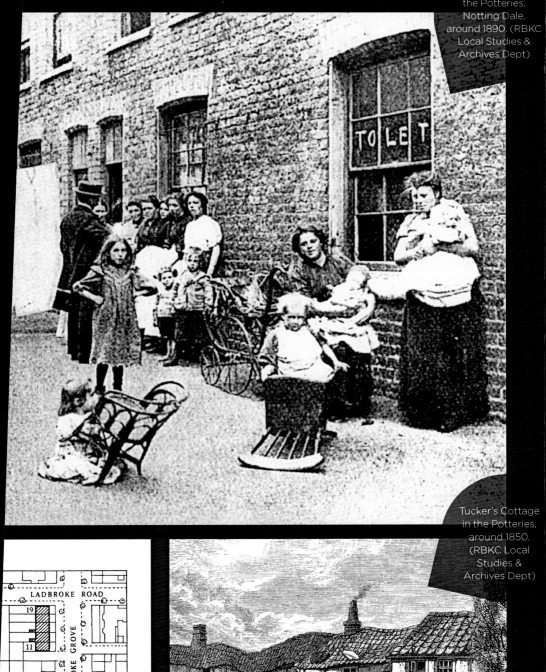

TO LET

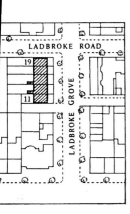

LADBROKE ROAD

LADBROKE GROVE

19

11

at Walter Carter's fish shop on the Portobello Road, around 1890. (RBKC Local Studies & Archives Dept)

Notting Hill Gate, around 1895. (RBKC Local Studies & Archives Dept)

Marks & Spencer's Penny Bazaar on Portobello Road, around 1900. (RBKC Local Studies & Archives Dept)

Milk cart Colville Gar Notting Hill, 1905. (RB Local Studi Archives D

Children playing
outside 10
Rillington Place,
1966. (Terry
Fincher/Express/
Getty Images)

Cover of *OZ*
magazine,
May 1968.
(Felix Dennis)

Squatters' protest at Powis Square, Notting Hill, 1972. (Marx Memorial Library/ Mary Evans)

The Si
Esta
the We
the bac
1988,
Local S
Archive

Ladbroke Grove during the Notting Hill Carnival, around 1980. (RBKC Local Studies & Archives Dept)

'The Commission has received continuously reports of a persistent feeling on the part of West Indians that the Police are not impartial,' but that conversely, the authorities did little to curb the migrants 'who have house parties of a disturbing character'.

The parties to which the commission referred often took place in 'shebeens' – unofficial nightclubs run by West Indians that were set up in private houses. On arriving in Notting Hill, John Edgecombe set up his own shebeen in Colville Terrace. He later described how it operated in his book, *Black Scandal*:

> It was a flat on the first floor. When it was full, we had about twenty to thirty people inside the flat. There was a front room where you could listen to the latest sounds, sitting on low chairs. In this room there was a bar, where we served every type of drink you wanted. Next door in the bedroom was the casino. The only furniture in the bedroom was a table with chairs, where people sat and played poker. Then there was the kitchen at the end, where the cooking went on. In the kitchen I employed a man called Bully. He cooked Caribbean soul food, which was rice and peas. In the front room would be some nice jazz going down, with people drinking and smoking dope. I would roll the joints myself and sell them for five shillings a spliff. While the men were gambling, the chicks sat around getting stoned and drunk … The shebeen had no fixed hours and just stayed open each day until the last people left. In any card game the house is always a guaranteed winner, and on a good week, my shebeen could earn up to £400.

Despite the fact that shebeens were clearly a good way to make money, they did little to endear the proprietor and his patrons to the other residents of the house.

By the latter years of the 1950s, the West Indians were understandably growing heartily sick of being blamed for the ills of Notting Hill. However, as they settled into the district and grew in numbers, their confidence also increased, and by 1957 they were ready to fight back. On Friday, 18 October, the *West London Observer* reported on a vicious altercation between local Teddy Boys and a rival gang of black youths:

Police Sergeant Robin Duff-Cole said it was 4.15 p.m. on Sunday when with other officers he saw approximately 50–60 coloured and white people gathered in Ladbroke Grove at the junction with Lancaster Road. There was a fight in progress. At the centre of the crowd, excitedly urging on the white combatant, stood 24-year-old William Bell, who lived in nearby Talbot Grove. Sergeant Duff-Cole and his fellow officers told Bell to go home, but he refused, shouting, '**** off you coppers. We will deal with these black ****s', before punching PC Desmond Condon in the face.

The incident in Ladbroke Grove highlighted the disturbing fact that Notting Hill's Teddy Boys had decided to take matters into their own hands and their adversaries no longer had any intention of turning the other cheek. A young black woman summed up the West Indians' mood when she was interviewed by the newscaster, Reginald Bosanquet. Defiantly, she told him, 'If they [white youths] attack my countrymen … then we are going to make certain that we get the last hit. If they don't attack us they have no fear of us, but if they attack, then we'll fight back.'

It was only a matter of time before the streets would descend into complete chaos, and the moment finally came the following summer when, during the August Bank Holiday weekend, Notting Hill found itself at the epicentre of London's first race riots.

The first signs of trouble occurred a week before the bank holiday. In the early hours of Sunday, 24 August, nine Teddy Boys armed themselves with coshes and iron bars and began cruising the streets of Notting Hill hell-bent on 'nigger bashing'. They found five unlucky victims: Matthew Lucien, John Pirmal, Joseph Welsh, James Etienne and MacDonald Waldron were all subjected to vicious and unprovoked attacks, during which they were beaten so badly that they required hospital treatment. Although the white youths were quickly arrested, their violent spree provided a catalyst for others to unleash their pent-up frustrations over the following weekend.

On the evening of Thursday, 28 August, with a four-day holiday ahead of them, groups of white youths – some only just out of school – began to congregate on the streets of Notting Hill looking for trouble. One such gang were hanging around outside Latimer Road tube station when they noticed Majbritt Morrison, a young white woman, striding up the road in the throes of a heated argument with a black man. They rushed to defend her, but were temporarily stunned into silence when she told them that the man was, in fact, her husband and that they should mind their own business.

Humiliated, the gang decided to beat up Mr Morrison anyway, but they did not bank on the fact that several of his friends were nearby. A violent scuffle broke out between the two factions and, although it ended as rapidly as it had started, news of the altercation began to spread through Notting Hill. As word was passed around, the Morrisons' petty argument morphed into something more serious and within hours, rumours were being circulated that a white woman had been raped.

The following evening brought much graver trouble to Notting Hill. As darkness fell, a mob of around 400 angry white youths made their way to Bramley Road, which was largely populated by West Indians. Although a police contingent was dispatched to the area in a half-hearted attempt to restore calm, the officers quickly realised that their presence would have little effect. PC Richard Bedford recalled how the mob shouted at him, 'We will kill all black bastards. Why don't you send them home?'

His colleague, PC Ian McQueen, tried to reason with the ring-leaders but was told, 'Mind your own business … keep out of it. We will settle these niggers our way. We'll murder the bastards.' Fearful that arrests would only make matters worse, the police stood by and watched while Bramley Road filled with people, many of whom directed their anger at them. PC Geoffrey Golding and several other officers were confronted by a furious group of Teds who demanded to know, 'Why are you helping the black bastards? You are a lot of nigger lovers … come on you f*****g coppers if you want to fight.' With that, a shower of bottles rained down on the policemen's heads.

As the siege at Bramley Road continued, word spread across London that Notting Hill was on the verge of riot. Soon, gangs of youths from across the capital were pouring out of the nearby tube stations, armed with a frightening array of weapons. Others came in cars and vans. Few stopped to think about what they were doing, or why they were doing it.

Patrick Short, who, along with his friends, was stopped by police after driving up and down Portobello Road shouting insults at black passers-by, told the officers, 'I know it sounds silly, but we were look-ing for fun.' Another young lad, who was in the gang who attacked Mr Morrison, told the police, 'It was just fighting which grew bigger and everyone joined in. We were bored.'

Although a few scuffles broke out on the Friday night, police man-aged to contain the violence. However, by the following evening, the sheer number of gangs on the streets of Notting Hill made the fighting impossible to control. Incidents broke out across the district and anarchy reigned supreme.

In Bramley Road, a group of youths threw a firebomb into the home of a 27-year-old Jamaican man, driving him and his friends out into the street, where they were set upon. In other incidents, windows of West Indian houses were shattered as iron railings and bricks were launched at the properties in a bid to rout the inhabitants.

Wisely, most of the people inside stayed put, but by the following evening they were growing weary of being imprisoned in their own homes. Consequently, Sunday night saw worse violence. At one point, an estimated 400 people were fighting on Bramley Road. Builder, Bert Harper, who had unwisely gone to see what was going on, received a 5in slash across his neck from a knife-wielding rioter. Other bystanders were also injured, including an elderly woman who was knocked over as the mob fled from police and a 10-year-old boy, who was hit in the face with a broken bottle.

When the mob could find no West Indians, they attacked the police instead. *The Times* reported that during Sunday night:

A jeering crowd threw bottles at a shop which was being guarded by a policeman ... Later skirmishes seemed to be between police and crowds of white persons ... a gang of 100 youths armed with sticks, iron bars and knives gathered under the railway arches at Latimer Road Underground Station. Police cars were hit by bricks flung by the crowd.

By Bank Holiday Monday, the mob showed no sign of dispersing and so the Metropolitan Police tried a different tactic, sending plain clothes officers into the fray to get intelligence on the ringleaders.

The officers' findings were chilling. One of the spies, PC Roy Fuller, remembered encountering a well-known thug named Brian Greenham on Latimer Road. Desperately hoping that the youth and his cohorts would not recognise him, PC Fuller tentatively went over to strike up a conversation. As he approached, he noticed that Greenham had a leather belt hanging round his neck, which had been studded with bolts and screws. When PC Fuller asked him what it was for, Greenham shrugged and told him he planned to use it on 'a bloke who done one of my mates up'.

Journalists also took to the streets of Notting Hill in a bid to get to the bottom of the violence. *Daily Express* writer Merrick Wynn was astonished at the ferocity of the atmosphere. He wrote:

> I have seen nothing uglier, or nastier, than this. A young man, coloured, a student, walks alone in the middle of a shabby road, Bramley Road, Notting Hill. It is three in the afternoon ... He looks about him, jumpily, wondering about the silent people, white people, crowding the pavements ... Suddenly a voice yells, 'Get him!'... The people sweep after him. Middle-aged people, but most of them young people. And many are children. They hit the student. A youth flings his cycle at him. He pleads and cries out, then breaks away into a greengrocer's shop. The greengrocer locks the door. The student stands trembling and says, 'They'll kill me.'

Author Colin MacInnes was so affected by the riots in Notting Hill that he wrote about them in his 1959 novel, *Absolute Beginners*, vividly painting a picture of the ominous atmosphere that pervaded the streets during the hot bank holiday weekend:

> Standing about on corners, and outside their houses, there were Teds: groups of them, not doing anything, but standing in circles with their heads just a bit bent down ... Also, I noticed, as I cruised the streets, that quite a few of those battered little delivery vans that

I've referred to – usually dark blue, and with the back doors tied with wire, or one door off – had groups around them, also, who didn't seem to be mending them, or anything.

As night fell, the Teddy Boys resumed their rampage, first targeting West Indian properties in Oxford Gardens, where they threw bricks, iron bars and any other missile they could lay their hands on through the windows. 'They didn't miss a house', a white resident told a *Times* reporter.

By 7.30 p.m., there were literally thousands of people on the streets of Notting Hill and incidents were breaking out across the district with intense frequency, stage-managed by groups of ringleaders who cruised the streets in cars directing the disparate groups of youths through the urban battlefield.

The police found it impossible to predict where the next wave of violence would take place as the mob changed direction seemingly at a whim. Walking down some streets, it was difficult to believe that the district was under siege, but unknown dangers lay around every corner.

Colin Eales, a journalist for the *Kensington News*, journeyed into the centre of the fighting on Monday evening. As he walked down Lancaster Road, he noted that passers-by seemed oblivious and unconcerned at the mayhem occurring literally streets away. As he made his way further down the road, he began to notice a few groups of Teddy Boys hanging around street corners, but nothing was to prepare him for the sight that met his eyes as he turned into Bramley Road – the riots' 'Ground Zero'. He later wrote:

I saw a mob of over 700 men, women and children stretching 200 yards along the road. Young children of ten were treating the whole affair as a great joke and shouting 'Come on, let's get the blacks' and '**** the coppers, let's get on with it'. In the middle of the mob of screaming, jeering youths and adults, a speaker from the Union Movement was urging his excited audience to 'get rid of them'. Groups of policemen stood at strategic points carefully watching the 'meeting', while police cars and Black Marias waited round the corner. Suddenly, hundreds of leaflets were thrown over the crowd, a fierce cry rent the air and the mob rushed off in the direction of Latimer Road, shouting, 'Kill the niggers!' Women grabbed their small children and chased after their menfolk. Dogs ran in among the crowds barking. Everywhere was riotous confusion. Police cars and vans wheeled out to cut off the mob.

Rapidly growing in numbers, the crowd surged towards Blenheim Crescent, planning to wreak havoc. Little did they realise that they had been ambushed. As they poured into the street, they were suddenly bombarded by a shower of milk bottles and petrol bombs being hurled by West Indian men who had climbed on to the roofs of the houses in a desperate bid to defend themselves and their property. The counter-attack surprised and frustrated the mob in equal measure. Colin Eales, who was following at a safe distance, recalled, 'One 18-year-old youth was led away with blood streaming from a head wound. Unable to get at their attackers, the inflamed rioters moved off to vent their wrath on other coloured men.'

The baying crowd made their crazed way to Westbourne Park Road, where there was a well-known West Indian lodging house. Grabbing any missile they could find, they smashed every window of the property, terrifying the inhabitants. Satisfied with their work they turned and moved on, swelling in number at every turn as more thugs joined their ranks. Colin Eales wrote, 'They came on foot, by train, bus, motor bike, car and lorry, shouting, "Alright boys, we're here!"'

By the end of Bank Holiday Monday, the race riots were threatening to spread across west London. The black South African actor and director, Lionel Ngakane, who was rehearsing for a BBC television play nearby, remembered, 'There were many black actors [in the play]. Things got so bad outside with the rioters that the BBC had to arrange for us to be bussed out of our rehearsal room with a police escort.'

In Kilburn Park, around 2 miles away from the centre of the riots, black families had petrol bombs thrown through their windows. However, as police despaired of ever getting the mob under control, the violence suddenly began to subside. In the end, the Notting Hill riots ceased simply because the bank holiday weekend ended and many of the ringleaders had to return to work. By the end of the week, the disturbances had almost completely petered out and the residents of Notting Hill set about repairing their shattered community. In total, fifty-five people were arrested during the riots. Only ten of them were black – proof, if any were needed, as to which side were the antagonists and which were the victims.

Determined that such violence would never be seen on London's streets again, the nine white youths who had run rampage on 24 August were made examples of by the courts. All of them were sentenced to four years in prison, with the judge, Mr Justice Salmon, stating:

> It was you men who started the whole of this violence in Notting Hill. You are a minute and insignificant section of the population who have brought shame upon the district in which you lived, and have filled the whole nation with horror, indignation and disgust. Everyone, irrespective of the colour of their skin, is entitled to walk through our streets in peace, with their heads erect, and free from fear. That is a right which these courts will always unfailingly uphold.

However, despite the court's best efforts, the Notting Hill riots left an indelible stain on the streets of west London. Ivan Weekes, who had arrived in Notting Hill from Barbados in 1955, recalled that the violence destroyed the West Indians' entire concept of Britain being the 'mother country'. 'Those of us who were on the front line were in psychological no-man's-land, thinking "what's next?"'

Mr Weekes' apprehension about the future was not unfounded. Racial hatred reared its ugly head in Notting Hill again in 1959. This time it ended in murder.

Just after midnight on 17 May, Kelso Cochrane, a young Antiguan carpenter, was walking home to Bevington Road, having spent the evening in St Mary's Hospital after breaking his thumb at work. As he reached the corner of Golborne Road and Southam Street, he noticed a gang of Teddy Boys hanging around on the opposite side of the road. On seeing him, the youths began shouting, 'Hey, Jim Crow!' (a reference to the racial segregation laws in America).

Cochrane ignored them and quickened his pace, but this only infuriated the gang and they chased across the street and attacked him. Unable to properly defend himself because of his broken thumb, he was easy prey, but regardless, one of the gang saw fit to pull out his stiletto knife, which he plunged into the young Antiguan's chest. On realising that their victim had been stabbed, the cowardly gang ran off into the night, leaving Kelso Cochrane dying on the pavement. A passing taxi driver rushed him to St Charles' Hospital nearby, but he died soon afterwards. His killers were never apprehended, mainly because witnesses were too scared to come forward with information.

Following Kelso Cochrane's brutal murder, the government finally woke up to the racial tension in London and organised an investigation into race relations. The chairman of the subsequent inquiry was well placed to lead the onerous task. Amy Ashwood Garvey, the first wife of Black Nationalist Marcus Garvey, had long been acquainted with Notting Hill and its grave social problems. In the years preceding the Second World War, she had lived in the district and had founded the 'Florence Mills Social Parlour', one of Britain's first Caribbean restaurants, in Carnaby Street. Returning to London after the Second World War, she helped set up the Afro People's Centre in Ladbroke Grove, which was a lifeline for West Indian newcomers as it provided them with companionship in a district that was often hostile and unwelcoming.

Ultimately, the race relations inquiry did little to make any practical improvements to the situation in Notting Hill. However, Kelso Cochrane's murder was not entirely in vain. Over in Brixton Claudia Jones, the editor of the *West Indian Gazette*, resolved to 'wash the taste of Notting Hill … out of our mouths'. In order to achieve this, she and her supporters organised a Mardi Gras style carnival in St Pancras town hall in January 1959. The event featured dance troupes and jazz musicians, including the popular singer Cleo Laine, and was filmed by the BBC. It proved to be a huge success and became an annual fixture, although the organisers were never completely happy that it had to be held indoors.

Their chance to change this came in the mid-1960s, when they heard about a new outdoor festival in Notting Hill, which was being planned by Rhaune Laslett, a co-founder of the London Free School – an adult education project based at 26 Powis Terrace. Laslett explained to *Grove* magazine her reasons for starting the festival:

'We felt that, although West Indians, Africans, Irish and many other nationalities all live in a very congested area, there is very little communication between us. If we can infect them with a desire to participate then this can only have good results.'

Rhaune Laslett's festival fitted perfectly with Claudia Jones' Mardi Gras and, thus, the two events merged and the Notting Hill Carnival was born. Its popularity vastly exceeded everyone's expectations – by 1976, around 150,000 people were attending the free event every year. Twenty years later, this figure had risen to an incredible 1 million and, despite tensions between revellers and the police, the carnival established itself as one of London's most popular events. Fittingly, it takes place over the August Bank Holiday – the weekend that, in 1958, saw the city's first race riots.

Who is in your home while you are away ?

Make sure that you don't leave any clues that your home is unoccupied

- Fit good locks to doors and windows
- Ask a neighbour or friend to look after your home
- Use a timer switch on your lights

Holiday tips

• If your milk or newspapers are normally delivered make sure you cancel them.

• Get a friend, family or neighbour to look after your home whilst you are away. You could do the same for them when they go away.

• Criminals don't like light! Put your lights on timer switches whilst you are away.

• Don't put your name and address on the outside of your suitcase. Put it inside.

Preventing a burglary

• Fit good locks to your doors and windows.

• Use an ultra violet pen to postcode all your valuables, and if possible photograph them.

For more information or advice, contact Community Safety on (020) 8871 0803 or the Police Crime Prevention Office on (020) 8247 8788

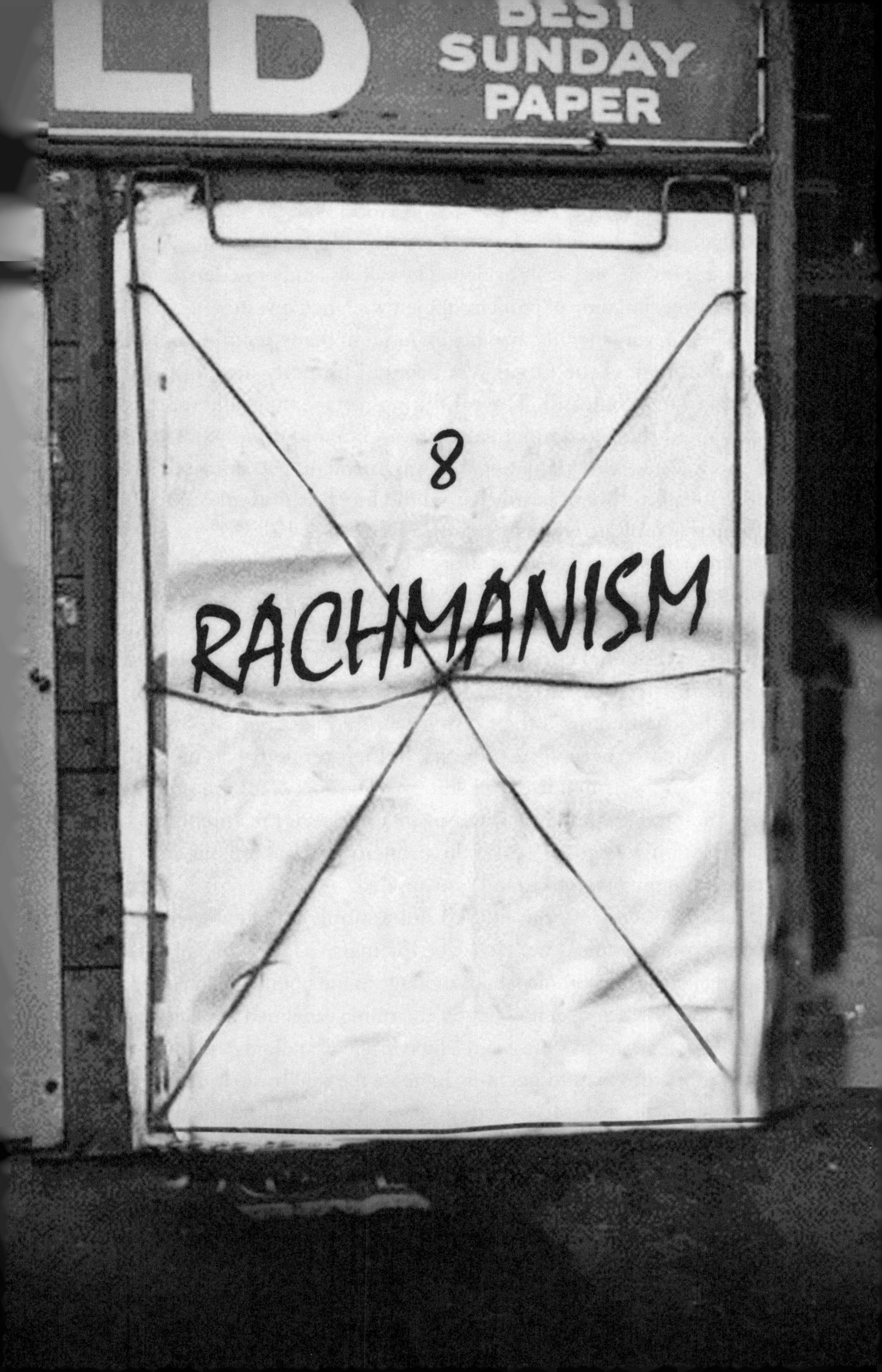

8
RACHMANISM

Without doubt, one of the root causes of the Notting Hill riots was the deplorable living conditions endured by the area's poorer inhabitants. As the already dilapidated houses became packed with people after the Second World War, the stress of living in such close proximity to total strangers created a tense and fragile atmosphere. This was ruthlessly exploited by callous landlords, determined to wring every last drop of profit from their wretched investments.

The rot, very literally, had begun to set in many years before, when the outbreak of the Great War brought property development in London to a standstill. The resulting shortage of available housing prompted rents to dramatically rise as demand rapidly outstripped supply. Faced with a situation that was threatening to spiral out of control, the government hastily passed the Increase of Rent & Mortgage Interest (War Restrictions) Act on 23 December 1915.

The ruling protected landlords by freezing the interest rate on mortgages for the duration of the conflict. However, it also restricted their right to evict tenants and prevented them from raising the rent unless exceptional circumstances prevailed. Thenceforth, landlords could only remove a tenant by applying to the courts with proof that they had not paid their rent for a prolonged period, were causing a nuisance to their neighbours, or their property was needed for the owner's personal use. In addition, the rents of all the properties to which the Act applied were frozen at the sum for which they had been let on 3 August 1914. If the property was not tenanted on that date, then the previous rental sum applied.

The Rent & Mortgage Interest Act was only intended to be a temporary, wartime measure. However, the massive loss of life during the conflict created a chronic labour shortage in the building trade for many years afterwards and, consequently, the ruling remained in place. In the 1920s the regulations were eased a little to allow landlords who improved their properties to retrospectively increase the rent by up to 25 per cent. However, with no reserve funds in place, few could find the money to make any renovations apart from those that were absolutely necessary.

The Act's effect on the cheaper end of London's housing market was devastating. Firstly, landlords saw no value in modernising their properties. This meant that, by 1945, much of the capital's old

Victorian housing stock was stuck in a time warp, with facilities and internal decoration that pre-dated 1915. Many properties had no indoor toilet, the utilities were woefully antiquated, roofs leaked, windows let in draughts and the only form of heating was an ineffective coal fire. Modern innovations such as telephones were unobtainable unless the tenants were prepared to pay for the line installation themselves. In Notting Hill, this deplorable situation was made worse by the fact that many of the properties' original ninety-nine-year building leases were coming to an end, which made them almost impossible to sell at any price. Unsurprisingly, the housing market collapsed.

By 1950, the government finally woke up to the fact that controlled rent was creating slums and quietly began to phase it out in favour of a self-regulating system. It was hoped that lifting the rent restrictions would persuade landlords to renovate their properties, but it actually had the opposite effect. Over in Notting Hill, the cheaper streets became overrun with avaricious investors determined to make a fast buck from the neglected streets before the leases expired.

The area's proximity to central London and its popularity among the new West Indian community (who were forced to pay higher than average rents) made it a perfect place for dubious new landlords to operate. The only problem was that many of the houses were filled with long-standing tenants to whom the old rent controls still applied. Known as 'stats' because they paid the statutory rent, they quickly fell prey to the new landlords, who were prepared to do almost anything to persuade them to leave.

The financial rewards of a 'stat-free' house were immense, as the vacated rooms could be let to West Indians paying double the previous rent, or better still, prostitutes who would pay considerably more. The *Daily Mirror*, which launched an investigation into the intimidation of 'stats', christened the new landlords 'slum emperors' and explained how they made a fast profit from their investments:

> One way is to jam people into slum houses – sometimes ten in one room – and charge each tenant at least £1 a week. The other way is to bully tenants out of a house, decorate the place, put in baths and let 'luxury flats' at £10 10s a week or more.

The shrewd slum landlords also quickly realised that Notting Hill's persecuted West Indian community could be used to unwittingly scare statutory tenants into vacating their homes. The notorious property magnate, Nicholas van Hoogstraten (who was gaoled in 1968 for paying a gang to attack a business rival), recalled that this intimidation of white tenants was colloquially known as 'de-stating with de-schwartzers'.

Despite their reputation, Notting Hill's slum emperors largely remained anonymous, which probably added to their fearsome reputation. However, a scandalous series of events in the early 1960s inadvertently led to the exposure of one – Perec 'Peter' Rachman. Although he was, by no means, a major player in the slum property market, Rachman came to epitomise the money-grabbing investor. Today, 'Rachmanism' remains the dictionary definition for the exploitation and intimidation of tenants by unscrupulous landlords.

Peter Rachman had a distinctly inauspicious early life. Born in Lvov, Poland, in 1919, the son of a middle-class Jewish dentist, he probably would have lived his life in comfortable obscurity had the Nazis not invaded his homeland in 1939. Leaving the rest of his family behind, Rachman managed to escape over the Russian border, but was soon caught and interned in a labour camp in Siberia. However, when Germany declared war on the Soviet Union in 1941, he joined the Polish Army and spent the remaining years of the war fighting in Italy and the Middle East.

The rest of his family almost certainly perished in Nazi concentration camps. Although he never spoke of them, their deaths must have affected Rachman greatly. Indeed, one of his girlfriends later commented that 'making money was a way of defending himself against insecurity and loneliness'.

Peter Rachman's army unit remained in Italy until 1946, when they transferred to Britain. With nothing but painful memories left in Poland, he decided to remain in England after he was demobbed in 1948, and for the next two years he worked at a succession of low-paid jobs while he perfected his English and ruminated over what he should do with his life.

During this period, he became intimately acquainted with a Paddington prostitute named Gloria, who complained to him that it was difficult and expensive for working girls like her to find rooms in which they could ply their trade. Knowing all too well how much Gloria charged for her services, Rachman quickly realised that good money could be made by providing prostitutes with accommodation, and he began renting £5 per week bedsits in the red-light district of Sussex Gardens, Paddington, which he sublet to hookers for double the price.

His dealings in the seediest end of the market convinced Rachman that investing in London property was one of the easiest ways to make a fortune. He also discovered that many people were prepared to hand over their money and ask no questions in return for a steady return on their investment. Two such people were Cyril and William Foux, professional property men who agreed to finance a deal in March 1954 to acquire a large townhouse at 6 Norfolk Square, a shabby genteel street close to Gloria's hangout at Sussex Gardens. The acquisition clearly proved satisfactory to all parties as, three months later, Rachman and the Foux brothers also purchased the house next door.

Over the ensuing months, Peter Rachman continued to present deals to the Fouxs and also started to do business with Lieutenant Colonel George Sinclair, a property investor and mortgage broker whom he had known since 1952 (when he had purchased a shabby old house in Paddington to use as a brothel). Emboldened by the success he had experienced with the buildings at Norfolk Square, Rachman agreed to buy thirty houses in Shepherd's Bush from Sinclair, who also arranged the finance. Again, these properties proved profitable, and early in 1955 Rachman moved into Notting Hill, buying six houses in Powis Terrace, a dilapidated thoroughfare off Westbourne Park Road.

The rotting properties rapidly became the most notorious slums in the district but, nevertheless, their rents netted their owner a handsome profit. Rachman went on to purchase numerous houses in Notting Hill, including decrepit dwellings in Colville Road, Colville Terrace, Powis Gardens and Powis Square. As his slum empire grew, he became an enthusiastic exploiter of the West Indian community to get rid of his stats. In one of the few interviews he ever gave, he told the *Empire News*, 'The government does nothing to house these West Indians when they come over here. Somebody must. That's why they come to me.' He then added cryptically, 'Some white people do object to the coloured people when they move in. They don't always like the way they play jazz records up to 1 a.m. and always loudly.'

Although rowdy West Indians did get rid of some statutory tenants, many proved more difficult to remove. The opening gambit of most slum landlords (including Rachman) was to offer alternative accommodation in a property that was worth less to them. If this did not work, full-scale intimidation was unleashed.

A team of journalists working for *The Times* compiled a dossier of ways in which stats were pressurised. It included the shameful story of two elderly sisters who, having lived in their flat for decades, were reluctant to leave. The landlord subsequently demanded two months' rent in advance, which the sisters duly paid in cash. However, the following month, the rent collector arrived at their door again, demanding more rent. The ladies explained that they had already paid it, only to be told that the house had been sold and the new owner had no responsibility for the earlier payments. Unable to provide a receipt for the previous transaction, the sisters reluctantly paid up and began looking for alternative accommodation.

Another case in the dossier concerned a middle-aged man named Mr Joseph, who had gone into hiding after being terrorised by his landlord's henchmen. *The Times* wrote:

> His furniture was smashed ... after he refused to move out of his flat. The previous Tuesday, four men arrived with an Alsatian and ordered him to leave. A police constable was called and he told them they could not evict without an order of court. Three days later, the man returned from work to find the furniture smashed and piled in the corridor. Floorboards were ripped up. He realised the price of refusing to go. Mr Joseph had no redress. He did not know the name of his landlord. How could he know the name? The property where he lived had changed hands 15 times since he moved in 18 months ago.

The case of Mr Joseph highlighted a common practice among the slum emperors. In a bid to hide profits from the tax man, the capital in one single property was often divided between numerous proprietors.

The head lease would be held in trust for an off-shore company, while the leases to the flats would each have different owners. In addition, tenants would pay rent to one company while another seemingly independent firm would carry out repairs.

Consequently, establishing the identity of the property's real owner was a massively time-consuming, frustrating and expensive business. With no obvious landlord to approach, the authorities were powerless to act on behalf of tenants. An anonymous landlord admitted to *The Times* that he could 'keep a defective drain going for four or five months without the legal penalties becoming uneconomic'. That period was sufficient to drive unwanted tenants out of the house.

In 1957, Peter Rachman and his fellow slum emperors had cause for major celebration when the Rent Act fully extricated private property from state interference. Although this was supposed to eliminate the problems caused by rent controls, the old statutory tenants remained protected, and this actually made the problem worse. John Silkin, MP for Deptford (another of London's most deprived areas), recalled that a multiple occupancy house in his constituency that might have sold for £1,800 before the 1957 Rent Act, was finally offered for £10,000 after the stats had been removed. He also noted that the Act provided 'full incentive to unscrupulous landlords to get the tenants out'.

John Silkin was entirely correct in his assessment. By the end of 1957, eviction teams known as 'heavy glove gangs' were being sent to properties with the express instruction to get the statutory tenants out using any means necessary. A member of Rachman's gang told *The Times*, 'We get paid up to £250 to clear houses of unwanted tenants … [those] who know what's good for them usually get out without giving trouble … Those who don't get roughed up and chucked into the street with their belongings.'

The heavy glove gangs were collectively referred to by slum tenants as 'the red ants' – a wry reference to their unwanted and troublesome presence in people's homes. The arrival of an eviction gang on a Notting Hill street corner sent up the cautionary whisper 'the red ants are here', and most residents knew better than to try to stop them carrying out their heinous duties.

A few, however, had the courage to make a stand. A west London heavy, known only as 'Jim', told the *Daily Mirror* how his gang dealt with a woman named Margaret who refused to leave her flat in Roseford Terrace, Shepherd's Bush:

> She was tough. Three of the Heavy Gloves went down to see her but she locked them out. Man, that's not the way to deal with the Heavy Gloves. They just smashed in the door and were all set to rough her up and throw her out into the street. But they saw a little baby lying sick in a cot, so they decided to let her off light. They just ripped out the electricity, cut off the gas and water and told her she had better get out quick.

Unbowed, Margaret brought an action against her landlord at West London County Court and was awarded £45 in damages. She also got a restraining order preventing the gang from entering her home.

Unfortunately, few shared Margaret's bravery. Most of the slum emperors' tenants were terrified of the heavy glove gangs and their intimidating methods. Serge Paplinski, one of Rachman's employees, collected rents around Notting Hill accompanied by vicious German Shepherd dogs. Another, named Peter Rann, was a champion wrestler and his cohort, Norbert Rondel, worked as a nightclub bouncer. 'I was a chucker-out of spades who were Rachman's tenants and causing trouble,' Rondel told the press, 'although I spent a lot of time just sitting around smoking cigars.'

Another man allegedly on Rachman's payroll was Michael de Freitas, a Trinidadian who lived in one of his employer's rundown properties on Powis Square. De Freitas had been born in Port of Spain in 1933, to Iona Brown and Emanuel de Freitas, a Portuguese sailor who kept a shop on the island. From an early age he developed a reputation as a troublemaker and, at 14, he was expelled from school, branded a 'thoroughgoing terror'.

Following in his father's footsteps, de Freitas went to sea and eventually wound up in Britain – first in Cardiff's Tiger Bay and then Notting Hill, where he met and married a Guyanese woman named Desiree de Souza and took up a new profession as a rent collector. The writer Michael Horowitz knew de Freitas and described him as a 'dapper yet piratical figure patrolling London's Westbourne Park/ Portobello district with a silver-topped cane, big hair and beard, glint of earring, often with other heavies and growling Alsatians in tow'.

Whether or not de Freitas initially worked for Peter Rachman is a moot point – by 1959 the pair were sworn enemies. By this time, the West Indians in Notting Hill had tired of being exploited and were beginning to organise themselves in a bid to fight back. Black Power groups such as the 'Lions of Judah' were formed, and their members launched a campaign against the slum emperors.

Over on Powis Square, Michael de Freitas persuaded his fellow tenants to go to a rent tribunal. It was the first time that Peter Rachman's name was identified with slum property in the press. On 28 May 1959, *The Times* published an article headlined 'Coloured Tenants Allege Intimidation'. It read, 'Allegations of intimidation were made in the course of a hearing yesterday of three appeals by coloured tenants in Powis Square, North Kensington, to the West London Rent Tribunal.' The tenants in question were Michael de Freitas, Edmund Jarvis and Marion Hall, and although each of them had a different landlord on paper, Michael de Freitas ensured that the true owner's name was revealed.

MP Arthur Skefflington, who represented the tenants, stated at the tribunal, 'We understand that Mr Rackman [*sic*] is the owner of all these three properties.' As the case progressed, Rachman was also shopped by one of the supposed 'owners' of the properties. Answering the charge that he had threatened Marion Hall with a knife after she complained about the deplorable condition of her flat, her supposed landlord, Vernon Hunte, told the tribunal, 'I am responsible for no decorations … Mr Rachman is the owner of the property.' Disgusted at the conditions in which the tenants were forced to live, the shocked court ordered a significant decrease in their rent.

Although he scored a small victory against Rachman at the rent tribunal, it later transpired that Michael de Freitas was, in fact, a far worse individual than his perfidious landlord. Having become heavily involved in the Black Power Movement, he later changed his name to 'Michael X' and set up 'Black House', a huge edifice on the Holloway Road sponsored by a host of luminaries including Muhammad Ali, Sammy Davis Junior and John Lennon.

Black House was supposed to be London's first arts and community centre for black youths, but ended up being, in the words of de Freitas' biographer John L. Williams, 'an intimidating establishment used as a base for various kinds of illegal activity'. After an inevitable police raid, its founder hastily fled to Trinidad where he set up a farming commune. However, the discovery of two bodies on the land led to de Freitas' arrest and subsequent conviction for murder. He was hanged on 16 May 1975.

Despite the horror of his later crimes, Michael de Freitas did succeed in exposing the shameful state of Notting Hill's slums. As a result, Ben Parkin, the MP for Paddington North, launched a personal crusade against the slum emperors, collecting evidence of intimidation from dozens of tenants. In addition, Kensington Public Health Committee launched an investigation into living conditions in Powis Terrace and was shocked to find 300 people living in just sixteen properties. Their report stated that, in addition to the extreme overcrowding:

> Litter is allowed to accumulate, food refuse is left in the communal kitchens and the bathrooms seem little used, probably through lack of hot water … So many dustbins are needed that there is no room for them all outside and some are kept inside flats. Some refuse is thrown out of rear windows, where it chokes the drains … Attempts at improvement have been frequently frustrated, mainly because of the difficulty of finding out the legal owner at any particular time.

Ben Parkin and the health inspectors' newfound interest in the Notting Hill slums, combined with the increasing belligerence of his West Indian tenants, prompted Peter Rachman to sell the vast majority of his west London property portfolio in 1959. However, as he signed over the crumbling houses to his rapacious successors, little did he know that in less than four years, his name would be used to epitomise greed and exploitation. The circumstances under which this happened were truly extraordinary.

Peter Rachman first stepped on to the path that led to his notoriety in the closing months of the 1950s. Keen to leave the slums behind him and establish himself as a major player in the property world, he had begun to frequent exclusive West End nightclubs where potential investors could be found and cultivated. One such place was Murray's Cabaret Club, a Soho nightspot owned by Percival Murray which prided itself as being the 'largest and most elaborate in town [with] the most beautiful show girls and dancers'. Murray's had a strictly controlled membership and, since its inception in 1933, had developed a reputation as a discreet place where the rich, famous and notorious could relax without fear of press exposure.

By the early 1960s it was rumoured that patrons as diverse as Princess Margaret and the Kray twins were enjoying the nightly floor show featuring topless dancers. These showgirls were expected to act as hostesses once their set was over, swelling the nightclub's coffers by encouraging the patrons to buy more drinks. Many of them were recruited from the chorus lines of West End musicals as they could work a shift at Murray's after the performance. Others were lured to the club via press advertisements that urged, 'If you are a really attractive and ambitious young lady, you should write for an audition'. One girl who answered the call was Christine Keeler, a pretty, dark-haired 17-year-old from the Middlesex suburb of Staines.

To her delight, Christine's audition at Murray's was successful, and by the autumn of 1958 she was working regular shifts as a dancer and had become hostess to two of the club's regular patrons: Peter Rachman and Stephen Ward, a middle-aged osteopath with connections to high society. Within just five years, all three members of this unholy trinity had become mired in disgrace and tragedy.

Christine Keeler's new acquaintances were diverse characters. While Rachman was a persecuted Polish exile, Stephen Ward was the quintessentially English son of Arthur Evelyn Ward, the canon of Rochester Cathedral. Uninterested in an ecclesiastical career, Ward had journeyed to America after leaving school, where he trained in osteopathy. After gaining experience treating injured officers during the Second World War, he returned to England where he worked for the Osteopathic Association Clinic in London's Dorset Square. During his time there he treated an impressive array of clients including Winston Churchill and Ava Gardner.

The money and status he acquired at the clinic enabled him to set up his own practice in Cavendish Square to which he attracted an affluent and influential stream of patients, one of whom was William Waldorf Astor – the immensely wealthy owner of Cliveden, an enormous, Italianate mansion set in sprawling grounds overlooking the Thames at Taplow, Buckinghamshire. Ward became good friends with his eminent client and was invited to use a cottage on the Cliveden estate whenever he wished. In return, he provided Astor and his associates with attractive female companions recruited from Murray's and other West End nightclubs.

Although they frequented the same London clubs, Stephen Ward and Peter Rachman barely knew each other. However, over the following years, their lives were to become inextricably linked by their mutual obsession with Christine Keeler and her alluring colleagues. Soon after meeting her, the infatuated Rachman installed Christine in a mews house he had recently acquired in Bryanston Mews West and the pair became lovers. Given that Rachman was short, overweight, balding and middle-aged, it is unlikely that she was attracted to him for his looks.

Nevertheless, what he lacked in physical allure was countered by his generosity and, thus, Christine lived the precarious life of a kept woman while Rachman's official girlfriend, Audrey O'Donnell, tried to ignore his frequent absences from the home they shared in Hampstead. However, within a few months, Christine tired of being Rachman's mistress and after she began to flirt with his considerably younger and more handsome cohort, Serge Paplinski, their relationship soured. In the summer of 1960, she moved out of Bryanston Mews and went to live with Stephen Ward in Orme Court in Bayswater, only seeing Rachman when he visited Murray's.

Soon after Christine moved in with Ward, a new girl arrived at the nightclub. Marilyn Rice-Davies (known as Mandy) was a 16-year-old blonde from the West Midlands, who had come to London to pursue her dream of becoming a model. She and Christine soon became firm friends, who shared the outlook that any man was worth sleeping with if he rewarded them with expensive gifts.

Taking full advantage of the girls' lack of morals, Stephen Ward and William Astor installed them in a flat at Comeragh Road, Barons

Court, and invited their friends round for sex parties. During this time, Christine introduced Mandy to her old flame Peter Rachman, no doubt telling her that he was extremely generous in return for services rendered. Thus, Mandy Rice-Davies began an affair that would later serve to blacken Rachman's name to the point of notoriety.

By March 1961, Mandy and Christine were getting bored of their louche life at Comeragh Road and both left the brothel. Christine temporarily took up with a Persian boyfriend, while Mandy moved into Rachman's house at Bryanston Mews West. Although he was now married to Audrey, Rachman was delighted to have Mandy as his mistress and showered her with generosity. She later told Rodney Hallworth, a journalist for the *Daily Mirror*:

> For two years, Peter was my life ... I never had to ask him for anything. In our two happy years, he gave me a mink coat, three mink jackets, three diamond brooches, two pairs of diamond and ruby earrings, a Persian lamb jacket, a big gold, diamond and ruby watch bracelet, two diamond rings worth about £500 each and a Jaguar car. For my 18th birthday he gave me £1,000 in cash. I spent it in two weeks on a pearl necklace and a bracelet with diamond clasps worth £700 and bags of clothes.

Blinded by greed, both Mandy and Christine gave little thought to the fact that they were getting deeply entrenched in a distinctly seedy and increasingly perilous life. Matters took a darker turn when, in the summer of 1961, Christine split with her Persian boyfriend and went back to live with Stephen Ward, this time in a West End flat he was renting at 17 Wimpole Mews.

By this stage, William Astor had taken to throwing sleazy sex parties at Cliveden and his eager-to-please friend was on the constant lookout for new girls to take there as escorts. Realising that the young women would be far less suspicious if they were invited to the parties by another girl, he asked Christine to help him with the recruitment process.

Their modus operandi was later revealed in the story of 'Miss R', a shop assistant who Ward had noticed while trawling Marylebone

High Street. He instructed Christine to go into the shop and tell the girl that her shy, love-struck brother would like to meet her after work. The girl reluctantly agreed and went to Wimpole Mews with Christine where, over coffee with Ward, it was suggested that she should accompany them to Cliveden.

At first Miss R refused but, after some persuasion, she capitulated and went to the country estate on several occasions where she was introduced to several men and a woman known as Maria Ella, who organised S&M parties. Miss R also revealed that Stephen Ward's girls were paid £15 for sex, out of which Ward would receive £6.

In addition to the Cliveden sex parties, Stephen Ward also organised similar gatherings at his flat in Wimpole Mews, and it was here that Christine began liaisons with two men that would eventually put her in a highly dangerous position. The individuals concerned were Yevgeny Ivanov – a Soviet naval attaché – and John Profumo, Conservative MP and British Secretary of State for War. At the time, tensions between the USSR and the West were at their height (the Cuban Missile Crisis occurred in October 1962) and Christine's relationships with these men did not pass unnoticed by other guests at Ward's parties. Soon, rumours began to circulate that British secrets were being passed to the USSR.

By January 1962, Christine Keeler's decadent and debauched lifestyle was beginning to take its toll on her mental state. Stephen Ward had introduced her to marijuana early on in their relationship, which he obtained from various dealers in Notting Hill. As the pair sank into a life of depravity, the dope began to control them. Christine recalled, 'We both went out to places to see if they had it. It was me who actually went in and asked for it. [Stephen] waited outside in the car.'

During one of her expeditions to Notting Hill, Christine was introduced to John Edgecombe, the erstwhile proprietor of Colville Terrace who has been described in the previous chapter. John Edgecombe and his West Indian friends were considerably younger and refreshingly different to Christine's usual middle-aged, lascivious companions and she began to spend an increasing amount of time in Notting Hill, where she could get stoned and temporarily forget about her sordid lifestyle. After a surprisingly long courtship, she and

Edgecombe finally got together in the early summer of 1962, after a late night party. He later remembered, 'Four of us had been drinking and smoking pot and at around two o'clock, I said I was going to split. Christine turned to me and said, "Do you have to go?"' The pair became inseparable for the next eight weeks.

Christine and John Edgecombe's time together was spent in a drug-fuelled haze. Too intoxicated to do much else, Christine talked at length about her degenerate life and numerous boyfriends, while Edgecombe casually listened, too lethargic to be jealous. However, one name did succeed in rousing him from his stupor. The man in question was a West Indian musician and club promoter named Aloysius 'Lucky' Gordon who had treated Christine very badly, holding her hostage for two days when she tried to end the relationship.

John Edgecombe already despised Lucky Gordon as he had threatened to tell the police about his shebeen, forcing him to close the lucrative enterprise down. Seizing the opportunity for revenge, he kept a sharp eye out for his rival. Their paths finally crossed that October in a West End jazz club. Edgecombe recalled:

> Tubby Hayes was playing, and I was standing up, diggin' the music with Christine and a few other people. At that moment, Lucky Gordon came in, looking very intimidating. There were about four people in our party and I was standing up by a rail, which separated the seating area from the dance floor. I was listening to the music when Lucky came up and punched me. I jumped over the table to go after him, but Lucky grabbed a chair. Then the bouncer grabbed Lucky and dragged him out of the club and into the foyer. There was a scuffle, during which Lucky got cut.

Realising he was in serious trouble, John Edgecombe fled back to Notting Hill and went into hiding in one of Rachman's old houses in Powis Terrace. Meanwhile, back at the club, the police arrived and quickly issued a warrant for his arrest.

Once the police became involved, Christine realised that, given her associations, it would be wise to quickly end her relationship with John Edgecombe. Having nowhere else to go, she was forced to return to

Stephen Ward's flat in Wimpole Mews where she found her old friend
Mandy Rice-Davies, who had walked out on Peter Rachman after he
refused to leave Audrey. Over the following weeks, the two women took
up their previous roles as escorts and they probably would have slowly
slipped into obscurity if events had not taken a series of shocking twists.

Mandy Rice-Davies was still hoping that Peter Rachman might
relent and leave his wife when, on 29 November, she was horrified to
discover that he had suddenly died from a massive heart attack. While
Mandy struggled to come to terms with the untimely death of her
sugar daddy, John Edgecombe desperately pleaded with Christine to
help him find a solicitor so he could give himself up to the police.
Weary, and feeling desperate herself, she refused and told him that
if he continued to pester her, she would give evidence against him.
Incensed and humiliated in equal measure, Edgecombe grabbed a
gun (apparently Christine's) and took a taxi to Wimpole Mews, determined to get her attention using any means necessary.

On arrival, he told the cab to wait while he hammered angrily on
the door to Ward's flat, ordering Christine to come out and talk to
him. She refused, and when Edgecombe told her the waiting taxi
was costing him money, she arrogantly threw a pound note out of the
window. This proved to be the last straw. Edgecombe recalled:

> I just went mad and blew my cool. I began shouldering the front door,
> but it was a really tough door, and after the first time, I knew the door
> wasn't going to budge. Like a gangster, I thought, 'OK, I'll shoot the
> door off.' So I whipped out my shooter and started firing at the lock.

This time, John Edgecombe had gone too far. The police were called
and he was subsequently taken into custody. His arrest set in motion
a chain of events that sent shockwaves through the corridors of power
and became known as the 'Profumo scandal'. The sordid story shattered the reputations of many, but perhaps none more so than Peter
Rachman who was no longer around to defend himself.

In March 1963, John Edgecombe was brought to trial for the shoot-
ing in Wimpole Mews. By this stage, the rumours about Stephen
Ward's girls sharing pillow talk with British politicians and Soviet

agents had reached fever pitch, and when Christine Keeler failed to appear as a witness, the press finally had an excuse to expose the scandalous speculation. At first, John Profumo denied having sexual relations with Christine, but by June the pressure on him to confess had become so great that he was forced to admit he had lied and promptly resigned from the cabinet. Three months later, Prime Minister Harold Macmillan also resigned on the grounds of ill health, which had worsened as a result of the scandal. He was replaced by Sir Alec Douglas-Home, but the damage to the Conservative Party's reputation was too grave for them to survive the general election the following year.

Soon after Profumo's resignation, Stephen Ward was arrested and accused of living off the earnings of prostitution and procuring under-age girls. A trial date was set at the Old Bailey for July; the prosecution's main witnesses being Christine Keeler and Mandy Rice-Davies.

As Stephen Ward's trial took its course it became clear that, although there was some doubt over the charge of procurement, he had indeed been living off immoral earnings for some time. With his reputation in ruins and his former friends refusing to speak to him, Stephen Ward had a devastating mental breakdown. The evening before the final day of the trial, he took an overdose of sleeping pills and fell into a coma from which he never recovered. He died on Monday, 5 August and his trial was closed with no sentence pronounced.

Stephen Ward's suicide should have brought the whole sorry affair to a close. However, the Profumo scandal was set to expose the sins of one more person before it finally subsided. While giving evidence at Ward's trial, Mandy Rice-Davies had been shockingly candid about her numerous relationships. When asked where she had been living before going to Wimpole Mews, she unhesitatingly named Peter Rachman, telling the court, 'He was a very rich man. He kept me amply supplied with money and presents, one of which was a Jaguar car.'

Mandy's casual comment finally gave Ben Parkin (the MP who had been tirelessly campaigning against Notting Hill's slum emperors for years) ammunition to force a government enquiry into the exploitation suffered by his constituents. He and his colleague, Michael Stewart (MP for Fulham), pressed for a debate on housing and reminded the House of Commons that some time previously,

Henry Brooke, then Minister of Housing, had promised to investigate Rachman's empire. They now demanded to know how far those investigations had gone.

Ben Parkin also felt that Rachman's influence and involvement in the Profumo scandal might not have been as minor as first thought. Citing a rumour that had been circulating for several months, he told the incredulous House of Commons that the landlord might not even be dead, as 'it would be a very easy thing to switch bodies' at the hospital, 'and a very useful thing, just ten days before all hell breaks out'.

Ben Parkin's sensational claims caused a press frenzy and journalists began to conduct their own investigations into Rachman's slum empire. Realising that defamation laws only applied to the living, they had free rein to demonise the former landlord as much as they liked without fear of repercussions. Thus the word 'Rachmanism' became synonymous with the exploitation of impoverished tenants, although there were many other landlords whose names would have been equally fitting.

The witch-hunt prompted Audrey Rachman (who had been in hiding since Stephen Ward's trial) to issue a statement through her solicitors, which read:

> It appears that the law permits the dead to be defamed with impunity, and that I have no legal remedy against the campaign of vilification which is being conducted against my late husband.
>
> As regards those participants in this campaign who are manifestly more concerned for sensation than for truth, there would be no purpose in my attempting to pursue and expose the droves of grotesque lies and absurdities which have been paraded to the public during the last fortnight.

Audrey did, however, take great pains to state that Rachman's houses had been sold in 1959 and, from that point onwards, he had ceased to own any slum property in London or elsewhere. In response, Ben Parkin countered, 'I am not conducting a campaign against a dead man. I am waging war against all the people in this dreadful chapter in the history of property owning.'

In the event, the true extent of Peter Rachman's property empire was never proved. However, the horrendous conditions in London's slums exposed by Ben Parkin and the press in the wake of the Profumo scandal did prompt the government to launch an enquiry into housing, headed up by Sir Milner Holland, a well-respected QC. The report agreed that Rachman was by no means the only landlord who used intimidation and violence to control and exploit his tenants.

Among the many cases cited in the 250,000-word report was that of the statutory tenant who found snakes in the bathroom of a flat he refused to vacate. Another concerned a Nigerian tenant who found a shrunken head and burned chicken feathers left outside the door of his home. Neither of these victims of intimidation lived in Rachman's properties.

Holland's report also found that there were 1,500 homeless families in London, around 45,000 slum properties that were so dilapidated that they were 'urgently requiring demolition', and a massive 10,000 cases received by councils every year concerning the ill-treatment of tenants by their landlords.

It concluded that the rent controls of the previous fifty years had heavily contributed to the problem, as landlords were unlikely to repair and maintain buildings when they had no opportunity to recoup their costs. Holland noted, 'this trend will not be halted unless investors can be assured that they will be free from the hazards of political uncertainty and able to obtain an economic return'. He sagely added, 'there will remain many thousands of families who are unable either to pay an economic rent for accommodation appropriate to their needs or to obtain a council tenancy. To meet their needs, a very great addition to the stock of assisted housing will be required.'

Ultimately, while Holland's report successfully identified the social and economic challenges that faced private landlords, they also highlighted the stark fact that London simply did not have enough homes for its inhabitants. As long as that problem existed, the city's most vulnerable tenants would always be in danger of exploitation.

Today, nearly fifty years after the report was published, London's housing shortage persists and some private-sector tenants still pay ludicrously large sums of money for pitifully low-grade accommodation.

9

'HE'S IN
LOVE WITH
JANIE JONES'

LIBRARY

HOW TO

Order items by
shelfmark not listed
in the Integrated
Catalogue

---

ck on '**Log in as reader
ss holder**'

---

ter your Reader Number
d Password

---

ick on '**Request List**'
the Navigation bar

---

ick on '**order by shelfmark**'
k; select appropriate
ollection

---

pply item details; some
lds are mandatory, see
e online Help

---

lick on '**Go**'

---

lick on '**Request List**' again

---

hange delivery date in '**Date
equired**' column (if necessary)

---

lick '**Request**' in the '**Action**'
olumn; see the online Help,
r the Integrated Catalogue
Guide, if you are ordering
ulti-part items

---

hoose a reading location

---

nter seat number for same
ay delivery, if applicable

---

lick on '**Go**'. The Status
olumn displays '**Requested**'

---

o Quit: Click on '**Logout**'
and then '**Finish**'

If requesting from the As
Pacific and Africa Collect
You may request Prints,
Drawings or Photographs
any time, but you must n
an appointment at the O
Reference Enquiry Desk t
see them.

To request items from the
Office Records, use an ob
to separate elements of th
shelfmark, e.g. **L/PJ/6/23**

If requesting Maps:

Detailed ordering advice i
in a separate folder in the
Reading Room

If you are having proble
using the system...

Online help: Click '**Help**'
in the utility bar

Printed guides: next to
each terminal

Induction Sessions:
Weekdays. Ask at the
Reference Enquiry Desk

Disability Support Offic
Ask at the Reference
Enquiry Desk

Although the slum emperors' grip on Notting Hill loosened after the shocking revelations of 1963, the area continued to be a hotspot for prostitution. While landlords looked the other way, desperate young women plied their trade in sleazy basement clubs and spit-and-sawdust public houses, taking clients back to their dingy rooms for an hour or so of miserable passion.

One such girl was Margaret McGowan, a 22-year-old Scot, who had escaped a life of grinding poverty in her homeland only to become ensnared in vice once she reached London. Margaret had known some of the girls who frequented the sex parties at Cliveden, and had given evidence at Stephen Ward's trial under the alias Frances Brown. Just over a year later, her naked body was found hidden under debris in a car park on Hornton Street, W8 (the site of today's Kensington town hall).

At first, rumours abounded that Margaret had been killed in a revenge attack for the part she played in the Profumo scandal. However, it soon became clear to police that she had been the victim of a serial killer. Since early 1964, the naked bodies of four other hookers known to work in the Notting Hill area had been discovered in west London.

The first victim, 30-year-old Hannah Tailford, had been found floating in the Thames near Hammersmith in February. Two months later, the body of Irene Lockwood (26) was discovered on the riverbank near Chiswick. Then, over the summer, the remains of two more women – Helen Barthelemy (26) and Mary Flemming (31) were discovered in alleyways in Brentford and Acton. The women were all of slight build, averaging just 5ft in height and had been stripped of their clothing and jewellery. This last detail prompted the press to name the killer 'Jack the Stripper'.

The girls' disappearances from the streets of Notting Hill caused great anxiety among their peers. Soon after her murder, Margaret McGowan's friend Paul Quinn trawled the district's underworld in an attempt to find out what had happened to her. He encountered one of her compatriots in a dreary Notting Hill pub in late November. The *Daily Mirror*, who had been shadowing him as he went from club to bar, reported, 'The girl … wore a red suit and black, calf-length boots. She sat at the bar, drinking big glasses of cheap red wine.' The woman admitted that the killings had frightened her and told Quinn, 'I'm afraid another girl will get murdered if the man isn't caught soon. And the next one might be me.'

Unfortunately, Paul Quinn's attempts to get closer to the killer failed to produce any firm clues and, in February 1965, the murderer struck again, this time killing a 28-year-old Irish woman named Bridie O'Hara before dumping her body under bracken near the Heron Trading Estate in Acton. The shocking discovery of Bridie's remains at last provided police with one key clue: specks of paint found on her body were traced to a transformer housed in a shed on the trading estate, which proved that she had been temporarily hidden there prior to being moved out into the open. Paint flecks had also been found on the bodies of two of the other victims, which suggested that they had been hidden in the same place.

However, despite this encouraging lead, the police were no closer to catching the killer and the trail went cold. After the murder of Bridie O'Hara, the killings abruptly ceased and to this day, the identity of 'Jack the Stripper' has never been established.

Although the murders were unnerving, they did little to curb the brisk trade in prostitution in 1960s Notting Hill. The area's proximity to the West End meant that call girls had access to an endless stream of wealthy clients who would pay top dollar for services rendered. The lure of money proved irresistible and, as the '60s began to swing, the thought of another scandal like the Profumo affair caused much anxiety in the corridors of power. On the other hand, the newspapers – which had experienced a surge in circulation as they reported the sensational exploits of Profumo & co. – were actively seeking out new, salacious stories. By 1966, they had found new quarry in the compact form of Janie Jones – a young woman from the north of England who unwittingly found herself at the centre of a sex scandal that, once again, involved some of the country's most influential and affluent men.

Like Christine Keeler and Mandy Rice-Davies, Janie had arrived in London in her late teens with big ambitions. After a brief stint waitressing, she landed a job as a showgirl at the Windmill Theatre where she performed in its infamous, semi-naked 'tableaux vivants', which got around obscenity laws by having the girls pose absolutely still, like statues. When the Windmill finally closed in 1964, she graduated to distinctly racier private members' clubs such as the Panama (which was opposite her previous workplace) and the Gargoyle – a nightclub on Meard Street that, since its inception in the 'roaring twenties', had developed a reputation for louche decadence.

While working at these clubs, Janie inevitably became intimately acquainted with the seedier aspects of West End life. In her 1993 biography, she recalled how she became intrigued with the city's sleazy underworld: 'I'd relax by going to a hairdressers in Soho with the local whores. I used to love chatting to them about their profession. I was endlessly fascinated by what made them do it.' Her time working in Soho also made her all too aware that sex sells.

In July 1964, Michael Klinger, the owner of the Gargoyle Club, invited Janie and her younger sister, Valerie, to the premiere of *London in the Raw*, a film about London's more tawdry nightspots. Janie seized the opportunity to gain some press coverage by persuading Valerie that they should both arrive at the cinema wearing topless dresses. She later recalled, 'The evening arrived and we got into the Rolls in our beautiful, long, topless dresses and fur wraps. The streets outside the theatre were jam-packed, and Valerie was scared stiff. I got out, and of course I opened my coat.'

Unsurprisingly, the dresses caused a frenzy among the waiting photographers, but also resulted in the sisters' arrests for indecent exposure. At their subsequent trial, both girls received a hefty fine. 'There are things you can do at the seaside, which you can't do in the town', announced the court chairman, Mr R.E. Seaton, quoting lyrics from an old music-hall ditty. He then ordered that the sisters should pay £15 15s costs each for 'indecently annoying bystanders'. The girls' lawyer, James Burge, protested, 'If a man says he is annoyed by a topless dress, he ought to see a psychiatrist.' Nevertheless, the fine was imposed.

By the time she appeared in court, Janie Jones was a seasoned veteran of the Soho clubs. The stories she heard in the dressing rooms on a nightly basis taught her that patrons were willing to pay good money to girls prepared to satisfy their weird and often comical sexual perversions. One man, an army colonel, hired girls to sit on his back as if they were riding a horse while they whipped his backside with a crop. Another Soho regular paid £100 each to showgirls who agreed to come to his house, stick feathers in their bottoms and strut around the room naked calling 'cock-a-doodle-doo!' Clearly, not only did sex sell, but the stranger the request, the bigger the price. Shrewdly, Janie turned down any such offers herself, preferring to simply flirt with the customers (who seemed willing to part with large sums of cash in return for empty promises) before passing them on to her more demonstrative colleagues.

After spending several years cutting her teeth on London's slightly dubious cabaret circuit, Janie Jones' efforts were finally rewarded in early 1966 when she secured a recording contract. Her first single, 'Witches Brew', described in the *Daily Mirror* as 'a comedy song about the lighter side of unrequited love', was released later that year. It peaked at number 46 in the charts and quickly joined the pantheon of songs that are so bad, they are good. Nevertheless, it did give Janie a route into more mainstream entertainment. Keen to exploit the modest success of her debut record, she appeared on numerous television programmes and 'Witches Brew' was quickly followed up by several other releases, none of which troubled the Top 40.

After a promising start Janie's singing career rapidly stalled, and in the autumn of 1966 she found herself in the press for very different reasons, when an affluent businessman, known only as 'Mr A', accused her of demanding money with menaces.

According to Mr A – a 'young and rich City director' with a penchant for sadism – he had first come into contact with Janie Jones after meeting a girl named Maureen at a West End club. Beguiled by her charms, he was persuaded to take her on a shopping spree, after which they called in at the Playboy Club before retiring to a flat in Kensington Park Gardens, Notting Hill. It was here that Mr A claimed he was introduced to Janie Jones (whom he understood to be the owner of the property), along with some other girls. Although he did not say exactly what went on at the flat that night, Mr A clearly enjoyed himself, as the next day he returned twice – once alone, and once with his brother and some male friends. The men had sex with the girls and Mr A claimed that he paid Janie Jones handsomely for the services rendered.

Just over a week later, Mr A went back to the flat, where he met with Janie and three other girls named Crystal, Janice and Tessa. According to his testimony, he had sex with all four of them before inviting them to the Playboy Club followed by the Blue Angel Club, where they had dinner before returning to Kensington Park Gardens for another sex session. During conversations, Janie Jones had discovered that Mr A was married and he claimed that, as he was preparing to leave, she announced that instead of the £200 fee they had agreed at the beginning of the evening, the cost for her and the girls was now £1,250. If Mr A refused to pay, she allegedly threatened to tell his wife and father what he had been up to. In order to play for time, Mr A wrote her a cheque, which he later stopped, and went to the police.

Detective Sergeant Victor Wilding was duly dispatched to question Janie Jones over Mr A's allegations and received short shrift from her. Denying that she was employing blackmail tactics, she told the officer, 'I am entitled to take steps to have the cheque met. All I have done is to get my debt paid, the same as any other business woman.' Unconvinced, the police decided to put the flat at Kensington Park Gardens under surveillance but gained little in the way of incriminating evidence. The best they could muster was Janie arriving home late at night with a man who gave her some money, a sighting of her 'in her panties' through a window, and recordings of Janie and her friend, Janice, 'laying on an orgy' for two American boyfriends.

These flimsy pieces of evidence were, however, used to justify a police raid at the flat on 19 September. During the raid, officers confiscated various items including some photographs, a face mask, a book entitled *The History of Orgies* and notebooks containing room numbers and telephone numbers of some of London's plushest hotels, alongside intriguing names such as 'Sir Charles' and 'Prince Farah'. The dossier compiled by the police was sufficient to warrant an Old Bailey trial, where Janie Jones stood in the dock accused of demanding money with menaces.

The trial did not go well for the mysterious Mr A. Janie explained to the judge and jury that, far from being a client, the man simply enjoyed her company. The cheque he had written was for a deposit on a flat she wanted to buy in Holland Park, while the supposedly incriminating notebooks found by the police contained nothing more than friends' contact details.

Two of the girls who Mr A claimed were working as prostitutes also appeared at the trial and successfully humiliated their accuser. Janice Steinberg (20) swore that she had never seen any activity at Kensington Park Gardens that could deem the flat a brothel, but did tell the court that Mr A had asked her to become his 'slave in chief' at a villa he was buying in Spain. The man's sexual deviances were also revealed by 18-year-old photographic model Christine 'Crystal' Dale, who claimed that Mr A had privately asked her if she would like to earn £200 a week.

'I asked him what he meant,' she told the court. 'He said it would entail visiting him once a week and becoming his complete slave. He did not want normal sexual relations but wanted to whip me. I said I did not want anything to do with it.' Despite her slightly suspect job description, Crystal was determined to portray herself as a proper young lady. When prosecution counsel Desmond Vowden asked her why she had not walked out on hearing Mr A's lewd proposition, she exclaimed, 'I did not want to seem rude to Miss Jones and I was having tea at the time!' She then astutely backed up Janie's story by adding that she knew Mr A was helping her to buy a property and she did not want to jeopardise the transaction.

While the police had been busy watching the flat at Kensington Park Gardens, persons unknown had been engaged in the simple task of bringing Mr A's character into disrepute. Photographs emerged of him whipping girls in a flat in Hampstead, and a tape recording surfaced of him telling a girl named Joyce that he liked to take young girls as amateurs and turn them into professionals. Defence counsel, Michael Eastham QC, appealed to the jury, 'Is it safe to rely on the evidence of a man of his moral character? He is abnormal.'

In the event, Janie Jones was acquitted on account of insufficient evidence. Mr A skulked back to his poor wife, although many people felt that he should have been named and shamed for his immoral and depraved behaviour. This should, by all intents and purposes, have been the end of the sordid matter. However, during the police raid on Janie's flat back in September, Janice Steinberg (who had been present) had panicked and tried to climb out of a window. She was

stopped by Superintendent David Helm, who may have been a little
heavy-handed as he prevented her escape. As Janice was led away
from the scene, she shouted to the police officers, 'I'll stir things up.
You just wait and see.' She later accused Helm of striking her and
throwing her across the room.

Although no official action was taken on Janice Steinberg's allegations, Superintendent Helm was perhaps motivated by revenge when
he rearrested Janie Jones in November 1966, after apparently receiving an anonymous phone call telling him that the flat was being used
as a brothel. Her trial was set for March 1967 and, once again, was led
by Desmond Vowden for the Crown, with Michael Eastham acting
as defence.

Much of the evidence compiled during the police surveillance was
reintroduced and dismissed by Janie Jones as 'a pack of lies from beginning to end'. Michael Eastham also noted that, during the period in
question, her 70-year-old mother had been staying at the flat. 'It is difficult to appreciate how she could have blatantly carried on the profession
of a prostitute without her mother's knowledge', he told the court.

Desmond Vowden then turned to the notebooks found by the
police, highlighting an entry that read, 'Abdullah, Royal Suite at the
Dorchester'. Janie responded by telling him that the entry referred to
an associate of King Faisal with whom she had become friendly after
meeting him at the Astor Club. Another Arabic name picked out by
Mr Vowden apparently referred to King Faisal's son, and when the QC
tried to delve deeper into the nature of his relationship with Janie, she
retorted, 'He is in town now. Why don't you ring him up and ask him?'

As the names in the notebooks failed to produce any damning
evidence, the jury struggled to reach a verdict. The judge ordered a
retrial, which began in May. Once again, the jury found insufficient
proof that Janie Jones was operating a brothel and she was acquitted.
After being released, she made a defiant statement to the waiting press,
warning that she was considering suing the police, and explaining:

> I have missed a full television series of 10 weeks because of this pros-
> ecution. The producer wanted to put me in but the heads would not
> have it. I have lost work in the Bahamas also. Defending the action

has cost me several thousand pounds – an awful lot of money. I have
had to sell my flat in Kensington Park Gardens and am now selling
my home in Holland Park to pay for it.

In a bid to make the most of the publicity from the trial, Janie's record
company released a new single called 'Tickle Me Tootsie Wootsies'.
Written by her sister Valerie, the song made the irresistible offer that,
'if you tickle me tootsie wootsies, I'll scratch your back for you'. Sadly,
it failed to make much impression on the charts despite a promotional
tour of Britain's nightclubs.

Undeterred by "Tootsie Wootsies" lack of success, Janie Jones continued with her singing career, concentrating on nightclub cabaret
performances. During this period, she met a young American song-
writer named John Christian Dee, a man with whom she was destined
to spend the next five years of her life. Born in New York State, Dee
had carved out a flourishing career as a singer/songwriter, penning hits
for the Pretty Things (for whom he wrote 'Don't Bring Me Down')
and the Fairies, as well as performing himself, either solo or as part of
a duo named Adam & Eve – described unkindly, but not unfairly, by a
reviewer as a 'poor man's Sonny & Cher'. By the time he met Janie
Jones, John Dee had acquired an enviable reputation as a commer-
cially successful composer. However, he was also a heroin addict.

Janie Jones first came into contact with John Dee at a Kensington
nightclub. He was feeling ill due to his drug addiction and so Janie suggested that he and his friend, Long John Baldry, accompany her back
to the quieter atmosphere of her new home in Campden Hill Road,
Notting Hill. On arriving at the house, Baldry confided in Janie his
concerns that Dee was slowly killing himself, and asked her if she
could put him up for a few days as he had spent all his money on
drugs. She agreed, and over the following weeks John Dee gradually
withdrew from his heroin addiction while becoming increasingly
attached to Janie. After only a matter of weeks, he proposed to her and
the pair married at Kensington Registry Office on 7 November 1968.
Their wedding rings and the reception were paid for by an old friend
of Janie's. Known only as 'Bob', this enigmatic man worked as a West
End antique dealer by day, but by night he liked nothing better than

a good whipping. This guilty secret would later play a significant role in Janie's downfall.

Following his recovery from heroin addiction, John Dee's career began to take off again. In 1969, he was signed by Gordon Mills, the manager of Tom Jones and Engelbert Humperdinck, for whom he co-wrote the song, 'Café'. He also released his own tracks including 'The World Can Pack Their Bags and Go Away'.

However, by the end of 1972, his marriage to Janie Jones was unravelling amid accusations of infidelity and threats of violence. As Dee's behaviour became increasingly erratic and menacing, Janie threw him out of the home they shared on Campden Hill Road and was forced to apply for a restraining order from the courts, after he began threatening that he would 'show her what torture is'. When she dismissed the talk as idle threats, he warned her, 'You won't laugh when I pull the trigger.'

Janie Jones and John Dee's marriage ended in April 1973 after he was arrested for breaking into her house and taking some papers. However, as the couple officially parted company, little did they realise that, in just over a month, they would both be embroiled in the midst of a sex scandal.

The seeds of the scandal had been sown back in 1971, when the *News of the World* ran a story claiming that various television producers and disc jockeys had been bribed with free holidays and invitations to sex parties, in return for giving certain recording artists exposure and air time. Janie Jones had become linked to the sensational affair when a *News of the World* reporter posing as a music business executive taped a record company boss saying, 'Janie Jones gives the most fantastic parties.' Although Janie did indeed throw wild showbiz parties at Campden Hill Road, she vehemently denied that influential guests were lured there on a promise of sex, explaining:

> The parties started from the Revolution Club, which was in Bruton Place, Mayfair … It was a very in-place, and I was one of the regular crowd there on Friday or Saturday nights, usually in a non-working capacity. We'd all have a drink, go to the club, and from time-to-time, a gang of us would end up back at my house. Quite a few of the guests would be stars I had got to know through working in shows.

That said, the mere fact that household names such as Engelbert Humperdinck, Cat Stevens and disc jockey *du jour* Simon Dee were on the guest list, was enough for the *News of the World* to ignore Janie's protestations. Even more worryingly, their findings were passed on to Scotland Yard, who (perhaps remembering Janie's narrow escape from previous allegations) considered the evidence sufficient to launch a two-year investigation into the goings-on at Campden Hill Road. The inquiry was headed by Chief Superintendent Richard Booker and Detective Inspector Roy Penrose.

At 6.45 a.m. on Thursday, 17 May 1973, Janie Jones received a knock on the door. Bleary eyed, she opened it to find a police team standing on the doorstep. The police announced that they were arresting her for controlling prostitutes and attempting to pervert the course of justice by threatening a potential witness. In confused dismay, Janie dressed and grabbed a hasty breakfast, before being carted off to Cannon Row Police Station along with her lodger, Eric Gilbert, who was suspected of aiding and abetting her and influencing potential witnesses.

Jones and Gilbert were not the only people to be arrested during the police swoop. Over in the West End, Janie's ex-husband, John Christian Dee, was put under arrest for attempting to pervert the course of justice by using threats of violence to induce a witness to make a false statement. Record promoters Roger Bolton, Tony Saxon and Clive Crawley were arrested and later charged with bribing 'agents' of the BBC, and Leonard Tucker, a theatrical agent, was accused of manipulating sales figures to compile a false record sales chart.

Throughout the morning of 17 May, the arrest count steadily increased while the charges became more and more bizarre. John Grossman, a 34-year-old man from Stanmore, was charged with conspiring with several other people to forge postcards, which were duly sent to the ITV talent show *Opportunity Knocks* and counted among the votes for New World, an Australian pop group who had won the show on ten successive occasions. Warrants were also issued for the arrests of the members of New World who were on a promotional tour of Scandinavia.

On their return, they appeared at Bow Street Magistrates' Court, where they were remanded on bail. A warrant was also issued for the arrest of Edward Kassner, the head of US-based President Records, who was alleged to have conspired with Janie Jones to bribe individuals to promote his label's artists by supplying them with the free services of prostitutes. The most extraordinary arrest was that of the singer Dorothy Squires, ex-wife of Roger Moore.

Early that morning, Ms Squires had noticed a Morris Oxford parked outside her home in Bexley and, unaware that the occupants were actually watching her house, she telephoned the local police to report it. Another car arrived shortly before 10.30 a.m. and three detectives led by DI Penrose went to the house. *The Times* later described the farcical scenes that followed: '[The detectives] had to wait while Miss Squires had a bath, dressed and had breakfast. [They] refused the offer of tea while they waited and at 11.40 a.m., they led the singer from the house to the back of a police car.' Like many of the other suspects, Dorothy Squires was taken to Cannon Row Police Station.

She arrived there around the same time as Jack Dabbs, a former producer of the BBC radio show *Family Favourites*, who had allegedly been induced by Miss Squires and Edward Kassner to play her new record after being promised free holidays to Malta and Gibraltar. After questioning, everyone except Janie Jones and Eric Gilbert were released on bail. As she left Cannon Row, Dorothy Squires told the assembled press scrum that she had fainted three times from the shock of her arrest, adding, 'I never realised this could happen in this country.'

The arrests on 17 May caused a sensation in the press, who quickly dubbed the affair 'The Payola Scandal' – a term first coined in America by the legendary disc jockey Alan Freed, who had been accused of accepting bribes to give certain records airplay in the 1950s. Of course, the journalists were not particularly concerned with Jack Dabbs' free holidays to the Mediterranean and, in the event, the majority of charges against the bit-part players in the sordid drama (including the charge against Dorothy Squires) were dropped, as the police concentrated on the accusation that Janie Jones had been running prostitutes. At the ensuing pre-trial hearing in July 1973, and the subsequent trial which opened in September, the newspapers' appetite for raunchy details of the goings-on at Campden Hill Road was more than satisfied.

At the opening hearing at the Mayor's & City of London Court, Michael Worsley, the Director of Public Prosecutions, set out the basic facts of the case. Janie Jones was accused of supplying call girls to a range of clients, some of whom were in the entertainment business. A few of these girls had lived with her at Campden Hill Road until the News of the World began to show interest in late 1970. The girls then left, but were allegedly warned by Jones, Dee and Gilbert not to speak to the press or the police. Nevertheless, some of them did and the News of the World published the findings of their investigation in 1971. Afterwards, the prosecution asserted that Janie Jones had black-mailed her clients, telling them that she needed money to keep their names out of the papers. At the time of her arrest, police had found a box containing thousands of pounds in cash, which they considered to be the proceeds of blackmail.

The prosecution's first witness was then called. Referred to in the subsequent press reports as 'Miss A', she explained that she had begun to work for Janie Jones after being introduced to her by a boyfriend in March 1969. Miss A was keen to carve out a career as an actress and her boyfriend was convinced that Janie could help her. 'He picked me up in a car and took me to a house in Campden Hill Road,' Miss A told the court. 'Janie opened the door. She wanted me to go and see this television producer and said that he did all the advertisements for Silvikrin and Smarties.'

Intrigued, and seemingly aware of the 'casting couch' method of auditioning, Miss A accompanied Janie in a cab to the producer's flat where she claimed she saw him hand her 'something, but I don't know what'. Janie then left, and Miss A followed the producer into his flat where they had sex. Afterwards, he sent her back to Campden Hill Road with £10. She was greeted by Janie who told her that 'television work was sure to come now'.

Despite Janie Jones' assurances, Miss A did not receive any offers of acting work over the following weeks. However, she did secure work of a different kind at Campden Hill Road. She told the jury of an occasion when she visited the house and Janie told her to put on a child's suit and carry a teddy bear. As the court listened in shocked revulsion, she explained that she was then instructed to go to an upstairs bedroom and act as a young girl while an older man, playing the role of her step-father, proceeded to rape her. The pair's sickening performance was watched by a man through a two-way mirror that had been set into the wall of an adjacent bedroom. Miss A explained what happened next. 'I pretended to fight him [the 'stepfather'] off. Then [the man watching] seemed to be getting excited and he came into the bedroom.' At this point, the 'stepfather' left and Miss A had sex with her voyeur.

Michael Worsley asked her, 'Did you at any time, as a result of these or any other meetings, get any employment in relation to television?'

'No,' admitted Miss A. She then went on to recount the story of a party at Campden Hill Road, thrown to promote John Dee's new song, 'Come Forward the Men'. According to the girl, several people working for the BBC were invited to the gathering and Janie Jones told her she wanted to 'wine and dine and f**k the BBC men to death'.

The following day, Michael Worsley called 'Miss B' to the witness box. She told the court that she had been recruited while working as a switchboard operator at a Regent Street theatrical agency. Apparently, Janie Jones telephoned the agency regularly and one day she asked Miss B if she would like to work for a record company. On saying that she would, Miss B was then told that she would have to 'be nice' and do the 'beddie-byes' bit, to which she presumably acquiesced, as a few days later she was summoned to Campden Hill Road to meet a television producer. She had sex with the man in one of the bedrooms and told the court that Janie paid her £5.

The prosecution then asked Miss B about the alleged sex parties at the house and she told the court that she had attended two or three, during which she and some other girls (including Miss A) had sex with some of the guests and performed lesbian acts while others watched through the two-way mirror. She also claimed that she had accompanied Janie to several central London hotels to service clients and, although she had quickly realised that no television work would be forthcoming, she had carried on working as a call girl because she enjoyed the financial benefits.

During her time with Janie Jones, Miss B explained that she had been asked to fulfil many bizarre and depraved fantasies, which regularly involved dressing up and role-play, including playing the part of a dominatrix who strutted around the room brandishing a leather whip. Her clients were from diverse walks of life, and at least one worked for commercial television; 'He had something to do with Kitkat ads,' Miss B told the court.

As the prosecution called more call girl witnesses to the stand, the two men who stood accused alongside Janie Jones took great pains to distance themselves from the lurid goings-on at Campden Hill Road. John Dee's lawyer made sure that his client was portrayed as a despairing husband struggling to come to terms with what was happening in his home. Prompted by careful questioning, he inferred that he had no idea what Janie Jones was up to until he became suspicious of telephone calls she received from mysterious men. Miss A recalled that Dee had once grabbed her by the hair and told her to 'get out of the house, you bloody whore'.

'I believe he said we were all lesbians trying to interfere with his marriage,' she told the court.

Meanwhile, Eric Gilbert's defence was determined to present him as a lovelorn fool. Under questioning, he explained that he had first met Janie Jones in 1963, when he saw her performing at a cabaret club called the Georgian. After the show, the shy court clerk plucked up the courage to ask for her autograph. 'She seemed very nice,' said Gilbert. 'I never had any girlfriends before and we became very friendly.'

Later, when he was transferred from his job in Southport to London, Janie apparently invited him to stay at Campden Hill Road in return for a monthly rent of £28. However, according to Gilbert's testimony, his lodgings came at a price: '[Janie] demanded that I help with the cleaning, housework and shopping. [She] was bossy. I was completely under her command.' He went on to claim that he was often forced to stay in the kitchen of the house until 4 a.m. because people were using his bedroom, and he was expected to serve Janie Jones and John Dee with morning tea while they lounged in bed. His assertions were backed up by Miss A, who told the court that he was never invited to the parties but, instead, was expected to serve tea and coffee and wash dishes. 'My view was that he was a frightened servant,' she told the court.

While Dee and Gilbert desperately tried to exonerate themselves from any blame, the evidence against Janie Jones steadily mounted.

Two more girls – Miss C and Miss F – admitted that they had worked for her as call girls, while Miss B recounted talk of 'heavies' being dispatched to go after girls who dared to speak to the police during their investigation. She also claimed that a doctor had been called to see her at Campden Hill Road so she 'could be taken to a mental hospital and I wouldn't have to give evidence in court'.

However, Janie did have some witnesses on her side. A businessman known as 'Mr X' – described as 'very gentlemanly, with dark hair and beautiful pinstripe suits' – testified that her girls were merely supplied as escorts and hostesses. Explaining that he would arrange for attractive young women to be sent to hotels to entertain foreign colleagues, he told the court, 'Something in the region of £3,600 was paid for twenty-five visitors between 1968 and the end of 1971, and possibly early 1972. Payment was made with travellers' cheques, dollars or £10 notes.' He went on to strenuously deny that the girls were supplied as prostitutes, and found it difficult to believe they had been bullied into working for Janie. 'It would hardly be appropriate for hostesses to be under that kind of pressure when they were entertaining. I never saw anything to suggest such.'

In addition to Mr X's statements, 'Miss K' claimed that John Dee was not quite the innocent, moral-minded man he was trying to portray. She admitted under oath that she had been persuaded to create false evidence to expedite Jones and Dee's separation with the full knowledge of John Dee, who had agreed to be caught by a private detective in a compromising position with her so he could get a 'quickie' divorce on the grounds of adultery.

Janie Jones' niece, who was referred to in the case as 'Miss G', portrayed Dee as a man with a very violent temper. Explaining that she had recently been living at Campden Hill Road, she said:

> He [Dee] does not like me being in what he says is his house. On several occasions in the last six months he has phoned me up, come round and told me he will bring his boys round if I don't get out. He has said several times he is going to shoot us – my boyfriend, my little girl and me – with a shotgun. Four times I have reported him to the police when I could not take any more.

Miss G also claimed that Dee had once thrown Janie down the stairs of the house at Campden Hill Road during a row, and on another occasion had hit her in the face with such force that she needed several stitches.

Janie Jones' trial dragged on through the remaining months of 1973 and into the New Year, as some twenty-two charges were systematically dealt with. Finally, on 17 January 1974, her time came to speak. Her defence counsel, Peter Dow QC, began by asking her how she had come to know the men she was accused of supplying with call girls. She told him that she had first become acquainted with them while working at two London nightclubs – Le Prince and the Don Juan Casanova Club. 'They were both society clubs and the people I met there were all millionaires or peers of the realm.' Janie denied having sexual relations with any of the patrons, although 'these people were very generous. It was nothing to be given £1,000 or £3,000 in cash from someone in the club.' Dow then asked, 'What did they get in exchange?'

'Nothing,' Janie replied. 'Promises.' Pressed further by the judge, she added:

> They obviously gave me the money because they thought there might be something at the end of it, but I would tell them that as far as I was concerned, there was no hanky-panky with me. They would give me money anyway, thinking I would change my mind, but I did not.

Janie then described how she met Mr X, 'a spender in the millionaire class'. Mr X constantly had business contacts visiting Britain and suggested that she find escorts for them. Nightclub owners were also on a constant lookout for new girls to act as hostesses and, thus, Janie began to supply them too. Peter Dow asked her, 'Was it on the footing that these girls should go to bed with the members?'

'Definitely not,' she replied.

Turning to the alleged orgies at Campden Hill Road, Janie admitted to throwing show business parties, but categorically denied that she paid girls to attend them. 'They couldn't get there quick enough when there was a well-known disc jockey or name in show business present,' she told the court. She also refuted the claim that the girls were instructed to sleep with the men invited to the parties, asserting that she only ever received money for providing escorts, not prostitutes. The two-way mirror in the bedroom was explained away as a practical joke designed to embarrass a party guest who insisted he only took girls upstairs to interview them.

During the lengthy court case, Janie Jones had also been accused of blackmailing both her girls to prevent them from talking to the press or police, and some clients, from whom she had apparently tried to extract money for spurious abortions and/or to keep their names out of the newspapers. Unsurprisingly, she denied both charges emphatically.

The trial of Janie Jones finally ended on 1 March 1974. After deliberating for more than nine hours, the jury returned a verdict of guilty on seven charges of controlling prostitutes and three charges of attempting to pervert the course of justice. Eric Gilbert and John Christian Dee were both acquitted and were discharged. However, as Janie Jones stood alone and dejected in the dock, it became apparent that the court had not quite finished with her. The judge announced that he was postponing sentencing, citing 'other matters outstanding'. Officially, these 'other matters' concerned allegations of blackmail made by two of Janie's clients – Mr Y and Mr Z. Unofficially, the judge was preparing to hang Janie Jones out to dry.

Three weeks after she had been found guilty of previous charges, Janie Jones appeared in court again to face the new allegations. The fact that Mr Y and Mr Z appeared for the prosecution was shocking, given the history they shared with the woman in the dock. Mr Z was none other than 'Bob' the antique dealer, who had paid for Janie's wedding to John Dee back in 1968. His fellow accuser, Mr Y, was an eminent member of high society.

Back in 1965, Janie had saved him from being blackmailed out of £6,000, when a girl he had met in the Robin Hood nightclub claimed that not only had he got her pregnant but also that she was only 14. Knowing full well that the Robin Hood did not employ underage girls, Janie immediately suspected foul play and, after persuading Mr Y to go to the police, the blackmailer was arrested. However, her help clearly counted for nothing six years later, when Mr Y's penchant for having sex with women dressed as 12-year-old schoolgirls was under threat of being exposed to the nation as part of the *News of the World*'s investigation.

Although his name was not mentioned, Mr Y knew the story referred to him as soon as he read it. So did Janie Jones, and the day after the article was published she allegedly rang him and warned him that his name would soon make headlines if he did not give her £3,000 to start a libel action against the paper. Terrified, Mr Y handed over the money, but during the following months Janie contacted him several more times, telling him she needed more cash. Eventually, Mr Y claimed he gave her £12,000 in total. This extraordinary amount of money was apparently supplemented by a much smaller sum that Janie had demanded from Mr Z, whose predilection for being whipped had also been exposed in the *News of the World* article. The bank notes found at the time of Janie's arrest were cited in court as being the remains of this money.

Mr Y and Mr Z's blackmail allegations forced Janie Jones into a corner. How could she say she was using the money to keep their depraved exploits out of the papers if she was not involved in the whole sordid affair? Weeping as she stood in the dock, Janie admitted to committing perjury during her previous trial by denying she ran a call girl service. 'I was covering up for Mr Y and myself, as I promised from the very beginning I would,' she sobbed.

As the trial drew to a close, it was clear that Janie Jones had been outwitted. However, before the case was adjourned prior to sentencing, her counsel, Peter Dow, asked the court, 'Do you think … she is all that worse than the sort of man she provided services for? So much worse than Mr Y, who benefited from her false affidavit in the libel action, as well as from the services of the girls she provided?'

As Janie Jones sat in the cells awaiting sentencing, it became clear that some people wholeheartedly agreed with Peter Dow. Paul Foot, editor of the *Socialist Worker* (and nephew of MP Michael Foot) felt so strongly aggrieved by the double standards displayed during the case that he exposed the identity of Mr Y in his newspaper, writing, 'Now Mr Y is not Mr Y at all. He is Lord Y, or to be specific Lord B**** brother-in-law of the Duke of *******.' Foot went on to make the point that if victims of rape were not afforded anonymity (which at the time, they were not) why were sexual deviants like Lord B**** protected? In response, the High Court fined Foot and his publisher

£250 each for contempt of court and ordered them to pay the prosecution costs, estimated at £7,500.

On 18 April 1974, Janie Jones was given a massive seven-year gaol sentence for controlling prostitutes and attempting to pervert the course of justice. Realising that the allegations had done their job and not wishing to open another can of worms, the judge cleared her of the blackmail charges. 'Thank God for Paul Foot!' she exclaimed.

During his summing up, Judge Alan King-Hamilton's description of Janie Jones was so harsh that anyone unfamiliar with the case would have thought she had committed mass murder. He stated:

> In my time, I have come across many men whom it would be right to describe as evil, but in all my time ... I have only come across one woman who merited such a description. You are the second and beside you, she was comparatively harmless.

Unsurprisingly, given the judge's merciless summing up, Janie Jones was also ordered to pay £4,000 towards the prosecution costs of her first trial in addition to the whole of her defence costs, or £12,000, whichever was the less. She served just over three years of her sentence before being released in May 1977.

During this time she had become a heroine of the anti-Establishment, and her cult status was sealed when the Clash included the song 'Janie Jones' on their eponymous first album. Janie later said, 'I bought the album and I listened to it, and when I realised the song was quite the opposite of the character assassination I'd imagined, I was thrilled to bits. It boosted my self-esteem and self-respect no end, at a very vulnerable time.'

While Janie had become something of a folk heroine, the life of her erstwhile husband, John Christian Dee, had unravelled during the years of her incarceration. After being discharged from court, he fled to Germany, where he had previously achieved some chart success with his Adam & Eve singing duo. However, in 1976, he was gaoled for six years after attacking his girlfriend, Angela Fronek, with a knife when she told him she wanted to end their relationship. After being released, he lived for a time in France before returning to London. He died in 2004.

Eric Gilbert, Janie's lodger, was sacked from his job as a clerk at Croydon Court despite being acquitted of all charges. Although he had delivered some damning evidence against her in court, Janie forgave him and he returned to live at Campden Hill Road after Janie's release from gaol. As for Janie herself, after a brief (and ultimately regretted) campaign to free the Moors murderer, Myra Hindley, whom she had met in gaol, she gradually sank into obscurity occasionally punctuated by high-profile projects.

In 1982, she recorded a new single, entitled 'House of the Ju-Ju Queen', under the deliberately provocative name 'Janie Jones and the Lash'. The song was very ably backed by members of the Blockheads and her old friends, the Clash, while production was overseen by the latter's frontman, the late Joe Strummer. Eleven years later, she released her biography, *The Devil and Miss Jones*, in which she publicly retracted her former support for Myra Hindley, branding her manipulative and sickening. More recently, in 2006, she appeared in the video for Babyshambles' cover version of 'Janie Jones', being chauffeured around London with the Clash's lead guitarist Mick Jones (no relation).

To this day, Janie Jones continues to vehemently deny that she ever ran prostitutes:

> I knew what was going on, of course – the girls used to brag about what had happened – but it was nothing to do with me ... [The women] were girls I knew, or girls I'd recruited through escort agencies. And if I were running a call-girl ring, then so was every escort agency in the West End.

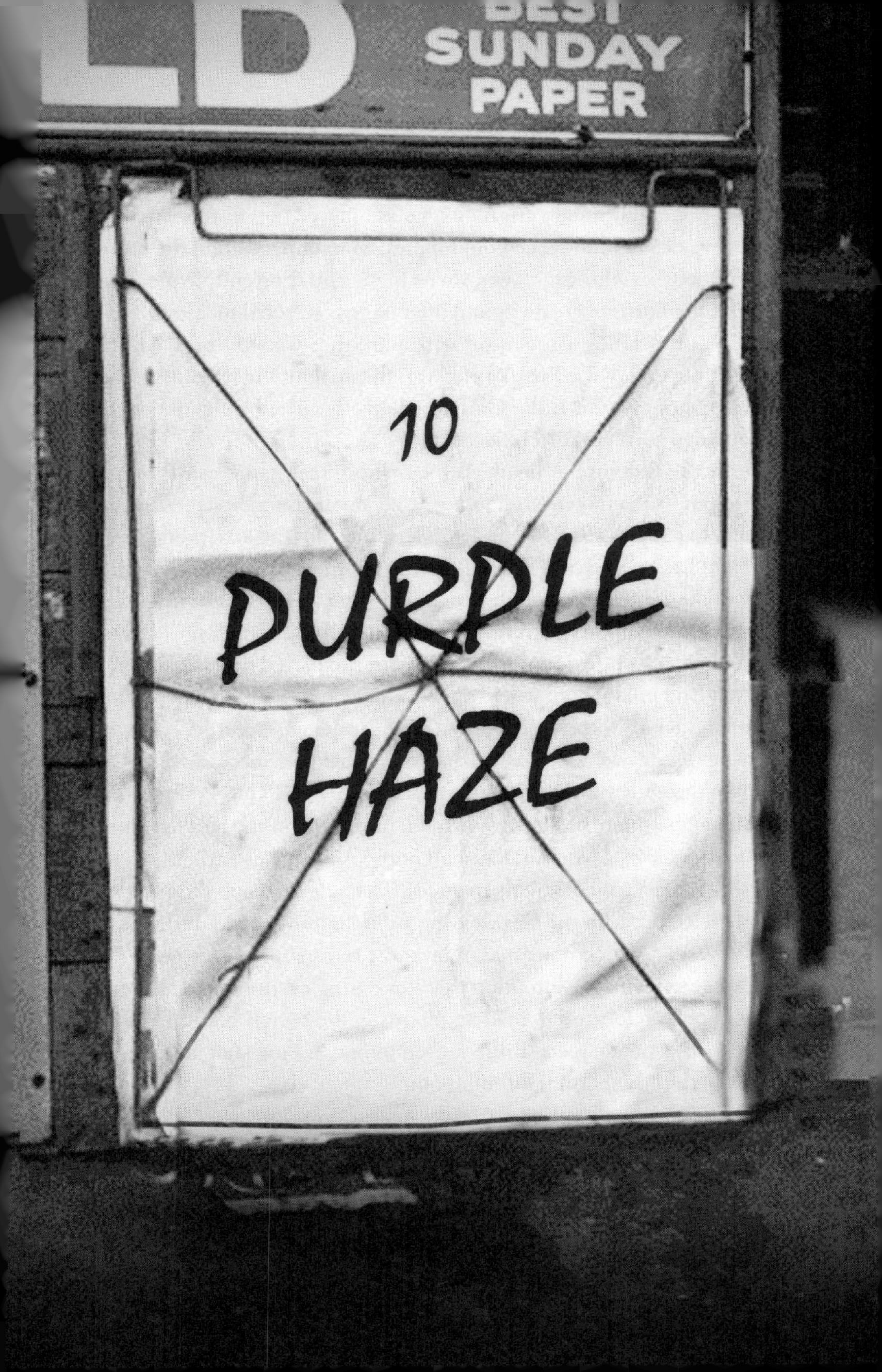

10

PURPLE HAZE

While Janie Jones was fending off unwanted police attention, Notting Hill was rapidly gaining a reputation for another vice. By the end of the 1960s the area had become a drug hub, and its crumbling houses played host to a sordid mix of furtive dealers and spaced-out hippies, who lounged amid the rotting grandeur searching for the ultimate high. This drug culture produced startling bursts of creativity and utter tragedy in equal measure.

Notting Hill's association with narcotics was not new. Shortly after the end of the First World War, the area hit the headlines when 22-year-old actress Billie Carleton died after overdosing on cocaine supplied by a Notting Hill dealer.

At the time of her death, Billie —whose real name was Florence Stewart – was enjoying a glittering career on the London stage. She had shot to fame in 1915 when she understudied for the actress and singer Ethel Levey, who had fallen ill during the run of a revue called *Mind Your Step* at the Empire Theatre in Leicester Square. The critics were impressed with her performance and soon Billie Carleton was in hot demand. Over the following three years, she played in a succession of West End productions where she became renowned for her good looks and vivacious wit. However, little did her audiences realise that much of her on-stage ebullience was due to her liberal use of cocaine.

In the early hours of 28 November 1918, Billie Carleton returned to her apartment at the Savoy Hotel, having spent the past few hours at a First World War Victory Ball at the Albert Hall with her friend Reggie De Veulle. Her appearance at the ball had caused quite a stir, not least because she was wearing a diaphanous gown, designed by De Veulle, which consisted of layers of transparent black georgette. Delighted with the attention that her daring costume had attracted and looking forward to reading reports in the society columns of the next day's newspapers, Billie retired to bed, telling staff at the hotel not to disturb her until the afternoon.

The Savoy complied with her instructions and after lunch dispatched her personal maid, May Booker, to see if she required anything. After tentatively knocking on the door several times but receiving no answer, May let herself into the suite. Her mistress was lying on the bed and at first she thought she was still asleep. However, as she drew closer, May realised to her horror that Billie Carleton was dead. The police were summoned and quickly found the cause of her premature demise: in her bag was a small, bejewelled gold box containing cocaine.

At the subsequent inquest into Billie Carleton's death, it became clear that both she and Reggie De Veulle were regular cocaine users. Their usual supplier was Don Kimful, a mysterious Egyptian who operated out of a Notting Hill flat, supplying addicts with liberal quantities of the drug, which he obtained from a chemist in Lisle Street, behind Leicester Square.

However, on the day of the ball, De Veulle had for unspecified reasons decided not to use Kimful's services. Instead he had gone to an opium den in Limehouse Causeway, where he bought a bottle of cocaine from a Chinese man named Lo Pingu and his English wife, Ada. Keen to get a fix, he had hurried back to his home in Camden Town but, on sampling his purchase, he realised he had been duped. Instead of pure cocaine, the contents of the bottle had clearly been cut with another substance, severely reducing its effects.

Frustrated and desperate to satisfy his cravings, De Veulle made his way to Lisle Street in the hope of seeking out Don Kimful. The Egyptian was nowhere to be found, but he did bump into Lionel Belcher, a movie actor and fellow addict. De Veulle knew Belcher from the Notting Hill drug den and, after complaining he had been ripped off by Lo Pingu, he asked if Belcher had any of Kimful's cocaine that he was willing to sell. Belcher said he did and told De Veulle that he would bring it to the Victory Ball that evening. It was this cocaine that ultimately killed Billie Carleton.

Following his revelations at the inquest, Reggie De Veulle was arrested and charged with manslaughter. At his subsequent trial he was acquitted, but pleaded guilty to the lesser charge of supplying cocaine and was sent to prison for eight months. During the trial it also transpired that Ada Lo was a regular pusher of cocaine and opium. Witnesses described how she would give drug tutorials at parties, where she would bring along the necessary ephemera and teach guests how to take the dangerous narcotics. Her activities earned her five months' hard labour, while her husband Lo Pingu escaped with a £10 fine. As for the enigmatic Don Kimful, all attempts to find him failed and the chemist in Lisle Street strenuously denied ever knowing such a character.

The tragic death of Billie Carleton contributed to the passing of the Dangerous Drugs Act (1920) which attempted to control the sale and possession of cocaine, raw opium, morphine and heroin by ruling that anyone dealing in the drugs had to be licensed by the Home Secretary. However, the Act merely succeeded in driving the trade underground, and over the following decades Notting Hill quietly retained its reputation as a place where suppliers could be found.

In 1965, an investigation by *The Times* found that the area was one of five 'drugs centres' in London, the others being the East End, Soho, Paddington and, rather surprisingly, Chelsea. By this time, the most sought after drugs had changed from opium and cocaine to the much cheaper marijuana and amphetamine tablets, which were readily available in countless cafés and clubs in the area. Amphetamines, known at the time as 'purple hearts' because of their shape, could be bought for around 1s 6d per tablet, while marijuana cost about £4 for half an ounce (enough to make thirty cigarettes when blended with tobacco).

One of the largest consumers of marijuana in Notting Hill at the time of *The Times*' investigation was the West Indian community, to whom smoking 'ganja' was very much a way of life. Marijuana had first been introduced to the Caribbean in the mid-1800s by contract labourers from the Indian subcontinent. Although they had been freed from slavery by this period, the black population of the islands still led relentlessly hard lives of grinding poverty and many quickly took to smoking ganja as a temporary release from their miserable existence. The drug became so popular that, in the early 1900s, it was officially adopted by the Rastafari movement, who used it to aid meditation. Unsurprisingly, when they migrated to Britain after the Second World War, many West Indians brought supplies of ganja with them and introduced it to the white population.

Although the psychological effects of marijuana did not appear to cause any permanent damage, it did encourage some users to experiment with harder drugs. By the closing years of the 1960s, lysergic acid diethylamide – commonly known as LSD – had become phenomenally popular with younger people as a recreational drug. However, although it was not addictive and could produce some truly mind-blowing 'trips' for users, LSD could also heighten feelings of anxiety and paranoia to the point where they became debilitating. Underlying psychological conditions such as schizophrenia and depression could also be made much worse by the drug.

Unsurprisingly, the authorities attempted to clamp down on the burgeoning trade in LSD and by 1967 the seedy abodes of known dealers in Notting Hill were subjected to regular police raids, some of which were more successful than others. In March 1970, *Daily Mirror* journalists Tom Tullett and Edward Vale accompanied Notting Hill's vice squad on a raid and described their experiences:

> A plain clothes policeman knocks discreetly at a front door and asks where he can find the 'scene'. The person who opens the door takes one look at the Hippie (imitation sheepskin coat, way-out shirt and drooping, Mexican-style moustache) and assumes he is inquiring about the others in the house. The police outside allow two min-utes to elapse, then move in. First through the door is two-year-old Fred, a black Labrador. He pounds up the staircase followed by his handler, ex-Navy boxing champion David Cadogan, a PC in civvies for the night. On the second floor, a door is already open. Several youths, barefoot and bewildered, are told to remain in the room until they have been searched. Mattresses are turned over, wardrobes are emptied. A quick sift through gramophone records. Socks are turned inside out and shoes shaken. Teacups are examined and tobacco tins sniffed at. All the time, Fred is poking his wet nose into everything, looking for something that concerns him. Eventually, one youth is cautioned about the Dangerous Drugs Act and asked to accompany the police to the station.

Once apprehended, Notting Hill's drug pushers were shown no mercy by the courts. In July 1967, 20-year-old Peter Bramwell Jackson of Blenheim Crescent was given a two-year prison sentence by Judge Alan King-Hamilton (Janie Jones' nemesis), who told him, 'Your determination to defy the law and continued dealing in drugs is matched by a determination of the courts to punish those who seek to profit by exploiting young people in their wretchedness and anxiety.'

Although individuals like Bramwell Jackson constantly ran the risk of arrest, their greatest threat came from the addicts they supplied. In January 1970, Thomas Ezelle, a 21-year-old American drug pusher, was stabbed to death in the Commune – a derelict school in Clarendon Road, Notting Hill – by drug-addled hippies who had plotted to steal the proceeds of his sordid trade.

Described as a 'big fish' in the west London drugs scene, Ezelle would frequent the hippie hangouts of Notting Hill, where his customers quickly realised that he carried huge amounts of cash – the proceeds of his numerous drug deals. On 10 January, he had already collected £950 when he was met near Clarendon Road by two teenagers named Andrew Timothy (commonly known as 'Jenk') and Michael Harper. The youths told him that they needed to score some dope and asked him to come to the Commune so they could do the deal in private.

Ezelle unwittingly followed them into the abandoned building where he was ambushed by Timothy, Harper and two other hippies – John Kenvyn and John Hughson, a 23-year-old from Yorkshire known to his associates as 'Jasper'. When Ezelle tried to stop the gang from taking his money, Hughson took out a commando knife and viciously stabbed him in the stomach. The youths then grabbed the money and left Ezelle dying on the floor.

All four of Thomas Ezelle's attackers were subsequently arrested and sent for trial. John Hughson admitted manslaughter and was gaoled for ten years. His cohorts all pleaded guilty to conspiracy to rob and each received three years in prison. The despairing judge sent them down to the cells telling them, 'It is appalling that youths of your upbringing should be brought to such an utterly demoralising state through drugs. I have the greatest sympathy for your parents.'

The Clarendon Road commune in which Thomas Ezelle met his fate was one of numerous squats that existed in Notting Hill at the end of the 1960s. A short distance away stood Centre House, a 'utopian community' run by self-styled guru, Christopher Hills – a hippie who believed that the Third World food shortage could be solved by feeding the starving with algae. Obsessed with the psychedelic power of colour, Hills trained his disciples to sense auras and encouraged them to take the Lüscher test, where their personality traits were revealed through their favourite hues.

Another commune of eccentrics could be found at the end of Colville Houses, a narrow terrace off Talbot Road. Set up by members of the Gay Liberation Front, 'Colvillia' (as it became known) was housed in an abandoned studio and provided a home for two hippies and their kids, an elderly homeless woman named Joyce and numerous transvestites. Bette Bourne, one of the 'queens of Colvillia', described how they transformed the abandoned studio into a theatrical wonderland:

> One end was the Arabian room and as you can imagine it was all bits of schmutter and silk and stuff draped like a tent. Then the next room was the wardrobe [with] hundreds of frocks that we found on Portobello [Market] … It was like living in this extraordinary kind of fairylike cocoon. Occasionally … we'd sit there and listen to Maria Callas all evening, you know, and on the acid and the dope.

Gay liberation activist Andrew Lumsden visited Colvillia during its heyday, and later recalled:

> It was like stepping off the planet. You went into a no-daylight zone where there were places to sleep strewn all over the floor, posters to do with pop groups, endless sounds always on, you were always offered dope or acid. The welcome was lovely. It was unstructured to a degree that was terrifying if you had led any kind of structured life … None of the ordinary ways of coping seemed to be there.

By the late 1960s, Notting Hill was the epicentre of the drug-addled underbelly of swinging London. However, although the destructive effects of hallucinogenic drugs were regularly reported by the press, the concept of psychedelia made it into the mainstream, where it was voraciously consumed by a public seemingly oblivious to the fact that it was inspired by hard drugs. While the Rolling Stones were banned from singing 'Let's Spend the Night Together' on television for fear it would corrupt public morals (they changed the lyrics to 'Let's spend some time together'), songs clearly influenced by LSD – such as the Small Faces' 'Itchycoo Park' and the Move's 'I Can Hear the Grass Grow' – received regular, unexpurgated airplay.

By the end of 1967, psychedelia had pervaded every corner of popular culture. Fashion labels used psychotropic, swirling designs in their clothing ranges, while magazines adopted the same designs and used them in graphic art and typography. Psychedelic imagery also regularly crept into children's television programmes – *H.R. Pufnstuf* and *The Banana Splits Adventure Hour* being two particularly trippy examples. Teen pop darlings the Monkees even made a full-length psychedelic feature film called *Head* (released in 1968).

The main reason behind the mainstream acceptance of psychedelia was innocence. At the time, mind-altering substances such as LSD were generally the preserve of affluent 18–25-year-olds whose parents had never been exposed to anything even remotely similar. The products of psychedelia – simple, childlike songs, cheerful colours and madcap films and television shows – seemed benign.

However, this naivety was not destined to last long. By the early 1970s, several idols of the psychedelic era had met untimely deaths and countless more were experiencing severe psychological difficulties. As newspaper headlines grimly announced the demise of seemingly immortal stars such as Janis Joplin and Jim Morrison, the darker side of psychedelia began to emerge.

One of its most high-profile victims was Jimi Hendrix, who met his end in Notting Hill on 18 September 1970, aged just 27. The circumstances surrounding Hendrix's death were mysterious and ignominious in equal measure. His final hours were mainly spent in the company of a girlfriend named Monika Dannemann, a 25-year-old German skating champion who was staying in a serviced apartment at the Samarkand Hotel in Lansdowne Crescent. The day before he died, Hendrix and Dannemann spent much of the day trawling round markets in Chelsea and Kennington, before visiting their friend Phillip Harvey, with whom they drank tea and smoked dope while the night slowly closed in.

According to Hendrix's biographer, Charles Cross, Monika stormed out of Harvey's house after becoming incensed that her boyfriend was flirting with other girls. Hendrix followed her and, apparently, a voluble argument ensued. However, Monika's version of events was considerably less dramatic. In an interview with Kenelm Jenour of the *Daily Mirror*, she claimed that she and Hendrix cheerfully returned to the Samarkand Hotel together after spending an uneventful few hours at Harvey's house.

Once back in her apartment, she cooked a meal and they shared a bottle of wine. 'It was a very happy atmosphere,' she told Jenour. 'There was no arguing or stress. We were just talking and listening to music.' Although Monika Dannemann took great pains to stress that she and Hendrix spent a contented evening together, at around 1.45 a.m. he decided to leave the hotel and go to a party being thrown by his friend Devon Wilson, to which Dannemann was not invited. Nevertheless, she agreed to drive him over to Wilson's flat. What happened next is, again, open to question. Monika claimed that she did not see or speak to Hendrix again until 3 a.m., when she returned to drive him back to the hotel.

However, party guest Angie Burdon recalled that Dannemann repeatedly buzzed the intercom to the flat while the party was in full swing. This caused so much irritation that eventually some of the guests went out on to the balcony and told her to go away. Monika apparently ignored them and eventually Hendrix relented, left the party and returned with her to the Samarkand Hotel. 'We went back to my flat and I made him a tuna fish sandwich,' Dannemann told the *Daily Mirror*. The pair then chatted in bed until around 7 a.m., when Monika fell asleep.

Monika Dannemann was the only witness to the terrible events of the following morning. According to her testimony at the subsequent inquest, she woke at around 10.30 a.m. and, seeing that Hendrix was fast asleep, she left him in bed and went out to buy some cigarettes. When she returned, she noticed that he had been violently sick and was unconscious. She told the inquest, 'I tried to wake him up but I couldn't. I then saw that he had taken some of my sleeping tablets.' Dannemann's tablets came in packs of ten and she quickly realised that nine were missing. 'He must have taken them shortly after I started to go to sleep,' she surmised.

In her testimony she stated that she quickly called an ambulance, hoping that the team on board would be able to revive Hendrix. The ambulance duly arrived and rushed him to St Mary Abbot's Hospital but he was pronounced dead on arrival, having choked to death on vomit. The hospital's surgical registrar, John Bannister, stated, 'He was cold and he was blue. He had all the parameters of someone who had been dead for some time.'

The inquest into Jimi Hendrix's death failed to reach a verdict, and this, combined with the conflicting reports of how he spent his final hours, prompted the rumour mill to go into overdrive. Had he taken nine sleeping tablets by accident, or had he planned to commit suicide? Had the sleeping tablets killed him, or was his death the result of overdosing on other drugs?

The flimsy evidence was ambiguous. Monika told the inquest that, although she knew Hendrix had taken hard drugs in the past, he did not use them habitually. Her statement was backed up by pathologist Donald Teare, who performed the autopsy on Hendrix's body. He asserted that, although barbiturate intoxication had led to his death, this could have been caused by the sleeping tablets alone. In addition, there was no physical evidence of drug abuse. 'The normal signs are marks on veins on the arms and hands,' Professor Teare explained. 'Once there, they never go. In this case, there were no marks whatsoever.'

Of course, not all drug addicts inject and the possibility that Jimi Hendrix delivered his fixes in other ways was backed up by guests at Devon Wilson's party, who claimed they had seen him taking amphetamine tablets. In addition, Hendrix's friend Eric Burdon was so concerned that police would find drugs at the Samarkand Hotel that (after presumably being tipped off by Dannemann) he raced round to the flat to remove incriminating evidence before the ambulance arrived. According to Burdon, Monika Dannemann then left the hotel with him, leaving the body of the man she supposedly loved abandoned and alone. Eric Burdon's version of events were backed up by a statement issued by the London Ambulance Service that read, 'There was no one else, except the deceased, at the flat when they [the ambulance crew] arrived.'

The evidence suggesting suicide was equally vague. During her interview with Kenelm Jenour, Monika Dannemann produced a poem Hendrix had written shortly before he died, that ended with the lines:

> The story of love is
> Hello and goodbye
> Until we meet again.

The verse clearly suggested that Hendrix may have been planning to end his life, and Dannemann unthinkingly went on to give more weight to the suicide theory by claiming that Hendrix 'would have had to get out of bed and go to a cupboard' to get the sleeping tablets. Surely if he had enough presence of mind to know where the pills were, he would also have been aware that taking nine would be extremely dangerous.

Frustratingly, Monika Dannemann did not reveal the existence of the poem until after the inquest. On learning of its content, a police spokesman said, 'Had I known about the poem earlier, I could have placed it with the coroner's office as evidence.'

The conflicting stories of Jimi Hendrix's last hours conspired to obscure the truth. In 1992, his friend Kathy Etchingham called for the case to be reinvestigated, but the sheer amount of time that had elapsed made it impossible to form any definite conclusions. However, what is known for certain is that the world prematurely lost one of the most innovative and talented musicians of the twentieth century on that fateful September morning.

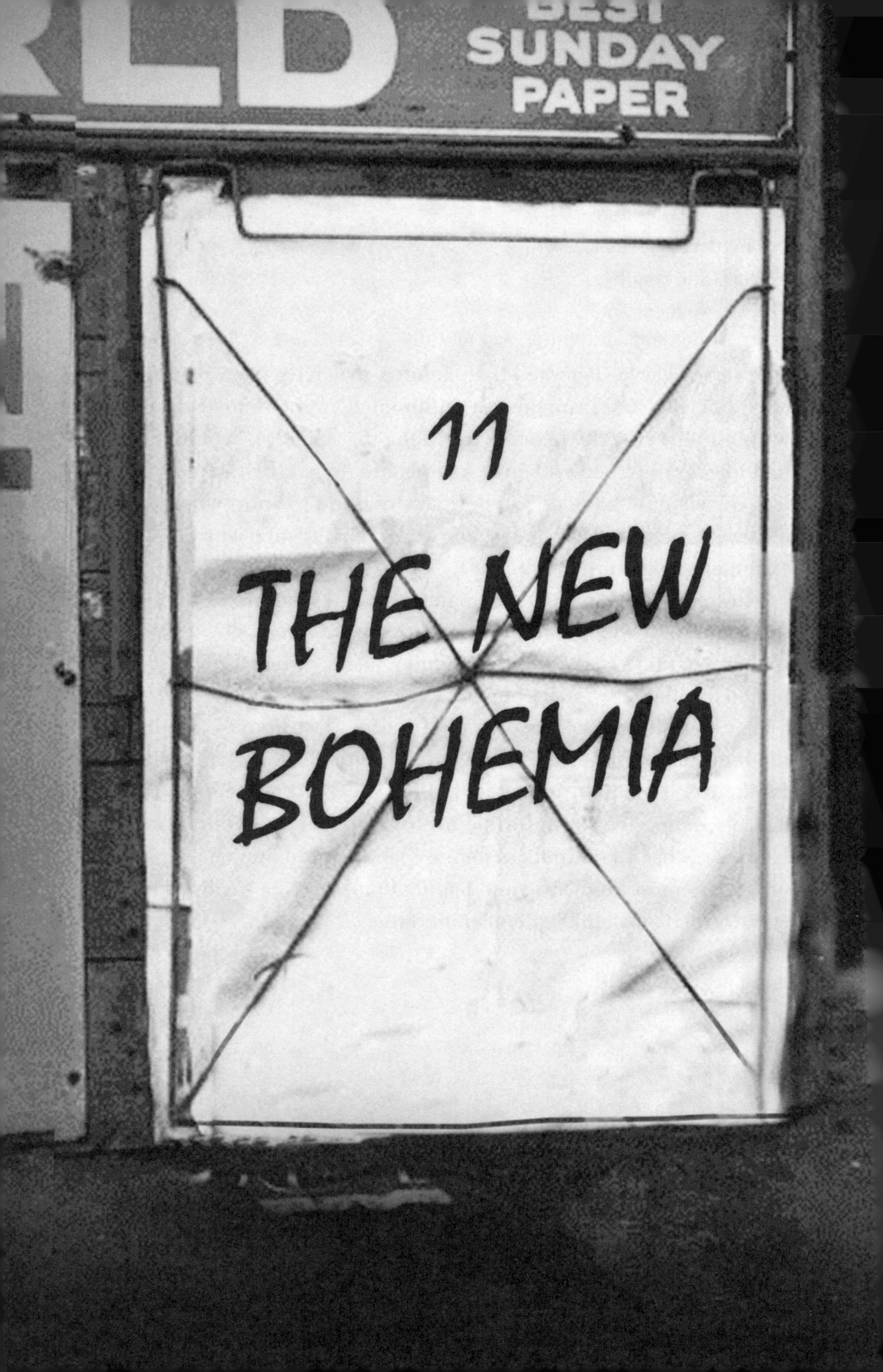
BEST
SUNDAY
PAPER
11
THE NEW
BOHEMIA

Although drugs played a destructive role in late 1960s Notting Hill, the counter-culture from which they sprang was not all bad. Indeed, psychedelia gave birth to a wave of creativity in the area that took many diverse forms. In 1966, journalist and political activist, John 'Hoppy' Hopkins, and community worker, Rhaune Laslett, drew inspiration from the Victorian Jewish Free School to found an adult education project in Notting Hill, which they named the London Free School.

Although it ultimately failed in its attempts at education, the enterprise did sow the seeds for the modern Notting Hill Carnival (as we have already seen) by organising two free, local festivals that were later described by Jeff Nuttall as 'models of exactly how the arts should operate – festive, friendly, audacious; a little mad'. Interestingly, the festivals played a significant part in the early, psychedelic life of Pink Floyd, who appeared at the 1966 event. Syd Barrett's whimsical song 'See Emily Play' was rumoured to be inspired by the sculptor Emily Young, also a patron of the London Free School.

Shortly after the first festival, Notting Hill's Bohemian culture attracted the attention of two art student brothers named David and Stuart Wise who were looking for people who shared their surrealistically nihilist political outlook. They found like-minded individuals aplenty amid Notting Hill's hippie communes and, in 1967, they formed 'King Mob', a radical underground movement and self-proclaimed 'gangsters of the new freedom'.

King Mob took its name from graffiti daubed on the ruined walls of Newgate Prison during the Gordon Riots of 1780. As the remains of the prison smouldered after being gutted by rioters, an anonymous wit attributed the destruction to 'His Majesty, King Mob'. Driven by 'sheer passion and the desire to live a life free of money', the twentieth-century incarnation of King Mob devised a provocatively surreal series of campaigns to promote their often obscure ideals.

In 1968, members dressed as a gorilla and a circus horse appeared in Powis Square and proceeded to pull down the high fence that surrounded overgrown gardens at its centre, declaring the space a new playground for local children.

Fittingly, given the history of their name, King Mob's most lasting contribution to Notting Hill and its surrounds was graffiti. At the soon to be demolished Rillington Place, they painted the slogan 'Christie Lives!' much to the bewilderment and disgust of the residents, some of whom remembered the atrocities committed in their midst during the 1950s. David Wise later made an attempt to justify the graffiti, stating:

> What we wanted to bring out was that these horrendous episodes were nothing more than can be expected from a necrophiliac capitalism where the dead labour embedded in the process of accumulation somehow toxically reacts on a starved psyche only De Sade had the guts to depict in all its utterly necessary rawness.

Blaming capitalism for the actions of a psychopath perhaps says far more about King Mob than it does about Christie.

The group's most memorable graffiti appeared on a concrete wall under the Westway, near Royal Oak underground station. It read, 'Same thing day after day – tube – work – diner [sic] – work – tube – armchair – TV – sleep – tube – work – how much more can you take – one in ten go mad – one in five cracks up'. Amazingly, the slogan survived into the 1990s and must have been seen by literally thousands of commuters using the Hammersmith & City line.

King Mob's reign proved to be brief. However, some members went on to join other underground movements. One – John Barker – joined militant group the 'Angry Brigade', and was eventually imprisoned for his role in a bombing campaign targeting embassies, banks, the homes of Conservative MPs and, memorably, the Miss World Pageant. The Angry Brigade's bombs only caused minimal damage (and no injuries), but that did not stop the courts from imposing heavy sentences on its members. John Barker was sentenced to ten years for his part in the campaign, while his cohort Jake Prescott, who was considered a ringleader, received a fifteen-year gaol term. Prescott later bemoaned the lack of commitment displayed by many of his comrades, humorously noting that while he was genuinely angry, his associates 'were more like the Slightly Cross Brigade'.

While King Mob waged their surrealist war on the mainstream, a Ladbroke Grove busker named Dave Brock became preoccupied with the idea of forming the ultimate psychedelic music group. In a bid to create the 'aural equivalent of an acid trip', he recruited four 'traditional' musicians – saxophonist Nik Turner, guitarists Mick Slattery and John Harrison, and drummer Terry Ollis – along with Michael Davies, an electronics operator and keyboardist, otherwise known as 'Dik Mik', who was tasked with providing the band with their trademark, psychedelic sound using an 'audio generator' – an electronic device and predecessor to the synthesiser.

Brock's new band played their first gig at All Saints Hall, Notting Hill, in 1969. At the time they had no name (they were billed as 'Group X') and as they had barely rehearsed, they opted to play just one song – an extended version of the Byrds' psychedelic anthem, 'Eight Miles High' – which lasted for a marathon twenty minutes. Despite the lack of preparation, the band produced an innovative sound that perfectly encapsulated the drug-fuelled hedonism of the era.

The influential disc jockey John Peel, who was in the audience, was so impressed that he persuaded the gig's organiser, Douglas Smith, to help the band secure a recording contract. Under Smith's guidance, they renamed themselves 'Hawkwind Zoo' and recorded a demo tape, which ultimately secured a deal with Liberty Records. The label shortened the band's name to 'Hawkwind' and their first, eponymously titled, album was released in 1970. A second album – 'X In Search Of Space' – was released the following year.

Both albums produced satisfactory, if not stratospheric, sales figures. Their success was largely due to Hawkwind's almost ceaseless tour schedule, through which the band built up a sizeable and loyal following. Their early gigs often featured another west London psychedelic band named the 'Pink Fairies', a group that took its name from a Notting Hill drinking collective. Formed in 1969, the original Pink Fairies' line-up comprised Marc Bolan's ex-bandmate, Steve Peregrin Took, Mick Farren (who had previously played with the Deviants) and drummer John Adler, commonly known as 'Twink'.

However, after just one chaotic gig at Manchester University, Twink and Farren decided to leave. Undeterred, Steve Took recruited new members and renamed the band 'Shagrat'. Twink promptly reclaimed the 'Pink Fairies' name, recruited new members and began supporting Hawkwind on tour.

The concerts, many of which were free, became known as the 'Pink Wind' gigs and gained legendary status. They finally ended in 1972, when Hawkwind's track 'Silver Machine' became a massive worldwide hit. This classic example of psychedelic rock was originally recorded live at the Roundhouse in Camden Town, with poet and band associate Robert Calvert providing vocals.

'To be honest, Bob's vocals were f*****g terrible,' recalled Douglas Smith:

> It was just this vibey sort of groove, and the audience used to go nuts every time they played it. I thought, we've got something here. We should try and get this out as a single. But Bob's voice was so sort of middle-class English – almost spoken word – it didn't fit at all.

Soon after the song was recorded, Calvert was hospitalised with severe depression and, seeing his chance, Smith wiped his vocal from the master tape and re-recorded the track with new band member Lemmy (who went on to found the hugely successful Motorhead). As a musician, Lemmy had little experience (he had previously been a roadie for Jimi Hendrix) and he was something of a last resort: 'They'd tried everybody else in the band and there was only me and the drummer left,' he recalled. Nevertheless, 'I sang it very, very well the first time and the others all f*****g hated it. Then it went to number one in the *NME* and they *really* hated it!'

'Silver Machine' was a colossal, international hit and the proceeds were sufficient to create 'The Space Ritual' – a spectacular live show that has rarely been equalled in its outlandish splendour. The band were regularly joined at performances by a rehabilitated Robert Calvert, the sci-fi author Michael Moorcock and a stripper/dancer named Stacia who gyrated around the stage illuminated by a migraine-inducing strobe light show. Designer Barney Bubbles

devised madly eclectic stage sets for the shows, which incongru-
ously mixed Weimar Republic graphic images with Art Nouveau and
aliens. Founder member Nik Turner described 'The Space Ritual'
as 'the culmination of all the creative input that all these incredible
people had put into the band'.

In addition to spawning hugely successful bands like Hawkwind,
Notting Hill's psychedelic counter-culture also played a huge part in
the unprecedented rise of alternative magazines. These quirky, irrev-
erent publications were a phenomenon of the late 1960s. Launched
during a period of financial affluence, they survived simply because
advertisers and backers had the confidence to experiment with titles
they would never have risked touching in tighter economic times.

Alternative, underground magazines were not restricted by the
editorial policies that constrained their mainstream counterparts and
so they could write about controversial subjects such as revolutionary politics, drugs and sex. Their edgy subject matter made them
extremely – and almost exclusively – popular with younger readers,
typically students between the ages of 15 and 25. In 1970, the journalist Geoffrey Wansell wrote in *The Times*, 'The underground press has
an estimated readership of one million people, most of them under
25. Yet for much of the rest of the population, it remains a mystery
glimpsed occasionally on the pavement news stand.'

The alternative press thrived for a brief and glorious period that
spanned the end of the 1960s and the first years of the 1970s. By 1972,
nearly all the titles had either disappeared or been forced to become
more mainstream in order to survive. However, during their short
heyday, they revolutionised magazine production, experimenting
with offset printing techniques and bold new graphic layouts that
influenced a whole raft of publications in their wake.

During this period, numerous titles came and went. However,
two of the most innovative and controversial were founded in
Notting Hill. In December 1969, Alan Marcuson, a former writer
for the music magazine *Rolling Stone* (UK), launched *Friends* – an
underground magazine that, in the words of historian Tom Vague,
was 'the literary equivalent of the Pink Fairies'. Marcuson had
grown disillusioned with *Rolling Stone* after its US owners took over

editorial control, leaving its London staff with little to do apart from sell advertising space. Seeing an opportunity to launch his own title and poach *Rolling Stone*'s British readers in the process, Marcuson got to work:

> I always had an idea that you could produce a paper with the underground commitment but which was well-organised and efficient and spread the word rather than be elitist and simply preach to the converted. *Friends* was a very early and naïve attempt to move out into that bigger market.

After persuading his father to lend him £400, Marcuson took a little office at the unfashionable end of Portobello Road and set about creating *Friends of Rolling Stone* magazine, unashamedly affiliating himself with the more widely known publication until its lawyers threatened to sue, forcing him to shorten the name to *Friends*.

Unfortunately, the project quickly ran into financial difficulties and, despite attracting some seriously talented contributors including the writer Rosie Boycott, Hawkwind collaborator Barney Bubbles and rock photographer Pennie Smith, by the beginning of 1971 *Friends* was in serious trouble. The magazine was forced to close the following May, and Alan Marcuson later admitted:

> *Friends* was just pandemonium and I was a rank amateur editing a two-weekly paper, basically saying 'thank God' because I had a bunch of talented people around me ... I had all the right instincts as an editor but of course I was too young and too inexperienced to really manage people.

As *Friends* faced financial collapse, another Notting Hill underground magazine was experiencing trouble of a different kind. *Oz* magazine had been launched in Australia (hence its name) in 1963 by law graduate Richard Neville and artist Martin Sharp. In 1966, the pair decided to transfer their operations to London where there was a significantly larger market and Oz Publications Ink Ltd set up shop at Princedale Road in Notting Hill.

Under Sharp's art direction, *Oz* became one of the most visually exciting magazines of its day, featuring ground-breaking graphic art and innovative printing techniques and formats. By the end of the 1960s it had become one of Britain's most successful alternative magazines, selling around 50,000 copies every month, and Sharp and Neville had been joined by fellow Australian, Jim Anderson, and Felix Dennis, an art school graduate who left his job as a West End window dresser to become *Oz*'s business manager.

Like all the underground publications, *Oz* traded on its controversial subject matter and, although much of the magazine's content could be described as 'sixth form common room' in nature, it was considered dangerously subversive by more conservative members of the public (who had probably never read a copy). As the popularity of the underground press gained momentum, the authorities found themselves under increasing pressure to restrict the magazine's content for fear that the nation's youth were being dangerously corrupted. As the most popular publication in the genre, *Oz* was the most closely scrutinised, and in May 1970 the authorities seized on the opportunity to make an example of its editors when they brought out their now infamous 'School Kids' issue.

The 'School Kids' edition of *Oz* had been published after Richard Neville received criticism from readers that the magazine was losing touch with Britain's youth. In response, he invited around twenty secondary school children to edit an edition. The results were a fairly predictable manifestation of schoolboy preoccupations. The cover featured images of naked women, while much of the editorial content focused on sex, including an obscene parody of the *Daily Express*'s family friendly cartoon, 'Rupert the Bear'.

Misinterpreting the title of the edition, the authorities accused the editors of attempting to corrupt school children, and Richard Neville, Jim Anderson and Felix Dennis were charged with conspiring with 'young persons' to produce a magazine containing 'divers obscene, lewd, indecent and sexually perverting articles, cartoons, drawings and illustrations with intent thereby to debauch and corrupt the morals of children … and to arouse and implant in their minds lustful and perverted desires.'

The *Oz* obscenity trial began at the Old Bailey on 22 June 1971 before Judge Michael Argyle QC, an elderly fellow who advised the jury not to worry if they failed to fully understand the content of the magazine, assuring them 'neither do I. We shall get a grip on it as we go along.' Brian Leary QC appeared for the Crown, while Jim Anderson and Felix Dennis were defended by John Mortimer QC, the creator of *Rumpole of the Bailey*. Richard Neville opted to defend himself.

Unsurprisingly, the prosecution decided to focus their case on the Rupert Bear cartoon. Brian Leary warned the jury, 'you may be familiar with him but not in the guise in which he appears in this magazine'.

As editor-in-chief, Richard Neville defended his decision to publish the 'School Kids' issue of *Oz* aggressively and adeptly. He told the court, 'If you convict us at the end of this trial, you are in reality convicting school children. And if you convict them, you yourselves must accept some of the responsibility for their guilt.'

When accused by Leary of deliberately putting pictures of nude women on the cover to attract the attention of children, he argued, 'If we had wanted to attract school children, we would have put a picture of the World Cup team on the cover.' Richard Neville was vociferously supported by defence witness George Melly, who told the court:

> My 16-year-old son Patrick reads [*Oz*] and I do not think it would corrupt or debauch him … It seems to me that young people today are less uncertain, less miserable and less tormented about sex than they were in my generation … Anything that can be done to alleviate the guilt complex about sex is good.

As the trial went on, the prosecution accused the magazine of promoting drug use. In response, the defence called Caroline Coon, the artist founder of Release, an association that assisted drug offenders. She told the court:

> [*Oz*] is a very good-looking, gutsy magazine. I would not be in this witness box if the underground newspapers were encouraging young people to take drugs … I think its attitude to drugs is very responsible.

We have cases of children saying that if they even mention drugs at home their parents threaten to report them to the police.

Michael Schofield, a psychologist, agreed with Melly and Caroline Coon that the authorities were giving *Oz* more credit than it was due for being a corrupting influence on the young. In his informed opinion, most youngsters would consider the magazine 'a giggle' and then quickly forget about it. The comedian Marty Feldman, who was also called as a defence witness, agreed that the whole affair was a storm in a teacup. 'There is more obscenity in the Bible than there is in this issue of *Oz*,' he controversially declared.

On 28 July 1971, after enduring the longest obscenity trial in British history, Richard Neville, Jim Anderson and Felix Dennis were convicted on four obscenity charges, but acquitted of conspiring to corrupt morals. All three subsequently received gaol terms. Neville was sentenced to fifteen months' imprisonment and recommended for deportation. Justice Argyle told him, 'You have very great ability and very great intelligence [but] I have come to the conclusion that you must go to prison.'

The judge then handed Jim Anderson a twelve-month custodial sentence, before turning to Felix Dennis, whom he sentenced to nine months in gaol, telling him, 'You are very much less intelligent than your two co-defendants and a much younger man, and I have taken this into consideration.' It transpired that the gaol sentences had been imposed purely for show. After just four days in gaol, all three men were released on bail.

Following the obscenity trial *Oz*'s circulation temporarily rocketed, but then gradually began to subside and the last issue was published in November 1973. Largely because of Martin Sharp's visionary art direction, some editions of the magazine now change hands for several hundred pounds and elements of *Oz*'s innovative graphic style can still be seen in print today.

Richard Neville was never deported, but eventually returned to Australia of his own free will where he became a successful author and public speaker. In the 1990s he published a memoir of his time at *Oz* entitled *Hippie Hippie Shake*, which has recently been made into a feature film.

Jim Anderson found the stresses of the trial to be particularly testing. After being released from prison, he suffered a breakdown and
left Britain in search of treatment. He lived in California until the
mid-1990s when he returned to Australia and pursued a successful
career as a writer and photographic artist. Contrary to Justice Argyle's
condescending expectations, the 'very much less intelligent' Felix
Dennis went on to become one of Britain's most successful publishers. Today, his company produces some of the country's most popular
titles including *Maxim*, the *Week* and *Viz*.

In 1995, Argyle, who clearly had an axe to grind, made several serious allegations about Dennis in *The Spectator*, claiming that he and
his fellow defendants had given school children access to drugs and
implying that they had made threats against his life during the obscenity trial. Dennis successfully sued *The Spectator*, which agreed to pay
£10,000 to charity by way of an apology. To his credit, Felix Dennis
resisted the temptation to sue Argyle personally, stating, 'I don't want
to make him a martyr of the Right. There's no glory to be had in suing
an 80-year-old man and taking his house away from him.'

12 GENTRIFICATION

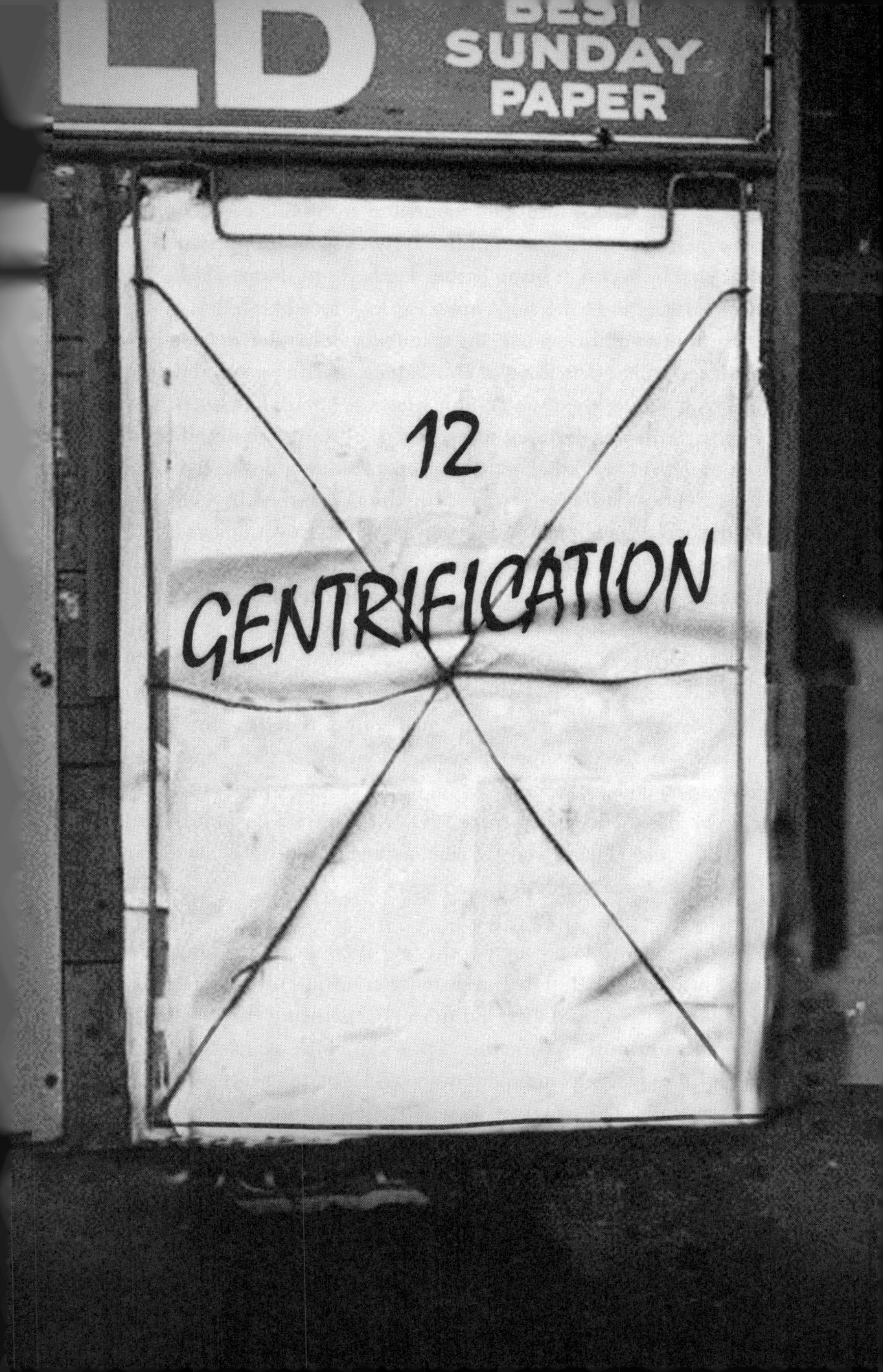

*D*uring the halcyon days of the underground press, Notting Hill began a slow transition from squalor to splendour. Elements of this remarkable transformation were documented in film. The grubby furnished rooms and crumbling edifices presided over by the slum emperors of the early 1960s were presented in all their shabby horror in Bryan Forbes' kitchen-sink drama *The L-Shaped Room* (1962) and Michael Winner's gritty *West 11* (1963).

By the end of the decade, the area's new Bohemian decadence was explored in Nicolas Roeg's *Performance*, starring a suitably louche Mick Jagger. By the time *Performance* was being shot, clues to what Notting Hill was destined to become had started to manifest themselves. David Hockney had acquired a studio opposite the London Free School on Powis Terrace – an area described by Christopher Isherwood as 'peeling houses, trashcans spilling over sidewalks'.

Soon after Hockney opened his studio, fashion designer Zandra Rhodes purchased a house close to a bedsit she was renting in St Stephens Gardens. She remembered:

> It was £22,000 and had sitting tenants so I could just afford to buy it. [The house] still had all the original cornices but there was a giant fungus in the corner of the ground floor. I said the people living there could have the top floor for the same rent, which was £1.50 a week. They'd been there since 1941. Then there was a little old lady on the second floor, who was fabulous and used to do all my ironing. I had the three dilapidated floors below.

Another migrant to the area in the late 1960s was David Bowie, who was initially attracted by the thriving counter-culture. He recalled, 'I moved to Notting Hill, living in sin, painting the ceiling blue; Swedish furniture.' While there, Bowie met the avant-garde dancer/ actor Lindsay Kemp and spent two years learning the art of mime with his company. The pair were drawn together through a mutual admiration for each other's work. '[Lindsay] was playing my music during an interval and expressed an interest in my writing,' he recalled. 'He said, "If you write music for me, I'll teach you mime."' This inspired Bowie to introduce theatre into his performances and while honing his act in west London's underground clubs, he developed his flamboyant alter ego Ziggy Stardust – the persona that launched him on the international stage.

While Bowie was practising his performance skills, over on the corner of Lancaster Road, Chris Blackwell, the founder of Island Records, established Basing Street Studios in an old, deconsecrated chapel. The facilities attracted a wealth of musical talent. In 1970, Led Zeppelin recorded the classic *Led Zeppelin IV* in one studio, while Jethro Tull laid down tracks for their critically acclaimed album *Aqualung* in another. Three years later, the building was simultaneously used by Bob Marley and the Wailers and the Rolling Stones. Other artists destined to record at Basing Street include Queen, Roxy Music, the Eagles and Dire Straits. The studios would also be used to record Band Aid's single, 'Do They Know It's Christmas?', in support of the Ethiopian famine in 1984.

As celebrities became a familiar sight in Notting Hill, the shabbily decadent atmosphere of the early 1970s began to change, along with the streets themselves. The seeds for this transformation had been sown many years previously. After the devastation of the Blitz, which succeeded in destroying vast areas of the old city, London County Council (LCC) explored ways to reconstruct the capital using an infrastructure that would sustain it in the future. Two town planners – Leslie Abercrombie and John Forshaw – were commissioned to draw up plans for this regeneration, focusing on two key areas: the removal of slum housing and the easing of traffic congestion. Both of these factors affected Notting Hill and, thus, the area was earmarked for intense redevelopment.

Abercrombie and Forshaw recommended that a new ring road circling the city should run straight through Notting Hill. The housing problem would simultaneously be resolved, as great swathes of slums in the district would have to be demolished to make way for the new highway.

Post-war austerity measures prevented Abercrombie and Forshaw's plans from being realised, but by the early 1960s the chronic traffic congestion that prevailed on the outskirts of central London prompted the council to revisit the ideas. By 1966, new plans had been drawn up for 'Ringway 1' – a huge motorway that would run around the perimeter of central London, with a series of smaller multi-lane highways radiating from it and taking traffic straight into the heart of the city. These new roads were set to cut a swathe through the city's inner suburbs, including Notting Hill.

The motorway proved controversial from the outset. Londoners quickly realised that communities would be literally divided in two and people living nearby would be subjected to unprecedented levels of traffic noise. As opposition to the motorway grew, the architect, Lord Esher, and transport economist, Michael Thomson, published a damning report entitled *Motorways in London* (1969), in which they calculated that the cost of construction had been massively underestimated, while the economic return would be virtually non-existent. In addition, the motorway would generate even more traffic in the already congested city and, if a second proposed road was built in the outer suburbs, up to 1 million Londoners would be forced to live within 200 yards of a motorway.

The report and the astronomical cost projections prompted both the Treasury and the Department of Transport to oppose the scheme, but nevertheless, the Greater London Council (GLC, the successor of LCC) decided to start work on some parts of Ringway 1, including the monstrous 'Westway' – an elevated concrete highway designed to connect motorway traffic with Marylebone Road at Paddington.

The residents of Notting Hill were devastated when they learned that the Westway had been approved as it was obvious that it would devastate a huge section of their community. One of the streets that would be badly affected was Acklam Road, a late Victorian residential thoroughfare that had been laid out on land once owned by Portobello Farm. The arrival of the Westway meant that the entire southern side of the road, which contained over fifty houses, would be demolished, while the residents on the northern side would have to adjust to living on the edge of one of the busiest roads in Britain.

As works got underway, local resident George Clark decided to take action and promptly set up the Golborne Social Rights Committee (Acklam Road was in the parliamentary Golborne Ward). In a bid to get the residents of Acklam Road rehoused, the committee conducted a survey of the street, which revealed that no less than 380 people would be affected by the arrival of the Westway. But this had little effect on the GLC's plans, work on the motorway continued apace, and on 28 July 1970 it opened amid bitter controversy.

Billed in the press as the 'three minute motorway' (a term that will amuse anyone who has been stuck in a traffic jam there), the projected usage – 45,000 cars every day – made depressing reading for anyone living near it. Unsurprisingly, the opening ceremony was blighted by dissent. *The Times* reported:

> [Parliamentary Secretary] Michael Heseltine cut the tape at Paddington separating the official part from a two-lane jam of local people bearing banners. 'Don't fly over people's lives', 'Shut the ramps' and 'Rehouse us now!' they ran and there was a cry of 'We'll be on your back, Minister.' Once the ceremony was over, the police cleared the protestors from the road and the party of officials boarded coaches to convey them along the elevated road. As they reached Acklam Road, they tried to ignore a large banner fixed to the parapet of the remaining houses that read, 'Let Us Out of This Hell'. A little further north, near the junction of the proposed West Cross Route, residents had erected more banners that read, 'Rehouse Bramley Road and Walmer Road Now'.

Many civil servants had great sympathy for the protestors. John Peyton from the Ministry of Transport issued a statement in which he asked those present at the opening ceremony to spare a thought for those people whose homes had been ruined by the Westway, noting that the 'frigid phrase of the planners – "injurious affection" – does not convey anything of what it means to those who live in its shadow and within range of its unceasing din'.

Unfortunately, the protestors' worst fears were realised when the Westway opened to the public. George Clark likened the noise to 'being in the middle of a factory'. George Burton, who lived with his wife and daughter in a flat on Acklam Road, found they could not sleep until 2.30 a.m. because of the interminable traffic noise. Desperate to get his neighbours rehoused, Clark contacted solicitors who advised him to put forward a claim from just one tenant, which could act as a test case for all the other residents.

The claimant selected was 79-year-old Marie Reeve, whose home lay just 32ft away from the motorway. The plight of Mrs Reeve caused outrage. Malby Crofton, leader of Kensington & Chelsea Borough Council, wrote to the Minister of Housing, pointing out:

> This is no time for bureaucratic niceties. In the name of just and decent government, I appeal to you personally to give this problem absolute priority ... I hope that both you and your colleague, the Minister of Transport, will be able to visit the affected houses and see for yourselves that the conditions are indeed intolerable for the inhabitants.

Although it took longer than everyone had hoped, George Clark's tireless campaigning on behalf of the residents of Acklam Road ultimately met with results. By mid-August 1970, the GLC had agreed to immediately rehouse all council tenants from Acklam Road and adjacent St Ervans Road, along with several households in Walmer Road. Thus, a small part of Notting Hill's community was erased forever.

Although the arrival of the Westway had made Acklam Road uninhabitable, some saw the protestations about the motorway as rather ironic. Ian Wilson, who lived in nearby Paddington Green when the motorway was being built, said, 'Honestly, most of the streets near the Westway weren't worth saving. People were getting het up about preserving houses that should have been demolished decades before.'

He had a point. At the beginning of the 1970s, housing in Notting Hill still left a lot to be desired, despite the publicity surrounding the slum empires of the previous decade. In 1973, the Notting Hill Housing Trust conducted a survey of nearly 700 families in the area and found that housing conditions were still woefully outdated: 87 per cent of those surveyed shared either a kitchen or a bathroom (or both) with other tenants.

However, matters were about to radically change. The prosperity of the late 1960s had created thousands of new jobs in London, particularly in the media and banking sectors where the financial rewards were enticing. As young people flocked to the capital in search of riches, household demographics experienced a significant change.

Previously, young people (especially women) had tended to live with their parents until they married. However, as London's job market boomed, wages rose, and young people found they could afford to move out of the family home, especially if they clubbed together and rented a flat with a couple of friends. But, they did not want to live in a dilapidated property with no modern conveniences. Notting Hill's close proximity to the West End made it an ideal location for 'young professionals' and, in response to demand, landlords began to renovate the crumbling houses and convert them into proper, self-contained flats.

By May 1972, the Colville and Tavistock Wards of North Kensington reported that house conversions had driven out 40 per cent of the previous residents, most of whom had been low-income families living in furnished flats. The report noted:

> They have lost their homes to make way for couples who are better off and for single people who are beginning to take over the stress areas because of the shrinking rented market in London. The young, usually professional people who move in will eventually be able to buy their own homes. But for most of the families displaced, alternative accommodation is another furnished flat, which may be converted in its turn, driving them out again.

The wards' report was backed up by a study conducted by the Notting Hill People's Association, which revealed that average rents in the area had risen from £4.80 per week in 1967 to £14.50 per week in 1972. Some of the larger conversions were attracting rents of £25 per week. The study also noted that the conversions were usually around a third smaller in size than the previous furnished flats. Before conversion, the average house in Notting Hill contained four units; afterwards it comprised an average of six units. Therefore, even if one of the displaced families could afford to move back in, the reduced amount of accommodation would make it impossible.

The forced departure of Notting Hill's poorer residents dealt a blow to the often troubled but vibrant community. The statistics made sobering reading. The People's Association researched the fate of fifty-four families displaced from a terrace of Notting Hill houses between 1969 and 1972. Sixteen of the families were rehoused in the area, either by the developers or housing associations. However, thirty-six more were forced to find new homes away from Notting Hill as the spiralling rents made even the smallest flat impossibly expensive. Two of the families from the terrace were made homeless and were forced into a hostel.

London Free School founder, Rhaune Laslett, was all too aware of the problems facing Notting Hill's poorer families as more and more streets were gentrified. As the organiser of a local playgroup, she got to know many parents in the area and was 'directly confronted and involved with the difficult living conditions and the terrifically high rents' they were paying. In response, she set up the Neighbourhood Service, an advice centre staffed by volunteers including legal professionals who could counsel tenants on housing matters.

Although there was little that Rhaune Laslett or anyone else could do to stop the developers, the Notting Hill People's Association tried to stem the tide by using desperate measures. In May 1973, Kensington & Chelsea Borough Council held a meeting in All Saints' Hall where they intended to explain housing plans to the local residents. However, the meeting was hijacked by the Notting Hill People's Association, who locked the doors and refused to free the councillors until they had agreed to place compulsory purchase orders on multiple occupancy properties in the area in a bid to save them from developers.

Of course, the councillors were in no position to agree to such a demand and the siege continued all night. Police eventually released the captives the following morning. Malby Crofton, who had previously helped residents of Acklam Road with their campaign to be rehoused, stood firm, telling the press assembled outside All Saints' Hall, 'I am not making any bargains with these bloody anarchists.'

The siege of All Saints' Hall was the last high-profile attempt at 'people power' in Notting Hill. Times were changing and nothing would stop the developers. At the end of 1973, the Notting Hill Housing Trust conducted an in-depth study of the private housing market and found that a developer buying and converting a £15,000 house in the Colville Square area would have to let the resulting flats at £25 per week simply to recover his costs. As 62 per cent of current residents in that area only earned £40 or less per week, it was clear that they would never be able to afford to live in the new properties. With the housing associations priced out of the market, it fell to the council to solve the problem of housing Notting Hill's low-income families. Clueless, and facing a shortage of funds themselves, they decided to redevelop Acklam Road – the very place that their tenants had demanded to be rehoused from.

As the gentrification of Notting Hill continued throughout the 1970s, the most high-profile remnant of the area's poorer but more socially conscious past became a thorn in the side of the new, middle-class residents. Every August Bank Holiday, the Notting Hill Carnival took over the increasingly affluent streets and, as each year passed, the event was met with a greater amount of annoyance, not least because it was rapidly becoming a thieves' paradise. Pickpockets moved stealthily through the enormous crowds that congregated to watch the carnival procession, while more organised crooks took advantage of the fact that many residents and business owners vacated their properties over the weekend to escape the general hubbub.

In 1976, the police decided that the best way to curb the thieves' activities was to make their presence felt. It was the worst course of action they could have taken. Before the carnival had even started, thousands of uniformed police officers were drafted into Notting Hill. Many had no knowledge of the area, or its troubled history, and had no idea why the West Indian festivalgoers found their presence extremely intimidating. As the carnival infolded, the atmosphere of tension gradually increased until finally, on the afternoon of Bank Holiday Monday, it erupted into violence.

The trouble began when a team of police officers noticed a man having an altercation with a youth who had apparently tried to relieve him of his wallet. Their heavy-handed response caused the already fragile atmosphere to shatter. Orman Edgar, who was standing close by, said, 'I was having a marvellous time dancing to the band when suddenly everything went wrong. There was a dispute between two coloured youths – one apparently a pickpocket. The police moved in in a hurry.' Old tensions quickly resurfaced as youths began to pelt police with bricks and milk bottles. In response, a team of officers charged the angry crowd and all hell broke loose.

In Westbourne Park Road, windows were systematically smashed by a mob hurling any sort of missile they could lay their hands on, while the terrified residents barricaded themselves in. Two policemen were trapped by the mob and were forced to find shelter in the home of Catherine Madden. 'I was sure the crowd were out to kill them,' she told the press. 'We slammed the door and stood holding it tightly shut. The crowd were baying outside. Some of them threw bricks and smashed my front window.'

Journalist Charlotte Innes (25) also got caught up in the riot. 'It was terrifying,' she said. 'Every time I tried to get out of the trouble area, I ran into more mobs.' In the end, Charlotte gave up and hid behind a van, hoping that the violence would soon subside. She had a long wait. The mob continued to rampage through Notting Hill into the night, burning cars and smashing windows as they made their crazed way through the streets.

As word spread that Notting Hill was under attack, the police attempted to stop more troublemakers coming into the area by setting up road blocks on Waterloo, Lambeth, Westminster and Vauxhall Bridges, shutting Notting Hill Gate and Ladbroke Grove Stations, and ordering all pubs in the area to close. Eventually their tactics worked and the mob dispersed, but not before over 100 policemen and around sixty civilians had been taken to hospital with injuries.

In the aftermath of the carnival riot, questions were inevitably raised as to why it had started. Jeff Crawford, a community relations officer for Haringey, who had attended the ill-fated festivities, felt that the unprecedented police presence was largely to blame as it had intimidated some of the youths. 'The Carnival is ten years old. Until this year the police managed to maintain a low profile,' he observed.

Rhodan Gordon, another community worker, agreed. 'It was obvious the police wanted trouble,' he told the press. 'How do you explain the presence of over 1,000 [officers] this year when in previous years there have only been very few?'

Daily Mirror columnist, John Pilger, concluded:

Nothing was more certain than violence when from the beginning, the police blocked streets, even private doorways, cut through processions, stopped and frisked people and then, when a species as old as London – the pickpocket – was sighted, charged in platoon strength to get him and were followed by a full battalion.

Pilger also echoed the view of many Londoners when he suggested that the police's reaction had been influenced by the fact that many of the people at the carnival were black:

> If this had been a Cockney carnival in the East End, would they have marched in with such severity? No. Are tourists, who every day have their pockets picked in the West End, protected by flying tacklers from Bow Street? No. Would they have sealed off Piccadilly and harassed people outside the Savoy? No. Notting Hill Carnival, although a unique, multi-racial affair, is a predominantly black festival; and if Sir Robert Mark [the police commissioner] is honest, he will say that this distinction alone is why he sent an army there, led by a superintendent with delusions of General Patton.

For his part, Sir Robert Mark flatly rejected any criticism levelled at the way the police had handled the trouble, pointing out that his officers went into action to uphold the law, and there was 'no question of abdicating our responsibility … We are not going to buy illusory peace by watching decent people being robbed by hooligans, even if it is to involve an element of risk going in to help.'

Despite the commissioner's protestations, the majority of Londoners firmly believed that the large police presence had fuelled the riot. However, most also felt that the event was rapidly spiralling out of control, mainly because the labyrinthine streets and back alleys of Notting Hill were almost impossible to patrol when the streets were full of revellers.

In 1977 the police deliberately kept a much lower profile at the carnival, but this did not stop rival gangs of youths beating one another to a pulp in fights that injured up to 250 people. In addition, 247 visitors to the carnival reported items stolen by pickpockets and,

on Portobello Road, a gang broke into a jewellery shop and made off
with £10,000 worth of goods.

The severe problems arising from holding the carnival in Notting Hill
prompted Conservative Deputy Leader Willie Whitelaw to call for
future events to be held in an area such as Hyde Park, which could be
policed more easily. This call has been echoed nearly every year since
but, to date, the Notting Hill Carnival remains in its original location.

Social problems in late twentieth-century Notting Hill were not
purely restricted to the carnival. By the early 1980s, All Saints' Road
had developed the unwelcome reputation as one of London's vice
hotspots, where virtually any type of drug could be scored from a
shady collective of pushers who hung around the street, alerted on
CB radios to the regular police patrols by scouts who lurked nearby.

In May 1982, Michael Parry visited the street and reported on what
he found there in the *Daily Express*. He wrote:

> As I turned into the street, pushers came towards me like wolves from
> a pack, all trying to get there first to do a bit of business. 'You want
> hash, man?'
>   'No thanks.'
>   'OK, you want grass?'
>   'No, thanks.'

As he tentatively made his way up All Saints' Road, Parry was
approached by a man offering him the services of a prostitute. He wrote,
'When I declined, another youth appeared and produced a flick knife,
which he started playing with. He repeatedly flicked out the silver
blade. I walked off casually, wondering whether the blade might end
up between my ribs.'

Despite the area's gentrification, Notting Hill's seedy underbelly
still existed throughout the remaining years of the twentieth century,
along with fragments of the old Bohemia.

One sobering story that combined both elements was that of Ossie
Clark. A pioneer in the 1960s fashion world, Clark had introduced
the idea of marrying his craft with rock and roll, to stunning effect.
By the early 1970s, his catwalk shows at Chelsea town hall were the

most sought after ticket in town and the audience regularly included such luminaries as Mick Jagger, George Harrison and Eric Clapton. Ossie's King's Road boutique, Quorum, was frequented by the likes of Sandie Shaw, Marianne Faithful and Marie Helvin. Fashion writer Ann Chubb recalled:

> By 1970, at 28, Ossie Clark was being hailed by the *Daily Express* as London's number one fashion designer. He single-handedly began all the major fashion trends of the era – from maxi-coats to snakeskin jackets, Thirties-style crepe, floating chiffon and use of multi-prints. He created the first paper dress, in J-Cloth type fabric. He gave me one in black edged with orange and lime green that I wore and wore.

By this stage, Clark had met and married the designer Celia Birtwell and the couple had set up home in a large house in Notting Hill. They went on to have two sons, but gradually Ossie's hedonistic lifestyle began to take its toll. His brain addled by too many drugs, he became increasingly temperamental in both his domestic and professional life.

In 1975 he separated from Celia and, soon afterwards, his business floundered. He was declared bankrupt in 1983 and, by the early 1990s, the once fêted fashion designer was living in a shabby Notting Hill council flat surrounded by fading memories of his halcyon days. It was in these sadly reduced circumstances that his body was found in August 1996. He had been stabbed to death by his lover, Diego Cogolato who, in a state of drug-induced paranoia, had believed that Clark was the devil.

The last vestiges of Notting Hill's Bohemia died with Ossie Clark. From thenceforth, the creative but edgy counter-culture that had thrived throughout the area for much of the mid-to-late twentieth century shrank back till it solely comprised just Portobello Market and a few shops around Notting Hill Gate. The inexorable rise of property prices completed the area's transformation and its transition from Bohemian ghetto to middle-class respectability would, once again, be documented in a film.

Three months after Ossie Clark's ignominious death, Richard Wallace of the *Scottish Mirror* revealed plans for a new, big budget movie starring Hugh Grant. Hailed as the £6 million sequel to the phenomenally successful *Four Weddings and a Funeral*, Wallace speculated that Richard Curtis' script would see Grant's character 'ditch his wimpy ways' and become a tough guy. Quite how this new persona would manifest itself was not explained and, in the event, Grant thankfully did not become Britain's answer to Steven Seagal.

The film itself, however, did live up to Richard Wallace's expectations, and went on to become one of the highest-grossing UK films of all time. It also cemented Notting Hill's reputation as one of London's most sought after places to live. To mark the film's release in 1999, David Robson went on a perambulation of Notting Hill's streets and was struck by the massive changes:

> Forty years ago, Notting Hill was totally undesirable, a place of bad landlords, vice and a still famous 'race riot'; 30 years ago it was the epicentre of the London underground … here the Age of Aquarius was glimpsed through a marijuana haze. 20 or even 10 years ago, people moved here to enjoy, at the periphery of their senses, a whiff of danger. The 'notorious' All Saints Road, heart of darkness, was a no-go area even to police. Today it is a go-go area, ravishingly mixed – a West Indian community centre, a bathroom shop selling challengingly smart glass washbasins, a long-running, wildly thronged bike workshop, an old-fashioned working man's pub, a West Indian mini-cab service, a wedding dress shop verging on chic and a restaurant offering a main course of 'Rare seared tuna with peanut chayote salsa, purple potato and coriander mojo' at £16. *Notting Hill* is a film. Living in Notting Hill is living in a film.

Over the years that followed *Notting Hill* the movie, the area changed little, and today it remains a highly sought after, although prohibitively expensive, place to live. Nearly 200 years after it was first developed, the area is finally attracting the type of residents that James Weller Ladbroke sought, and much of Notting Hill's not-so-illustrious past has vanished.

All trace of John Whyte's Hippodrome has been erased, the only clues to its existence being a small mews and adjacent place bearing its name. Green's Lane, the track that once led to Notting Barns Farm, and later to the infamous Potteries, has been subsumed into short sections of Portland Road, Pottery Lane and Walmer Road. The Potteries themselves are also long gone, and the area that caused so much death and misery for its nineteenth-century inhabitants is now one of the few parts of Notting Hill that contains a large amount of social housing. Outside the entrance to Avondale Park – the successor to the stinking Ocean – one last surviving bottle kiln still stands, a testament to the area's long-disappeared industry.

The most upmarket streets in Notting Hill have seen the least amount of change. Janie Jones' homes at Kensington Park Gardens and Campden Hill Road look much the same as they did three or four decades ago, as does the Samarkand Hotel, in prestigious Lansdowne Crescent, where Jimi Hendrix met his untimely end. The old hippie hangout of All Saints' Hall is still used for concerts, and together with the adjoining chapel forms the Tabernacle Arts Centre. Over on Acklam Road, the residents of the council's redeveloped estate still live in the shadow of the Westway.

Elsewhere in the district, much has changed. The site of Christie's atrocities is now obscured by the deliberately confusing footprint of a quiet housing estate. On Bramley Road, much of the backdrop to the 1958 riots has been demolished, and today the street displays architecture from virtually every wave of development: original Victorian shops and warehouses face modern apartment blocks, while further towards the concrete behemoth of the Westway, ugly 1960s flats face older, post-war low-rise blocks. Slightly further south, the centre of Rachman's slum empire has been transformed into highly priced private accommodation – flats in Colville Road and Powis Gardens now regularly change hands for well over £1 million.

Without doubt, Notting Hill has undergone one of the most staggering transformations ever witnessed in London, but a price has been paid for its success. The ordinary, working people that made the area a vibrant and cosmopolitan place during the second half of the twentieth century have either been forced out of the area or are stranded in the pockets of social housing, gazing out over the affluent streets that, within living memory, were the resort of the very poorest Londoners and which earned the area the unflattering nickname of 'Rotting Hill'.

ACKNOWLEDGEMENTS

With many thanks to the people who helped bring *Streets Of Sin* to fruition, especially my agent Sheila Ableman, the staff at The National Archives, Metropolitan Archives & RBKC Archives and Mark Beynon and Naomi Reynolds at The History Press.

SELECT BIBLIOGRAPHY

Books

Ackroyd, P., *London: The Biography* (Vintage, 2001)

Baker, T.F.T. (ed.), *A History of the County of Middlesex* (Victoria County History, 1982)

Carr, G., *The Angry Brigade* (PM Press, 2010)

Davenport-Hines, R., *An English Affair: Sex, Class & Power in the Age of Profumo* (Harper Press, 2013)

Denny, B., *Notting Hill & Holland Park Past: A Visual History* (Historical Publications, 1993)

Edgecombe, J., *Black Scandal* (Westworld International, 2012)

Gladstone, F., *Notting Hill in Bygone Days* (Bingley, 1969)

Glinert, E., *Literary London* (Penguin, 2007)

Green, S., *Rachman* (Hamlyn, 1981)

Hobhouse, H. (ed.), *Survey of London: Volume 37, Northern Kensington* (Continuum International Publishing, 2004)

Hodgson, V., *Few Eggs & No Oranges* (Persephone Books, 1999)

Hyde, R. (introduction), *The A–Z of Victorian London* (Harry Margary/Guildhall Library London, 1987)

Hyde, R. (introduction), *The A – Z of Georgian London* (Harry Margary, 1985)

Jenkins, V., *Where I Was Young* (Harper Collins, 1976)

Jones, J., *The Devil & Miss Jones* (Smith Gryphon, 1994)

Kennedy, L., *Truth to Tell* (Bantam, 1991)

Lachman, G.V., *Turn Off Your Mind* (Disinformation Company, 2003)

Lewis, W., *Rotting Hill* (Black Sparrow, 1986)

MacInnes, C., *The Colin MacInnes Omnibus: His Three London Novels* (Allison & Busby, 1985)

Mitchell, N., *World Film Locations: London* (University of Chicago, 2011)

Moore, T., *Policing Notting Hill: Fifty Years of Turbulence* (Waterside Press, 2013)

Glinert, E., *Literary London* (Penguin, 2007)

Oates, J., *John Christie of Rillington Place* (Pen & Sword, 2013)

Povey, G., *Echoes: The Complete History of Pink Floyd* (Mind Press Publishing, 2007)

Selvon, S., *The Lonely Londoners* (Penguin Classics, 2006)

Walford, E., *Old & New London: Volume 5* (Cassell, Petter & Galpin, 1891)

Webster, W., *Imagining Home* (Routledge, 1998)

Wheatley, H.B. & Cunningham, P., *London Past & Present* (Nabu Press, 2011)

White, J., *London in the 19th Century* (Vintage, 2008)

Williams, J., *Michael X: A Life in Black & White* (Century, 2008)

Online Resources

Ancestry.com
British History Online
British Newspaper Archive
Charles Booth Online Archive
Dictionary of Victorian London
Financial Times Historical Archive
Family Search Internet Genealogy Service
The Guardian and *Observer* Archive
Daily Mirror and *Express* Archive
Oxford Dictionary of National Biography
Picture Post Historical Archive
Proceedings of the Old Bailey
The Times Online Archive
Who's Who & Who Was Who

INDEX

Also from The History Press

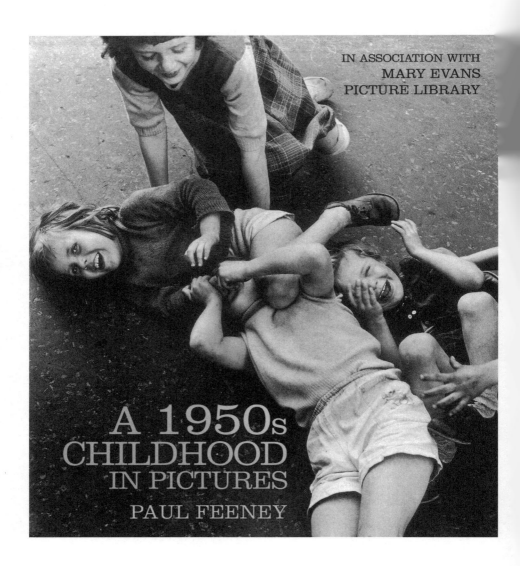

IN ASSOCIATION WITH
MARY EVANS
PICTURE LIBRARY

A 1950s
CHILDHOOD
IN PICTURES

PAUL FEENEY